Congressional Spending

Congressional Spending

A TWENTIETH CENTURY FUND REPORT

Dennis S. Ippolito

CORNELL UNIVERSITY PRESS

ITHACA AND LONDON

First published 1981 by Cornell University Press.
Published in the United Kingdom by Cornell University Press Ltd., Ely House, 37 Dover Street, London W1X 4HQ.

International Standard Book Number (cloth) 0-8014-1463-6
International Standard Book Number (paper) 0-8014-9230-0
Library of Congress Catalog Card Number 81-67971
Printed in the United States of America
Librarians: Library of Congress cataloging information
appears on the last page of the book.

For George M. Underwood, Jr., and
Nancy Chambers Underwood

Foreword

In the mid-1960s, when Lyndon Johnson was pursuing both the war in Vietnam and the war on domestic poverty, federal spending, which of course almost always increases, began expanding at a breakneck pace. Despite Richard Nixon's vows to economize, spending rose rapidly during his administration; moreover, he engaged in numerous disputes with Congress, which was then controlled by the Democrats, about whether the executive or the legislative branch was responsible for the excesses. In truth, there was more than enough blame for both. But the dispute helped to bring about passage of the Congressional Budget and Impoundment Control Act of 1974, which was an attempt to resolve the traditional problems of the legislature in approving budgets, controlling federal spending, and dealing with factional disputes. At the time, the new legislation seemed to be returning to Congress many of the powers of the purse that had been allegedly usurped by the executive branch.

When it became clear that spending was not being affected to any discernible degree by the new legislation, the Board of Trustees of the Twentieth Century Fund approved a proposal by Dennis Ippolito to evaluate the act and to make recommendations for strengthening it. The Trustees welcomed an examination to determine what had gone wrong and what could be done about it.

Ippolito has done a painstaking job of investigating the history of the federal budget process, analyzing the two major difficulties that Congress has always faced—fending off executive encroachments on its powers and setting up an effective process for making critical budget decisions. He has assessed the most recent efforts at achieving reform and has compared the budget processes in the two houses of Congress since the 1974 legislation went into effect. He evaluates the institutional processes established under the legislation and goes on to appraise the politics of spending controls, explaining how and why Congress spends and demonstrating that procedural devices, no matter how well devised, cannot have much of an influence on the congressional proclivity to keep on spending more.

While Ippolito's historical analysis is solid and useful, the major contribution he makes is in putting forward his ideas for controlling spending as a means of promoting economic stability. Even with the advent of an administration determined to cut back on federal spending, Ippolito believes that it is necessary to impose a formula solution—namely, a constitutional spending limit—if Congress' capacity for spending is to be contained. Arguing that entrenched constituencies exist for every individual spending program, Ippolito believes that only a spending limit will work.

We are delighted by the dedication of this young scholar and grateful for both his careful analysis and the clarity with which he has presented his views. His book is a notable contribution to the continuing debate over congressional spending, and the Fund is proud to have sponsored it.

M. J. ROSSANT, Director
The Twentieth Century Fund

Contents

Tables

Tables

Figures

Preface

There is serious and widespread alarm about federal spending—its uncontrollable growth and accompanying deficits, its economic and social effects, its political implications. The Reagan administration has pledged to bring federal spending under control and has announced ambitious plans to alter the size and shape of the federal budget. Predictably, its initiatives are being treated as unprecedented and self-executing. They are, in truth, neither. All of the past several administrations have promised to slow the rate of growth of federal spending, to eliminate deficits, and to reduce the relative size of the public sector. The most recent set of budgetary proposals is perhaps bolder, but it is certainly not unique.

Like his predecessors, Ronald Reagan will inevitably confront an unpleasant institutional reality. The executive branch, whatever its pretensions, does not control budget policy. The balance of influence now lies with Congress, which has protected its favored spending programs with statutory mandates and automatic increases. Unless Congress agrees to major changes in existing laws, spending policy will remain largely immune to the president's direction or intervention. The congressional dilemma is painful. Members of Congress feel political pressures to reduce spending totals, but they also feel the pressures of the well-organized and powerful constituencies behind individual spending programs.

What can we expect from Congress? Will it finally tame spending pressures, or are fiscal responsibility and congressional spending incompatible? These questions define the scope of this book. The particular focus is the Congressional Budget and Impoundment Control Act of 1974—the historical background and institutional factors

Preface

that shaped it, its subsequent implementation by the House and Senate Budget committees, and, most important, its impact on budget policy.

The authors of the 1974 budget law believed that improved organization and procedures would rationalize Congress' control of the budget, and Congress overwhelmingly ratified this generous endorsement of its policy-making capabilities. Now, with the congressional budgetary process seemingly unable to control spending or deficits, Congress' power of the purse is under attack. There is growing support for constitutional and statutory formulas that would govern spending or define the balance between spending and revenues. The framers of the congressional budget passed in the fall of 1980 conceded that "the time is right for considering revisions and modifications . . . to improve the congressional budget process."

Before Congress embarks on yet another reform effort, it might be wise to analyze why congressional spending problems have developed. It makes a great deal of difference whether current fiscal difficulties result from temporary economic dislocations or particular political coalitions, as opposed to endemic weaknesses in congressional control of the purse. The cure, after all, should fit the disease.

I am greatly indebted to the Twentieth Century Fund, not only for financial support of this study, but also for assistance at virtually every stage of its research and writing. Carol Barker provided encouragement and advice, particularly during development of the research design. James A. Smith has worked with great patience and enthusiasm in shaping the manuscript. His experience and judgment have been invaluable. Beverly Goldberg has been a skilled and sensitive editor. Wendy Mercer has kept the project within its budget, thus demonstrating that fiscal discipline is not an altogether outmoded concept.

Several individuals, including Joel Havemann, Charles O. Jones, and Bruce I. Oppenheimer, commented on an early version of a portion of the manuscript. Edwin L. Dale provided an immensely helpful comprehensive critique. I hope the book does justice to their insights.

Since they were promised anonymity, I cannot thank by name the many members of Congress, as well as committee and agency staff members, who shared their expertise and experience with me. Some of them will, I think, recognize their contributions. All of them will, I trust, find my portrayal of the congressional budgetary process to be honest and objective, even if they cannot agree with my conclusions.

Finally, I am especially grateful to several people at Emory University. Karen Bussell typed numerous drafts of this manuscript, discovered many of my errors, contributed none of her own, and displayed her customary intelligence, speed, and precision. Patricia Mills and Deborah Barrow were able research assistants. Thomas Walker has created a department in which it is a pleasure to work but impossible to take one's work too seriously. Since the budget provides little in the way of humor, this last contribution has been indispensable.

DENNIS S. IPPOLITO

Atlanta, Georgia

Congressional Spending

CHAPTER 1

Introduction:
Congressional Budget Reform

During the early 1970s, Congress was the target of much criticism. Critics believed that congressional operations were obsolete and undemocratic. Legislators, they said, were preoccupied with reelection to the detriment of their lawmaking responsibilities. The twin foundations of congressional authority—the power of the purse and the power to declare war—had eroded, and Congress no longer stood as a proud, equal branch of government.

These charges were accepted by members of Congress, who readily admitted to having been overwhelmed by the "Imperial Presidency" and perhaps sought absolution for past policy failures. These confessions of institutional failure proved unsettling, however, and Congress quickly, perhaps too quickly, initiated an unusually broad set of reforms designed to bolster its reputation and power. Some reforms, such as ethics legislation and the democratization of procedures and organization, were a response to internal congressional problems. Others, such as the statutory curbs on the president's war powers and the new congressional budgetary process, were designed to redress a perceived imbalance between presidential and congressional powers.

Congressional reform measures were, predictably, applauded by academics, journalists, and, of course, members of Congress. Now the applause seems to have been too loud and to have come too soon, not only in the case of budget reform, which has been buffeted by economic and political challenges, but also in terms of congressional performance. In fact, Congress' ability to govern is still in question.

The Budget Reform Initiative

Among the wide-ranging reform efforts, changes in the budgetary process represented a unique challenge to the executive branch. In the mid-1970s, Budget committees and the Congressional Budget Office were established to aid Congress in setting fiscal policy and budget priorities. Congressional budget resolutions would stand as formal alternatives to presidential budgets. Impoundment controls would ensure that the executive branch carried out congressional spending decisions. The Congressional Budget and Impoundment Control Act of 1974 was perceived by legislators as the key to making Congress "a more respected institution and a more effective partner in Government." Congress passed, by an overwhelming margin, "one of the most monumental reassertions of congressional prerogatives" and "the most significant reform of the 20th century."[1]

Despite nearly unanimous support for budget reform, there were disagreements about what it might mean for actual budget policy. Liberals and conservatives debated what would, and should, happen to budget growth rates, deficits, and the competing claims of defense and social welfare. Democrats and Republicans had different perceptions about the immediate impact of budget reform on relations with the executive branch. Ideological and tactical considerations aside, the belief that Congress would deal with fiscal issues in a responsible fashion now that the 1974 budget act had given it the proper machinery was widespread. Virtually everyone agreed with the chairman of the House Appropriations Committee, George Mahon, that "Congress should be in the driver's seat on fiscal matters."[2]

The "proper machinery," however, has been in operation since 1975, and there are complaints that it has failed to force fiscal discipline on Congress and control federal spending. Within Congress, there is growing support for statutory controls and even constitutional amendments that would limit Congress' discretion over the federal purse. Many congressmen today are skeptical about the effects of reforming only procedure and organization to ensure congressional fiscal responsibility.

Spending control* and the issues that surround it define contem-

---

*As used here, "spending control" means holding down government expenditures. Spending control can also imply higher spending, with control mechanisms being used to

22

porary debates on budget policy and must be examined before we turn to the institutional and policy issues related to congressional budget reform. The federal budget has no doubt always been a political document, but its widening economic and social impact over recent decades has magnified its political importance. The changing character of federal budgets reflects not only an expanding federal role but also a more complex controversial decision-making environment.

Spending Control

Public concern about the federal budget usually focuses on the growth in federal spending and the steady accumulation of large deficits. In attempting to assuage this concern, policy makers in Congress and the executive branch face a formidable problem: the budget they are dealing with has become increasingly hard to control.

Spending Increases

Actual government spending during a fiscal year is reported as budget outlays.* Outlays have been increasing for many years, of course, but recent growth has been exceptionally high. During the 1950s, for example, total federal outlays were just over $690 billion. Over the next decade the total nearly doubled, to over $1.3 trillion. For the 1970s the total came to some $3.3 trillion, an almost fivefold increase over a thirty-year period. In recent years, spending growth has been unusually high. The yearly increase in outlays since 1970, for example, has averaged 11 percent (see Table 1.1).

The federal budget has also grown more rapidly than the economy. As a percentage of gross national product (GNP), federal outlays have risen from 18.5 percent in fiscal 1960 to 20.5 percent in fiscal 1970 to levels of 23–24 percent in fiscal 1981. The relative

---

ensure more orderly and rational growth on priority items. The 1974 budget act can be analyzed from either perspective, but the more important issue at this time obviously is whether Congress can reduce the rate of budget growth, not accelerate it.

*When spending figures are reported, there is often some confusion about outlays and budget authority. Outlays represent actual expenditures or payments during a fiscal year. Budget authority is the statutory basis that allows an agency to incur obligations and make payments. The budget authority enacted for a given fiscal year's budget is divided between authority that will result in outlays during that fiscal year and authority for future years. Outlays, in turn, will be drawn partly from budget authority enacted during a fiscal year and partly from budget authority conferred in previous years.

Table 1.1. Federal outlays and annual increases, fiscal years 1970–80

Fiscal year	Total outlays (billions of dollars)	Increase over previous year (percent)
1970	$196.6	6.5%
1971	$211.4	7.5
1972	$232.0	9.7
1973	$247.1	6.5
1974	$269.6	9.1
1975	$326.1	21.0
1976	$366.4	12.3
TQ*	$ 94.7	—
1977	$402.7	9.9
1978	$450.8	11.9
1979	$493.6	9.5
1980	$579.6	17.4
Average annual increase		11.0

*Transition quarter, necessitated by the switch in the period covered by the fiscal year from July 1–June 30 to the current October 1–September 30. The change was part of the Congressional Budget and Impoundment Control Act of 1974.

SOURCE: *United States Budget in Brief, Fiscal Year 1982* (Washington, D.C.: Government Printing Office, 1981), p. 91.

size of the federal budget is now considered excessive by many experts; both Gerald Ford and Jimmy Carter advocated a gradual reduction in spending as a percentage of GNP* (a commitment that Reagan shares) but failed to achieve this goal because economic growth during their tenures remained sluggish and required spending cuts were not made. If the relative size of the federal sector is to be reduced, the rate of increase in government spending must be held below the GNP growth rate. Since 1 percent of GNP now represents almost $30 billion, it is apparent that even modest reductions in the government spending–GNP relationship will require effective and sustained control of spending.

*In its fiscal 1980 budget, for example, the Carter administration projected a drop in spending to 20.3 percent of GNP in two years. Carter characterized this "reduction in the share of our national product spent by the Federal Government" as a "fundamental goal of my policy, equally as important as reducing the deficit" (*Budget of the United States Government, Fiscal Year 1980* [Washington, D.C.: Government Printing Office, 1979], p. 4). This "fundamental goal" did not reappear in the next year's budget message.

Uncontrollable Outlays

Reducing the rate of budget growth, not to speak of cutting the budget from one year to the next, is extremely difficult, since the "uncontrollable" portion of the budget includes more than three-fourths of all federal spending. "Controllability" is the extent to which outlays in a given year can be increased or decreased under existing law. "Relatively uncontrollable outlays" are those mandated under existing law or required to fulfill previous contracts. The spending is *automatic* unless Congress makes legislative changes, and even then only certain spending would be affected.

Current levels of uncontrollable spending are proportionately well above those of previous years (see Table 1.2). The major growth has been in payments for individuals, which include income security and various other entitlement programs. About half of the entire budget is allotted to these income transfers, and since all major entitlements are automatically adjusted or indexed for increases in the cost of living, future spending is difficult to control or even to estimate accurately.

The uncontrollable classification is to some extent misleading because there are varying degrees of discretion within this part of the budget. Certain outlays, such as interest on the debt, cannot be

Table 1.2. Uncontrollable federal spending, fiscal years 1967–81, by category (in billions of dollars)

Category	1967	1971	1975	1979	1981*
Payments for individuals	$41.8	$ 77.6	$149.2	$224.9	$298.5
Net interest	10.3	14.8	23.2	42.6	54.8
General revenue sharing	—	—	6.1	6.8	6.9
Farm price supports	1.7	2.8	0.6	3.7	1.7
Other programs, fixed costs	3.0	4.9	7.8	8.0	8.3
Spending for prior- year contracts	37.0	40.2	50.7	80.0	101.4
Total	$93.7	$140.4	$237.6	$366.1	$471.6
Percentage of total outlays	59.2%	66.4%	72.8%	74.2%	76.6%

*Estimated.

SOURCE: Figures for 1967 are from *Budget of the United States Government, Fiscal Year 1976* (Washington, D.C.: Government Printing Office, 1975), pp. 354–55; all other figures are from *Budget of the United States Government, Fiscal Year 1981* (Washington, D.C.: Government Printing Office, 1980), pp. 598–99.

avoided. Contractual obligations can sometimes be deferred or canceled, but the controllable margin is minimal. Theoretically, Congress has greater discretion over entitlement programs and aid to states and localities. Legislative changes in eligibility requirements or benefit levels can reduce short-term spending. Even more substantial future savings are possible through legislative initiatives that eliminate indexing formulas or at least modify them. Political considerations may hinder such changes, of course, but Congress can curb at least some uncontrollable spending, thereby bringing more of the budget under *annual* control. Until now, Congress has not considered substantial changes in benefit formulas. The Carter administration's modest proposals relating to social security, for example, were ignored during the "budget-cutting" spring of 1980.

Conversely, the remaining one-fourth of the budget that is classified as controllable creates a misleading impression about the actual flexibility of the budget. A large segment of the defense budget, for example, is supposedly controllable, but any reduction here would depend on dramatic and improbable changes in national security policy. Similarly, personnel and operating costs in other areas cannot be radically decreased over the short term.

It is unrealistic, then, to assume that one-fourth of the budget can be substantially cut because it is controllable. It is also erroneous to treat the rest of the budget as untouchable. Marginal changes in uncontrollable programs may involve high political costs, but they are possible and would certainly strengthen Congress' control of spending. The controllability problem is to a considerable degree defined by political factors.

Budget Priorities

Over the past twenty-five years the priorities accorded defense and social welfare in the budget have changed dramatically. As recently as the late 1950s, the defense budget accounted for over half of all federal spending; today, its share stands at about one-fourth of the budget. This shift has been offset by increases in the share for social welfare programs.

Changing budget priorities have been the impetus for most of the real growth in the federal budget, as shown by constant-dollar comparisons that eliminate the effects of inflation. The category "payments for individuals and grants," unlike other expenditure catego-

Figure 1.1. Federal budget outlays, fiscal years 1950–82, by category (in constant 1982 dollars)

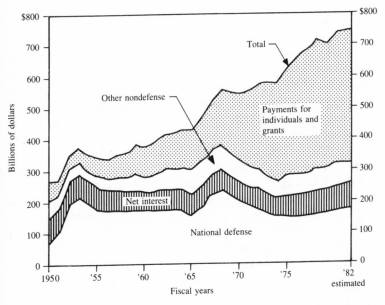

SOURCE: *United States Budget in Brief, Fiscal Year 1982* (Washington, D.C.: Government Printing Office, 1981), p. 19

ries, has benefited from very substantial real increases over the past thirty years (see Figure 1.1). By way of contrast, constant-dollar spending for defense in fiscal 1975 was below its fiscal 1955 level. With real spending increases now being provided for defense, however, the budgetary slack of previous years has disappeared. Rather than reversing the shift to social welfare, the attempts to limit overall budget growth will intensify direct competition between defense and social welfare.

Deficits

Over the past two decades, budget surpluses have been recorded twice, the last in fiscal 1969. Since then, an unbroken string of deficits has been incurred, averaging about $35 billion annually. If we take into account all federal outlays (including those of so-called off-budget entities), the average yearly deficit since fiscal 1975 has been close to $60 billion. At the end of fiscal 1980, the total federal debt stood at over $900 billion, compared with less than $400 billion in fiscal 1970.

This record is disturbing and provides a ready target for public discontent over the federal budget. Large, continued deficits are believed to have increased inflation and to have had other undesirable economic effects. While economists remain divided over just what impact deficits have, many public officials are convinced that the government must balance its budget in order to demonstrate its fiscal responsibility.

Attempts to control spending in order to balance the budget, however, run up against problems. In the spring of 1980 the Carter administration and Congress proudly announced plans to balance the fiscal 1981 budget. Even as these plans were unveiled, it was apparent that actual spending in fiscal 1981 would substantially exceed the amounts estimated. Congress was faced with three unpleasant options: it could increase taxes in an election year, cut spending, or accept an eventual deficit. With a recession under way, the deficit option had the attraction of being defensible as fiscal policy, but Congress was still reluctant to admit the inevitable, and postponed action until after the fall elections.

High rates of budget growth, the lessening controllability of budget outlays, and the dominance of social welfare priorities reflect the flourishing of congressional spending. Congress has deliberately created a good deal of automatic spending, which is easier to allow than to curb. If it were not for the deficits and disconcerting totals, this type of spending would not be under any serious pressure. Sooner or later, however, Congress will probably be forced to balance the budget; at that time, it will find that the budget is not easily controlled or balanced.

The Scope of Budget Policy

Since the 1930s, the explicit purposes of federal budget policy have become increasingly encompassing. Up until the New Deal, government expenditures were largely confined to defense and limited "public goods" that the private market did not provide. However necessary these expenditures were, they appeared to be economic burdens, and small, balanced budgets were considered essential for financial stability. Budgets still serve this public-goods function, but they are also used to manage the economy and to redistribute income among individuals and groups. In addition, the definition of public goods has expanded to embrace an unprecedented range of government activities. These individual expansions in the scope of budget policy are not unrelated, of course, and they serve to justify budgets that are neither small nor balanced. There is no longer a "fiscal constitution" that requires spending restraint.[3]

Fiscal Policy

The federal budget and the nation's economy are closely linked. The economy has certain direct effects on the budget. Government purchases of goods and services rise with inflation, as do the costs of benefit programs indexed to a cost-of-living standard. The costs of unemployment compensation and tax revenues fluctuate with the unemployment rate. It is currently estimated, for example, that each percentage-point increase in the unemployment rate translates into well over $20 billion in federal revenue losses and increased spending. Moreover, since the costs of financing the debt are tied to the interest rate, a sizable portion of each year's budget is determined by the state of the economy.

There is another and more complex but equally important link between the budget and the economy. With its impressive budget, the federal government can influence aggregate spending through its own purchases of goods and services, through transfers to individuals, and through tax policies that increase or decrease the amount of disposable income left to businesses and consumers. Aggregate spending, in turn, affects economic output, employment, and prices. When the economy is operating at less than full capacity, conventional fiscal policy dictates increased spending, tax cuts, and deficits to stimulate output and employment. When production is at or near capacity, spending cuts, tax increases, and budget surpluses are presumably available to reduce demand and weaken inflationary pressures.

In recent years, conventional fiscal policy solutions have lost some of their luster. Periods of simultaneous high unemployment and high inflation have created an obvious dilemma for fiscal policy theorists and government policy makers. There is a growing realization that government has limited ability to "manage" an enormous and complex economy, especially since political considerations cannot realistically be separated from fiscal policy choices.

In addition, conventional fiscal policy creates spending biases, at least as it has been applied by federal policy makers. They justify deficits in terms of economic stimulus, thereby severing the connection between spending and taxation that provides a potential check on spending. When the economy needs a stimulus (and it usually seems to need one), spending programs can be initiated or expanded on that ground alone. Once the programs are in place and new spending constituencies have been created, it is difficult to reduce or eliminate them. In effect, it is much easier for government to follow Keynes's prescription to stimulate demand than his equally important remedy of reciprocal restraint. Finally, fiscal policy makers have usually considered spending increases to be more stimulative than tax cuts. Since individuals may save part of a tax cut, so this reasoning goes, equivalent spending increases are a better and more certain means of injecting additional demand into the economy. Here, too, once the spending is initiated, reducing or eliminating it is difficult if not impossible.

A realistic appreciation of the limits of fiscal policy as an economic management tool does not mean it can or should be disregarded. Fiscal policy management is still considered vital by economists and policy makers, and the federal budget is so large that its economic impact cannot be ignored. At the same time, the inseparability of fiscal policy and politics suggests that greater attention should be directed toward those problem areas, such as spending, where the conjunction of the two creates undesirable effects.

Redistribution

While most taxing and spending decisions have at least some impact on income distribution, a substantial portion of the budget has direct redistributive objectives. It includes various income transfers and in-kind benefits, tax policies, and subsidized employment in the public sector. While the typical emphasis of redistributive programs is on demographic groups, interest in the impact of such programs on states and regions has been growing.

The expansion of income-transfer and benefit programs has had an enormous effect on federal spending. Since the mid-1960s, nearly half of the total growth in budget outlays has been concentrated in a few programs—social security and disability, health-care services, public assistance and other income supplements, and training and employment programs. Between fiscal 1975 and 1979, these programs increased by over $75 billion, while total budget outlays grew by about $170 billion.

The redistributive emphasis of federal income and in-kind benefit programs differs. Social security, for example, is a contributory program for which recipients have qualified through prior payments. Since benefits are only partially related to these payments, however, social security transfers income within and among generations. These transfer effects have been strengthened by recent legislative changes in benefit formulas, and the resulting tax burdens on current workers have increased so rapidly that painful choices between benefits and costs appear inevitable.

A second category of redistributive policy includes noncontributory programs designed to reduce poverty by providing cash or in-kind benefits to the poor and disabled. Among the cash programs are Aid to Families with Dependent Children and Supplemental Security Income, which provides assistance to the needy blind, aged, and disabled. The in-kind programs include medicaid, food stamps, and housing assistance. The impact and incidence of poverty have been considerably reduced through these and related programs. Between 1959 and 1976, according to the government's measure of poverty status, the number of families below the poverty level dropped by almost three million, and the percentage of all persons living in poverty declined by about half, to less than 12 percent of the population.[4] An adjusted definition of household income that includes the value of in-kind benefits would reduce the official poverty rate even further.[5]

Nevertheless, antipoverty programs are under continual attack for fraud and waste, inadequate coverage and benefits, and negative effects on work incentives and family stability. One persistent criticism is that the program-by-program approach is ineffective and should be replaced by a comprehensive cash-benefit or guaranteed-income approach. Thus far, however, cost constraints have worked against major attempts at welfare reform, and it is likely that these constraints will become more severe in the future.

Public Goods

The growth of the federal budget is not solely the result of redistributive efforts aimed at the poor. Indeed, certain income-transfer and benefit programs provide assistance for middle-income and even upper-income individuals. Social security benefits, housing subsidies and loans, medical care, child nutrition programs, and the like are not restricted to the disadvantaged. With perhaps one-third of the population benefiting from various income-security and income-assistance programs, it is apparent that many Americans besides the poor have a vested interest in federal spending.[6]

In addition, the federal government's charge is no longer limited to defense, public roads, and the post office. The federal budget has become a major source of funding for hundreds of educational, agricultural, energy, and environmental programs that presumably benefit the entire population. It is also a primary source of revenue for state and local governments and thus helps to finance their services. The range of what we consider public goods has broadened, and federal involvement in supplying these goods has become much heavier. The federal budget reflects the spending effects, if not the regulatory cost implications, of this enlarged federal role. In fiscal 1966, for example, federal aid to education totaled $2.7 billion. For fiscal 1981, the estimates exceed $14.4 billion. Over the same period, antipollution outlays have grown from less than $160 million to more than $5 billion, community and regional development outlays have risen from $1.5 billion to $8.8 billion, and federal energy programs have increased from less than $0.5 billion to over $8 billion.

For each of these and similar federal efforts, two spending constituencies are created—a direct clientele group, which receives federal funds for the goods and services it provides, and a substantial portion of the population, which supports active federal involvement in these specific areas. This piecemeal expansion of the federal sector has been accomplished with surprisingly little controversy, largely because budgets have grown sufficiently to accommodate popular programs without pitting them against one another. The central point, however, is that the direct and indirect beneficiary groups for federally provided public goods embrace much of the

32

population. The resulting overall spending increases may be unpopular, but concern with totals and deficits has thus far been unequal to the task of forcing choices among our redefined public goods.

The Challenge of Budget Reform

Because political choices must be made when budget policy is set, it is very difficult to control spending. On the presidential side, centralized control of the formulation of budget policy has facilitated the handling of difficult policy choices and provided an opportunity for initiatives to control spending. Presidential decisions on economic policy and program priorities establish the broad outlines of the executive budget. Staff agencies, primarily the Office of Management and Budget, then translate the president's decisions into detailed spending requests for agencies and programs. When the president's budget is submitted to Congress each January, its prominently displayed totals—spending, revenue, and deficit (or surplus)—suggest a carefully considered and coherent program.

The annual presidential budget was mandated by the Budget and Accounting Act of 1921. After decades of resistance, Congress finally accepted the necessity of presidential budgeting to control spending and reduce the debt from World War I. Over the years, other objectives have become associated with presidential budgeting—administrative management and planning, fiscal and priority choices, and occasionally political gamesmanship. If actual centralization and discretion in the executive budget process have perhaps been exaggerated by outside observers, including members of Congress, it is apparent that the president's exclusive jurisdiction over budget totals gave him an advantage over Congress for half a century. Before 1974, Congress was unable to match what the president and his advisers did as a matter of routine—develop a single, coordinated plan for economic policy objectives, overall budget priorities, and spending allocations among departments and agencies. In fact, the congressional budget process was almost the reverse of the executive model. When Congress received the president's budget each January, it apportioned pieces among its revenue, authorizing, and appropriations committees. Congress made no preliminary decisions about totals to guide its committees, nor were the committees required to coordinate their work on the separate pieces of the budget.

This lack of centralized control was a recurring theme of congressional critics, and the 1974 budget act was an attempt to reconcile the institutional need to set revenue and spending totals with the needs of individual legislators to support popular spending programs. Congressional totals, it was hoped, would blunt unfavorable comparisons with the executive budgetary process and counter the impression that congressional spending was "out of control." The setting of totals, however, could not guarantee lower rates of growth in spending or smaller deficits, nor was it certain that Congress would adhere to even its own totals if they seriously impinged on spending. The results ultimately depended on whether Congress was serious about controlling spending or simply intended to carry on business as usual behind a protective facade of spending ceilings and revenue floors. The historical background provided by previous congressional reform efforts and the final compromises on the 1974 legislation were not very reassuring. Nevertheless, newspapers, radio, and television orchestrated a chorus of praise for Congress' courage in passing the 1974 budget act, and the self-congratulation in Congress was only slightly less euphoric.

The issue of spending control has not disappeared, however. It is now, if anything, an even more serious policy problem and institutional challenge than it was in 1974. During the 96th Congress (1979–80), some two hundred proposals were introduced to require balanced budgets or to limit federal spending. Bolstered by the 1980 elections and a sympathetic Reagan administration, fiscal conservatives in Congress will undoubtedly increase their efforts to impose statutory or constitutional limits on the federal budget. Before possible cures can be intelligently debated, however, it is necessary to analyze the dimensions and causes of the spending problem. In particular, we need to understand whether or not Congress, which controls the federal purse, *can* exercise fiscal responsibility.

PART I

THE RISE OF
CONGRESSIONAL SPENDING

CHAPTER 2

The Legislative Power
of the Purse

The legislative character of the powers to tax, spend, and borrow was easily accepted by the framers of the Constitution, who considered an independent "power of the purse" to be a cornerstone of stable and effective national government. James Madison, in *The Federalist* 58, grandly declared legislative control of the purse to be "the most complete and effectual weapon with which any constitution can arm the immediate representatives of the people, for obtaining a redress of every grievance, and for carrying into effect every just and salutary measure."[1]

Although the first Congress, convened in 1789, possessed a broad and largely unqualified authority over the federal purse, it confronted immediate questions about how to exercise and safeguard that authority. In addition to controversy over the establishment of the Department of the Treasury, which reflected concern that executive officers might usurp congressional power, there was confusion about the manner in which Congress should develop its own fiscal plans.

The problems of how to resist executive encroachments and how to organize an effective *congressional* budgetary process that would control spending have frustrated members of Congress for almost two centuries. Before the 1974 reforms, Congress made periodic and unsuccessful attempts to improve its handling of the budget, leading some observers to conclude that Congress could not sustain a coordinated and comprehensive budget system or control spending, and that therefore the president should have the major responsibility for budgetary policy.

The historical record does not inspire confidence in Congress' ability to handle the federal purse. In particular, it shows the political dilemmas that legislators face in making spending decisions. Although individual spending programs rarely lack enthusiastic supporters, finding people who will defend all such programs and the tax policies necessary to support them is not easy. The immediate political needs of individual congressmen often produce results that threaten the long-term institutional interests of Congress.

The declared purpose of the 1974 budget act was "to assure effective congressional control over the budgetary process," including "congressional determination each year of the appropriate level of federal revenues and expenditures."[2] This was a departure from the usual congressional approach to budget decision making, as it required a degree of central control and coordination. Failure to control congressional spending in the past, however, clearly illustrates the difficulty of maintaining centralized authority over budget policy.

An Overview of Congressional Spending, 1789–1921

Before the 1920s, spending requests from the executive departments and agencies, along with plans and estimates of government revenues, were transmitted by the secretary of the treasury to Congress in the "Book of Estimates"; there was no national budget. Although several presidents and secretaries of the treasury attempted to influence departmental requests, Congress refused to grant statutory authority to revise these requests and to develop a national budget.[3] After receiving the Book of Estimates, Congress proceeded to act separately on spending and revenue legislation. During much of the nineteenth century, Congress dealt with financial matters through a relatively centralized process. By the 1890s, however, centralized spending control had eroded, and the congressional budgetary process was in disarray. Large budgetary increases and mounting deficits prompted efforts to establish an executive budget system and to reform congressional procedures.

The Pre–Civil War Period

Congress first created permanent (or standing) committees with jurisdiction over spending and revenue bills in 1789, when the House established a Ways and Means Committee to provide advice on fiscal matters. The committee was abandoned after the first session. In 1795, Ways and Means was revived, and in 1802 it became a standing committee with jurisdiction over appropriations and revenue bills. The committee's authority over appropriations made it responsible for the actual funding of programs and agencies that had been authorized by law.* In 1816 the Senate created a counterpart to Ways and Means, the Committee on Finance, which gradually assumed exclusive jurisdiction over appropriations legislation as well as revenue bills. The "money committees" maintained their broad responsibilities until the 1860s.

Combining revenue and spending jurisdictions within a single committee in each chamber allowed Congress to maintain a coherent approach to the nation's finances. The number of appropriations bills gradually increased during the 1790s, but the single-committee procedure allowed these spending decisions to be coordinated. During the early nineteenth century, moreover, the financial requirements of the federal government were modest, and revenues derived from customs duties usually proved more than enough to meet these needs. From 1789 to 1849, revenues exceeded expenditures by $70 million. Total expenditures over these six decades were less than $1.1 billion, as compared with $15.4 billion from 1850 to 1900.

Congressional control of actual expenditures presented persistent problems, however.[4] Funds appropriated for one purpose were on occasion diverted to other uses by executive officials. In some instances, these "transfers" were justified on administrative grounds and duly reported to Congress. But executive officials frequently sought to evade congressional spending directives. Expenditures frequently exceeded appropriations, and Congress was forced to correct the deficiencies. Here, too, the record was mixed; some deficiencies were unavoidable because of inadequate or late appropriations, while others were deliberate attempts to gain additional funds. Congress experimented with various statutory controls—such as highly detailed appropriations bills and prohibitions of transfers—to restrict

---

*Congress has generally used a two-step process in dealing with spending. An authorization bill establishes or continues an agency or program, while an appropriation bill provides actual financing. Authorizations are handled by legislative committees and may be for one year, a specified number of years, or indefinite. Appropriations may be for definite or indefinite amounts and for specified or unspecified time periods. There have been problems in keeping these two stages distinct, especially in restricting authorizing committees and appropriations committees to their respective jurisdictions.

the spending discretion of executive officials, but its efforts proved ineffective and occasionally counterproductive. Congress' "extreme of rigor" in attempting to control spending typically led to the "extreme of laxity."[5]

The House of Representatives had anticipated these difficulties in 1802, when it directed the Ways and Means Committee to oversee expenditures and ensure that they conformed to law. This expedient proved insufficient, and in 1814 the House transferred oversight responsibilities to a new Committee for Public Expenditures. Two years later, six additional expenditure committees were created to supervise specific departments.

The expenditure committees did not significantly improve congressional oversight of executive spending. Their reports were irregular and usually inadequate, in large part because committee members had neither the technical expertise nor the interest to do the job well.[6] Members of Congress were then, as always, "too much taken up with the making of plans for the future to allow of much examination of the transactions of the past."[7]

Throughout the early nineteenth century, Congress frequently had to compete with executive officials for effective control of the purse. While the Ways and Means and Finance committees provided coordination of spending and revenue decisions, Congress was unable to devise satisfactory means of enforcing its detailed spending preferences. It was evident that executive officials, particularly the president, could not realistically be excluded from all financial decision making by Congress, but the extreme emphasis on congressional prerogatives prevented any formal acknowledgment of executive responsibility.

The Appropriations Committees

The unprecedented growth in both federal expenditures and the federal debt during the Civil War prompted Congress to revise its budgetary process. By the end of the war, the federal debt was $2.7 billion, compared with less than $65 million in 1860. In 1866, interest on the debt alone was $133 million, a sum substantially above *total* federal expenditures during any prewar year.

In 1865 the House responded to the need to cut expenditures and to reduce the debt by establishing the Appropriations Committee, which assumed the responsibility for spending legislation previously exercised by the Committee on Ways and Means. Representative Samuel Cox, who sponsored this "division of labor," explained that the new committee would "investigate with nicest heed all matters connected with economy" and would be expected to restrain "extravagant and illegal appropriations."[8] According to Cox, the Ways and Means Committee alone could not cope with the financial emergency brought on by the war.

There were objections to the separation of finance and appropriations. Thaddeus Stevens, chairman of Ways and Means, complained that "the two subjects seem to be very properly connected" and had "some doubts as to the propriety of separating them."[9] But the House agreed to the division of committee duties, and two years later the Senate also established a Committee on Appropriations.* Congress also provided the Appropriations committees with effective controls over actual spending; statutory prohibitions wer² enacted to prevent transfers of funds and the carryover of unexpended funds from one year to the next. In addition, executive officials were forbidden to make current or future obligations in excess of actual appropriations.

Over the next decade, the Appropriations committees succeeded in significantly reducing federal expenditures. Between 1867 and 1875, an unbroken string of surpluses reduced the federal debt by $550 million. Annual nonmilitary expenditures, including veterans' pensions, increased by only $20 million during this period, while military spending and interest payments dropped by more than $100 million.

The centralization of authority over spending within committees that "guarded the Treasury" effectively restrained pressures to spend, but it also generated tension between these committees and the legislative or authorizing committees. The latter were typically more sympathetic to the funding needs of departments and agencies within their jurisdictions and resented the overriding emphasis on economy that characterized the Appropriations committees. In 1875 the House Appropriations Committee further alienated these committees by sponsoring a rules change, called the Holman amendment, that allowed an appropriations bill to change existing law if such action was germane and retrenched expenses, and thus autho-

---

*The House and Senate also established Banking committees, which assumed jurisdiction formerly exercised by the Ways and Means Committee in the House and the Finance Committee in the Senate.

rized the Appropriations Committee to invade virtually at will the jurisdictions of other committees in its desire to economize.

The counterattack against the Appropriations Committee, which had begun to incorporate a mass of general legislation into appropriations bills, began in the House in 1877, when the Commerce Committee wrested away control of the rivers and harbors appropriation bill, which was a prime example of pork-barrel legislation. In 1880 the Committee on Agriculture was granted similar authority over agriculture and forestry appropriations. Five years later the House voted overwhelmingly to remove six of the remaining twelve appropriations bills still controlled by the Appropriations Committee and to distribute them among the legislative committees.[10]

The debate over these changes in the appropriations process reflected congressional tension over spending policy. Supporters of the Appropriations Committee argued that fragmented control would inevitably lead to increased expenditures. Samuel J. Randall, chairman of the Appropriations Committee and a personal target of many of the committee's attackers, warned, "If you undertake to divide all these appropriations and have many committees where there ought to be but one, you will enter upon a path you cannot foresee the length of or the depth of until we find the Treasury of the country bankrupt." Randall went on to recount how, several years earlier, former Representative James A. Garfield had defined and defended the guardianship role of the Appropriations Committee:

> It is a fact within the experience of every member who has been here long that the Committee on Appropriations always finds itself confronted with a demand from each of the committees having a special subject in charge for larger appropriations than the Committee on Appropriations think should be made. There never was a time within my knowledge . . . when the Committee on Military Affairs did not resist the tendency of the Committee on Appropriations to cut down the appropriations for the Army. The Committee on Naval Affairs has always been found resisting the reduction of the naval appropriations bill. For this reason, I say that if each of these several committees had charge of getting up the appropriation bills on these several subjects, . . . they would outgrow the grasp of the House and there would be no unity in the appropriations of public money.

Randall noted that during the four years before his Appropriations Committee lost control of the rivers and harbors bill, annual appropriations had averaged $7.4 million; over the next four years, the average appropriation jumped to $13.6 million: "No one knows better than I do the pressure from within and from without in connection with river and harbor appropriation bills. There is hardly a member on this floor who does not feel it and know it. . . . *We ought to have some way . . . to protect us from ourselves.*"[11]

The economy mood of the House, however, had evaporated. One critic of the Appropriations Committee accurately summed up the prevailing sentiment that economy had been carried too far: "Increase of the expenditures has been the argument that has been used again and again. . . . I will ask is there a basis for this apprehension. I am not afraid of a reasonable expenditure. I am sometimes afraid that in the intense zeal of the gentleman who sits at the door of the Treasury in this House he forgets there is another word in the English language, and that parsimony sometimes passes for economy."[12]

A similar, if more gradual, disintegration of Appropriations Committee control occurred in the Senate. In 1877 the Senate Committee on Commerce gained jurisdiction over rivers and harbors appropriations. Efforts to distribute other appropriations bills to legislative committees gained momentum during the 1890s, and in 1899 the Senate removed six more bills from its Appropriations Committee.[13]

The budgetary "process" that arose out of these changes was chaotic. Since the various appropriations bills were considered by different committees and at different times, there was no way to coordinate spending decisions with one another or with revenue decisions. Moreover, spending pressures within Congress were extremely strong. Despite the efforts of such party leaders as Speakers Thomas Reed and Joseph G. Cannon to restrain spending, it was difficult to maintain limits on politically popular spending, notably rivers and harbors bills and military pensions. Occasionally the president stepped in with his veto power to check congressional spending. Grover Cleveland, for example, vetoed 241 general and private pension bills during his first term, and when he returned to the presidency in 1893, he continued to fight against abuses of military pensions.[14]

The fragmentation of the appropriations process signaled a decline of congressional guardianship. Members of Congress no doubt recognized that fiscal responsibility was necessary, but they also were aware that federal spending provided benefits to their constituents which could serve their electoral interests. It was not entirely coincidental that the push for higher spending accelerated as membership turnover in Congress began to drop dramatically. Between 1875 and 1901, for example, the percentage of first-term House members dropped from 58 percent to 24 percent.[15] By the turn of the century, the average congressional tenure was close to double the pre–Civil War level.[16] Congress was becoming a career for many members, and they naturally became increasingly preoccupied with reelection strategies. If spending programs had electoral benefits, the drive for economy was likely to be less than overwhelming.

The combined effect of a fragmented appropriations process and electorally related spending decisions increased expenditures. Table 2.1 shows expenditures by ten-year periods between the Civil War and World War I. When the appropriations process was dominated by the Appropriations committees, as it was between 1866 and 1885, total expenditures declined by more than 20 percent, and nonmilitary expenditures grew only slightly. Later, as the power of the Appropriations Committee was reduced, nonmilitary expenditures increased sharply. Outlays for veterans' pensions, for example, more than doubled in the ten years after 1885.

In fiscal 1894 the federal budget registered the first deficit since the Civil War. During the next fifteen years, ten more deficits were recorded, and criticism of Congress increased accordingly. The

Table 2.1. Federal military, nonmilitary, and interest expenditures, 1866–1915, by decade (in billions of dollars)

	Nonmilitary Expenditures				
	Veterans' compensation and pensions	Other	Military expenditures	Interest	Total
1866–75	$0.3	$0.7	$1.1	$1.2	$3.3
1876–85	0.5	0.7	0.6	0.8	2.6
1886–95	1.1	1.1	0.7	0.4	3.2
1896–1905	1.4	1.3	1.9	0.3	5.0
1906–15	1.6	1.9	3.1	0.2	6.8
Change	$+1.3	$+1.2	$+2.0	$−1.0	$+3.5

SOURCE: Data from U.S. Department of Commerce, Bureau of the Census, *Historical Statistics of the United States, Colonial Times to 1957* (Washington, D.C.: Government Printing Office, 1960), p. 718.

"spending heyday" had become Congress' "national scandal."[17] Representative Randall's prediction had proved accurate.

Congress moved slowly and reluctantly to revise its budgetary procedures. In 1905 and 1906 it took the first step, passing legislation that required executive agencies to apportion appropriations during the fiscal year, in an attempt to curb the widespread practice of spending all appropriations before the fiscal year was over, leaving Congress with little choice but to provide additional funds.[18] In 1909 Congress authorized the secretary of the treasury to recommend reductions in expenditures or increases in revenues if deficits were forecast. The following year Congress provided funding for President William Howard Taft's Commission on Economy and Efficiency, which was charged with making recommendations to improve the budgetary process. Although the commission's recommendations for a national budget system were ignored by Congress, they did focus attention on critical weaknesses in the existing process. The commission stated that a presidential budget would provide the executive branch with administrative control and political responsibility. According to the commission, an annual presidential budget would give Congress a "definite, well-considered, comprehensive program" on which to act.[19]

Institutional jealousies and partisan differences blocked Taft's attempt to implement a presidential budget, but there was considerable support for efforts to improve control of federal spending. Both the Democratic and the Republican party platforms of 1916 contained proposals for budgetary reform. The Republican party supported immediate adoption of an executive budget, while the Democrats advocated as an interim step the restoration of spending authority to the Appropriations committees.

World War I generated spending levels and financial pressures that strengthened the case for revision of the budgetary process. Spending rose from less than $750 million in 1915 to about $18.5 billion in 1919, and debts incurred during the war exceeded $23 billion. The prewar need for economy was supplemented by the postwar requirement for management and reduction of the federal debt. In 1919 Woodrow Wilson's administration declared its support for a comprehensive executive budget, and with eventual passage of a national budget ensured, Congress decided to reorganize its own procedures.

In 1920 the House restored exclusive spending powers to its Appropriations Committee, a move that was bitterly resisted by the leaders of several legislative committees. A spokesman for the Agriculture Committee denounced it as a return to an especially "malignant form" of "autocracy."[20] Representative James W. Good, chief sponsor of the proposal, admitted that the Appropriations Committee was unpopular, but declared that if "it becomes popular I for one shall question the quality of its work."[21] He went on to distinguish the purposes of the different committees:

> A legislative committee is appointed to guard the interests of a particular department committed to its care . . . even to the extent of taking up new projects that involve additional expenditures at a time when there should be rigid economy and a retrenchment in expenditures. This is not true of the Committee on Appropriations. It has no particular department to defend, no particular project to advance. It stands as the impartial arbiter of all the legislative committees.[22]

The following year the Budget and Accounting Act was signed into law, giving the president statutory responsibility for preparing and submitting a national budget to Congress. And in 1922 the Senate followed, returning all appropriations bills to the jurisdiction of the Appropriations Committee.*

The recentralization of spending authority within Congress was a significant step, although perhaps less significant than its advocates intended. In the House, for example, the original plan was to have the Appropriations Committee combine the individual bills considered by its subcommittees into one measure to be considered by the House at one time.[23] Instead, Congress acted on various spending bills one at a time. Nevertheless, by attempting to revive strong Appropriations committees, Congress was once again accepting the responsibility for guardianship of the budget. The struggle between

---

*The Senate also provided, however, that members of designated authorizing committees could have ex officio seats on their counterpart Appropriations subcommittees. This practice was eliminated by the 1977 Senate reorganization, which restructured the committee system and limited the number of committees and subcommittees on which senators could serve. Before this change, nearly half of the Senate directly participated in Appropriations Committee work, since the regular committee membership was supplemented by three ex officio members from each of eight legislative committees. See Richard F. Fenno, Jr., *Congressmen in Committees* (Boston: Little, Brown, 1973), p. 149.

the authorizing committees and the Appropriations committees appeared to be settled in favor of the latter.

The Deterioration of Spending Controls

During the 1920s, both the executive branch and Congress used the budget strictly to control expenditures. The national consensus that government spending should be restrained and the public debt reduced governed budget policy until the New Deal, when the Roosevelt administration, in a bold new step, adopted a policy of planned deficits in an attempt to bolster the economy. Major changes in the organization and authority of the Bureau of the Budget also facilitated the use of the budget for presidential policy leadership.

Congress did not respond immediately to these extensions of presidential power. Unable to define its own budgetary role during an economic crisis clearly, Congress granted the president greater authority over federal spending. Detailed or line-item appropriations were gradually replaced by broader appropriations categories, contingency funds were established for presidential use, transfers were allowed, and emergency appropriations were frequently provided, particularly during World War II.

Dissatisfaction with the congressional budgetary process was growing, however. During the 1920s, the emphasis on retrenching expenditures together with an expanding economy had produced large yearly budget surpluses. Beginning in fiscal 1931, however, the federal budget fell into a pattern of annual deficits that continued through the decade and reached unprecedented proportions during World War II.

Thus, just as the spending increases and debt accumulations of the Civil War and World War I led Congress to revise its budgetary procedures, World War II provided the stimulus for another attempt at budgetary reform. As part of the 1946 Legislative Reorganization Act, Congress established a legislative budget that was designed, according to its co-sponsor Representative Mike Monroney, finally to "give the Congress an over-all viewpoint on its fiscal policy."[24]

For years we have been operating our revenue-sharing committees and our revenue-spending committees completely and apart from any relationship one with the other. . . . Today we start out without any idea of how much we will spend, or where the money is to come from. We wind up the year wondering how many billions we are in the red or in the black. Surely it is not asking too much to consider these two important things, income and outgo, together.[25]

The Legislative Budget

The Legislative Reorganization Act created the Joint Committee on the Legislative Budget, which included the members of the Ways and Means and Finance committees and the House and Senate Appropriations committees. These four committees were to meet at the beginning of each session to prepare estimates of total receipts and expenditures for the fiscal year commencing on July 1. By February 15, their report, along with a concurrent resolution setting an overall spending limit, was to be submitted to the House and Senate for consideration. Spending could not exceed estimated receipts unless the resolution also specified a corresponding increase in the public debt, or in the event that a budget surplus was estimated, the Joint Committee was to recommend a reduction in the public debt.

Congress attempted to enact legislative budgets in 1947, 1948, and 1949, but its revenue and spending estimates were often inaccurate, spending ceilings were violated, and the House and Senate repeatedly disagreed over the content of the concurrent resolutions;[26] as a result, the procedure proved unworkable. The early deadline for reporting a spending ceiling was a major problem, as it did not allow the Joint Committee adequate time to study the president's budget and to specify where budget cuts should be made. And as no provisions were made for amending the ceiling, Congress was unable to take into account subsequent changes in economic conditions or other circumstances affecting the budget as it made its decisions on spending and revenue bills.[27]

In 1947 the House and Senate could not agree on the size of the reduction in the president's budget or on the disposal of the anticipated surplus, and no legislative budget was enacted. In 1948 the House and Senate agreed on a $2.5 billion reduction in the president's budget requests. Where the cuts were to be made, however, was not specified, and Congress then breached its own spending ceiling by appropriating $6 billion more than the legislative budget allowed. The following year Congress was unable to meet the February 15 deadline and changed it to May 1. Since most appropriations bills had been passed by that date, no legislative budget was adopted. By 1950 the legislative budget concept had been abandoned.[28]

The legislative budget procedure failed because of political as well as technical difficulties. The congressional parties disagreed with respect to the size and substance of budget cuts and the merits of tax cuts or debt reduction.[29] Moreover, the House Appropriations Committee was hostile to the legislative budget procedure. Representative Clarence Cannon, chairman of the Appropriations Committee, called it a "well-meant but hopeless proposal," which required a joint committee to set budget totals without adequate study or expertise. The process, he claimed, was akin to picking a figure out of the air and "merely the expression of a pious hope."[30]

Omnibus Appropriation Bill

Representative Cannon's solution for Congress' need "to exercise its important power of the purse with care and wisdom" was the consolidated or omnibus appropriation bill.[31] In 1949 Cannon reorganized the Appropriations subcommittees, restricting each committee member to one subcommittee and each subcommittee to one appropriation bill, revising the staffing and reporting system, and permitting all subcommittees to sit simultaneously. All of the annual appropriations bills were then reported out of committee and passed by the House within ten weeks after subcommittee hearings began. The next year Cannon announced that the committee would abandon the practice of reporting separate appropriations bills at different times and would submit the annual appropriations in an omnibus bill. The actions of the various subcommittees would be coordinated and the actual omnibus bill drafted by an eight-member executive committee within the Appropriations Committee.

During the spring of 1950 the House and Senate Appropriations subcommittees held parallel hearings on the various fiscal 1951 spending bills to facilitate preparation of the omnibus bill. The House Appropriations Committee was able to gain House approval of the omnibus bill on May 10, although Senate delays held up final passage until late August. Congress still completed action on the budget earlier than in previous years, and the omnibus bill cut more than $2 billion from President Truman's budget. This reduction was soon erased, however, by deficiency and supplemental appropriations during fiscal 1951, with a major spending increase resulting from the outbreak of the Korean war.

While Representative Cannon considered the omnibus approach a success, the members of his committee were less enthusiastic. Subcommittee chairmen viewed the omnibus bill procedure as a threat to the power and independence of their subcommittees, and in 1951 the committee voted to abandon it. Later attempts to revive it were unsuccessful.

Over the next two decades, other revisions in the congressional budgetary process—such as separate budget sessions, joint budget committees, and expenditure ceilings—were proposed, but none was both acceptable and effective. The major responsibility for controlling federal spending continued to rest with the Appropriations committees. And the Appropriations committees continued their traditional practice of reporting the more than one dozen spending bills at separate times.

Limiting Appropriations Control

The failure of the legislative budget and omnibus appropriation experiments left Congress without formal mechanisms to set budget totals and coordinate decisions on revenues and expenditures. Throughout the 1950s and 1960s, however, the Appropriations committees, especially the House committee, consistently held spending below the levels requested by the executive branch.[32] The committees generally considered the president's budget to represent an upper limit on spending, assuming that executive agencies could be expected to advocate maximum increases in spending and that the executive budget would reflect these spending pressures.[33] According to the dominant sentiments of Appropriations Committee members, their role as "guardians of the Treasury" meant assisting Congress by restraining its appetite for spending.

As Table 2.2 indicates, budget guardianship was characteristic of the appropriations process for almost two decades. Almost 90 percent of all regular appropriations bills for fiscal years 1952–69 reduced appropriations below the amounts requested by the president. Each year this action produced a net reduction, often substantial, in total appropriations. Most amounts requested for supplemental and

Table 2.2. Congressional increases and reductions in appropriations requested by president in regular bills and in supplemental and deficiency bills, fiscal years 1952–69

Fiscal year	Regular appropriations bills				Net increase or decrease, supplemental and deficiency appropriations bills (billions of dollars)
	Number reduced under president's budget	Number increased over president's budget	Number unchanged	Net increase or decrease (billions of dollars)	
1952	11	0	0	$ − 2.2	$ − 2.5
1953	10	0	0	− 6.4	− 2.2
Truman estimates	11	0	1	− 12.4	− 1.7
1954 Eisenhower estimates	11	0	1	− 3.1	− 1.4
1955	8	2	1	− 2.2	− 0.4
1956	10	3	0	− 1.4	− 0.7
1957	7	6	0	− 0.5	+ 0.3
1958	14	0	0	− 4.1	− 0.4
1959	10	4	0	− 0.1	− 0.4
1960	14	1	0	− 1.5	− 0.4
1961	11	1	0	− 0.2	0.0
1962	12	1	0	− 1.4	− 3.6
1963	11	1	0	− 3.8	− 0.9
1964	12	0	0	− 6.3	− 0.2
1965	12	0	0	− 3.7	− 0.5
1966	12	0	0	− 1.7	− 0.8
1967	10	2	0	− 0.5	− 0.4
1968	14	0	0	− 5.5	− 0.4
1969	13	0	0	− 13.9	− 0.7

SOURCE: Compiled from *Congressional Quarterly Weekly Report,* various years.

deficiency appropriations (several such requests were ordinarily made each year) were also reduced. Only once, in fiscal 1957, did congressional actions result in a net increase in the spending authorized by these emergency bills. If we look solely at the appropriations process, it appears that the fiscal conservatism of the Appropriations committees was governing Congress' decisions on spending.

In reality the situation was more complex. In the early 1950s most requests for federal spending went through the Appropriations committees. Two decades later, less than one-half of the budget was under annual review by these committees, and the portion that could actually be controlled through the appropriations process was considerably smaller. Over time the effect on the total budget of the cuts made by the Appropriations committees diminished.

The basis for this change was the rapid growth in uncontrollable spending, particularly entitlements. There had always been some spending that could not be controlled on an annual basis (for example, interest on the federal debt), but uncontrolled spending escalated rapidly during the 1960s and early 1970s. By 1967 almost 60 percent of the budget was classified as relatively uncontrollable; five years later this figure had climbed to over 70 percent. The composition of the uncontrollable share of the budget was also changing. Payments for individuals (such as social security, public assistance, and other entitlements) accounted for approximately 45 percent of all uncontrollable spending in 1967. This proportion increased to almost 60 percent by the mid-1970s. By fiscal 1973 over 40 percent of the *entire* federal budget was accounted for by payments for individuals.

The changing composition of the budget represented an important shift of power within Congress. The authorizing committees had gained control over the bulk of federal spending.[34] In the 1880s the authorizing committees had directly attacked the jurisdiction of the Appropriations committees. In the 1960s they adopted a more gradual and subtle strategy, circumventing the appropriations process. By sponsoring legislation that automatically created financial commitments—such as increases in social security benefits and various entitlements—the authorizing committees had once again decentralized control of spending.

This shift in power did not mean that the congressional budgetary process was "out of control." In fact, Congress determined the level and composition of spending, but it was becoming increasingly responsive to those committees that had traditionally advocated spending. As long as the Appropriations committees were responsible for most federal spending, the lack of coordination within the budgetary process was not a critical problem. The guardianship role assumed by these committees and the opportunities for informal coordination among their subcommittees served to restrain pressures for spending. The authorizing committees had no guardianship role. Indeed, they were expected to be proponents of agencies and programs within their jurisdictions. With responsibilities for spending dispersed among many committees likely to promote increased spending for their special charges, the possibility of even informal coordination was slim. Moreover, since the growth of uncontrollable spending was increasingly concentrated in the "payments for individuals" category, Congress was making long-term commitments to expenditures that were politically impossible to reduce. In effect, more and more of any future budgetary growth was being either explicitly or implicitly "reserved" for uncontrollable spending.

Once again Congress had demonstrated its ambivalence toward spending—general sentiments for economy and reductions on the one hand and intense support for particular spending programs on the other. The power of the Appropriations committees fluctuated accordingly. When Congress was dominated by general sentiments for retrenchment—for example, after the Civil War, World War I, and World War II—the Appropriations committees became extremely influential. As these sentiments waned, and they inevitably did, Congress responded more favorably to the spending psychology of its authorizing committees.

When Congress becomes an advocate of spending, however, it risks paying a heavy institutional price. And this is precisely what occurred during the early 1970s. The Nixon administration charged Congress with fiscal irresponsibility and challenged its power of the purse in an unprecedentedly broad fashion. The apparent success of these attacks provided the immediate stimulus for another attempt at congressional reform.

Unlike earlier efforts to reform the budgetary process, the 1974 budget act was not aimed simply at cutting spending (although this was the hope of a good number of its supporters). Its purpose was to strengthen Congress' influence over budget policy. This could mean higher or lower spending than a president desired, larger or smaller deficits than he recommended, and similar or dissimilar priorities from those he advanced.

Nevertheless, beneath the lofty purposes of the 1974 budget act lurked the still unresolved question whether legislators could deal responsibly with fiscal matters, especially spending issues. In the past, Congress' inability to maintain effective control over spending had damaged its image and reputation and promoted advocacy, even within Congress, of greater presidential authority over spending. For any congressional budget reform to succeed in protecting the power of the purse, it would eventually have to demonstrate what had long eluded Congress—stable, effective spending controls.

CHAPTER 3

Redefining Budget Control

An examination of Congress' early experiments with budget reform reveals similarities among them. The reform efforts shared a common and single objective: control over spending. Each was a response to the financial emergency created by a great war. Each sought to tighten internal spending controls in order to cut postwar budgets and reduce the debt. Each eventually succumbed to decentralizing forces that boosted congressional spending.

The 1974 budget act was different. Although Congress was uneasy about the great increases in spending and persistent deficits, its overriding concern was to protect Congress' budgetary powers against incessant attacks by Richard Nixon's administration. In the aftermath of the 1972 Nixon landslide, impoundments mounted, and the executive branch justified them with expanding claims of authority. Prominent legislators concluded that Congress had to strengthen its control of the budget in order to avoid continued encroachments by the executive; budget reform became a matter of institutional self-defense.

The meaning of "budget control," however, was unclear. Fiscal conservatives used the term to mean reductions in spending and balanced budgets. In their view, spending ceilings and internal controls had only one objective, to limit congressional spending. Congressional Democrats, particularly liberals, were interested in budget control as a means of countering the president's impoundments of funds and extending Congress' influence over fiscal policy and budget priorities. From their vantage point, more effective congressional budget control did not mean (and probably would not mean) lower spending but rather the ability to enforce spending preferences more effectively.

54

Because of these differences, initiatives toward congressional budget reform and impoundment control were originally separate, and each eventually bogged down. Finally they were united to break the deadlock. The result was a fairly neutral reform with respect to congressional spending (the spending-control provisions of the original budget-reform plan were substantially weakened in the course of negotiations), but a bold attempt to match presidential policy leadership.

The Prereform System Spending Ceilings

In the final years of Lyndon B. Johnson's presidency, Congress insisted on annual spending ceilings. Despite the questionable effectiveness of such ceilings, Congress resorted to them again during the first two years of the Nixon administration. Congressional enthusiasm for spending limits diminished, however, as pressures for domestic spending increased. Indeed, the immediate catalyst for budget reform was Nixon's demand for a ceiling on spending in fiscal 1973, which Congress refused to enact. This episode further discredited statutory ceilings that depended on cooperation between the president and Congress.

Budget Policy under Johnson

The Johnson years produced major shifts in budget policy. Budget growth was relatively low during the first half of the 1960s. Then the combined effects of the war in Southeast Asia and the Great Society programs caused the budget to expand rapidly. The Johnson administration eventually recommended tax increases to finance that expansion, but Congress chose at first to rely exclusively on a statutory spending ceiling. After a year-long dispute between the White House and Congress, a ceiling was enacted that applied a percentage cut to most controllable programs during fiscal 1968 and allowed the president to decide where specific reductions would be made.

Not everyone in Congress approved of this solution. Using language that others would resurrect five years later, George Mahon, chairman of the House Appropriations Committee, deplored the "abdication by Congress," which gave "the Executive the final authority to make reductions of several billions of dollars . . . without giving him any guidance." This state of affairs, declared Mahon, was "completely contrary to the time-honored claim that Congress has control of the purse." Perhaps uncharitably, Mahon went on to point out that just as Congress was congratulating itself on the spending ceiling, it was also approving "additional authorizations right and left . . . we have the audacity to talk about cuts, cuts, cuts, and saving money while we go on authorizing additional expenditures."[1]

Congress set a spending ceiling again in fiscal 1969, although this time it agreed to enact Lyndon Johnson's tax surcharge as well. Congress wrote in protections for some popular controllable programs as part of the ceiling and, as in fiscal 1968, provided a general exemption for uncontrollables. Even though unanticipated growth of the uncontrollables offset much of the anticipated savings from the ceiling, the growth of outlays was held to about 3 percent. And with a revenue boost from the tax surcharge, the budget registered its first surplus since 1960.

Although the 1968 and 1969 ceilings restrained spending, in general ceilings were not an effective solution. They did not govern uncontrollable spending, whose budgetary impact was widening. As in fiscal 1969, Congress was susceptible to pleas for favored controllable programs, thus concentrating the burden of spending reductions on a narrowing slice of the budget. For ceilings to be practical, additional discretion over spending had to be conferred on the executive branch. Lyndon Johnson did not use this authority to cripple programs that were popular in Congress. But when Richard Nixon became president, he took a decidedly less conciliatory approach, and Congress began to reconsider the boundaries of executive discretion over spending.

The Nixon Challenge

For both fiscal 1970 and fiscal 1971, President Nixon recommended low-growth budgets with small surpluses. Congress seemed to agree that restrictive budgets were necessary, passing spending ceilings that roughly matched the president's totals. The ceilings turned out, however, to be unrealistically low. Uncontrollable programs grew more rapidly than anyone had anticipated, and congressional add-ons to presidential budget requests pushed spending even higher. Nixon's revenue projections, in turn, were much too optimistic. Instead of the consecutive surpluses that had been projected, the budget registered deficits of nearly $3 billion in fiscal 1970 and $23 billion in fiscal 1971.

Outlay totals alone, however, did not account for the rapidly widening breach between the White House and the Democratic-controlled Congress. It was not just the size of the budget but the details that were at issue. Congress was not about to follow Nixon's lead in limiting the growth of spending on social welfare, nor was it willing to settle for modest cuts in the defense budget. It was not inclined to pursue the administration's recommendations for program cuts and terminations. Nixon's characteristic response was to attack Congress for its lack of fiscal discipline and to use vetoes and impoundments to dramatize his resistance to the pressure toward increased spending exerted by Congress. Although he suggested that part of the problem was "the hoary and traditional procedure of the Congress which . . . permits action on the various spending programs as if they were unrelated and independent actions,"[2] Nixon continually cast his budget dispute in partisan terms, attempting to brand congressional Democrats as the fiscally irresponsible culprits.

The Election-Year Controversy. Midway through his first term, in response to the recession that took hold in 1970, Nixon announced a shift in policy from restrictive to stimulative budgets. The change to an expansionary fiscal policy failed to resolve conflicts between the president and Congress over spending, but the controversies that surrounded the fiscal 1972 budget were relatively mild compared with those that occurred the following year. Indeed, the fiscal 1972 budget was overshadowed by the imposition of wage and price controls and related anti-inflation measures that the president announced on August 15, 1971.

When the fiscal 1972 deficit started to run higher than expected, Nixon stepped up his attacks on Congress. His budget message for fiscal 1973 warned that inflation would worsen "if Congress adds to my recommendations for domestic spending as it did last year." He also cautioned Congress against "the dangerous course of trying to match domestic spending increases with cuts in vitally needed defense programs."[3] The shaping of election-year budget politics was well under way, and Nixon dominated it.

Early in the spring, the administration raised its spending estimates for fiscal 1973 to $250 billion, and this figure came to define the budget debates leading up to the fall election. As Nixon no doubt expected, congressional add-ons for fiscal 1973 were substantial. In June, Congress passed a 20 percent increase in social security benefits. Other domestic legislative initiatives threatened to raise fiscal 1973 spending even further above the $250 billion mark, despite the expected sharp cut in the amount requested by the president for defense.[4] On July 26 Nixon called on Congress to enact a $250 billion ceiling and left no doubt that unless it did so, congressional spending would be a campaign issue. Administration spokesmen provided a taste of what was to come by charging that failure to limit spending would lead to tax increases and higher inflation. Congressional Democrats called this charge political blackmail but were hard-pressed to fashion a response.

Nixon's initiative was particularly effective in the House. Despite strenuous opposition from the Democratic leadership, the House voted by a wide margin to grant the president's request for unrestricted authority to cut controllable programs in order to stay within the $250-billion ceiling. The Senate proved less pliant. It would not agree to unrestricted authority and insisted that guidelines be part of any ceiling. The impasse was never resolved. Congress did agree, however, to establish a joint study committee to examine spending-control problems.

The president's reaction to defeat of the spending ceiling was predictable. Shortly after the Senate rejected it, Nixon vetoed an authorization of $25 billion to control water pollution and promised he would unilaterally limit spending under the bill even if Congress overrode his veto. Congress promptly did so, and Nixon eventually impounded nearly 40 percent of the allotments for fiscal years 1973–75. On October 27 nine more measures, including a reworked appropriation for the departments of Labor and Health, Education, and Welfare which had been vetoed several months earlier, were rejected in pocket vetoes. In a combined veto message, the White House declared that these measures would "breach the budget" and were therefore unacceptable.[5] Over the next several months the administration enforced the ceiling that Congress had rejected and implemented the program cuts it had ignored by impounding the funds authorized for a wide variety of domestic programs.

The Retreat. In the midst of congressional outcries about a constitutional crisis, Nixon submitted a fiscal 1974 budget that guaranteed additional confrontations. As part of this "dramatic document," Nixon insisted that Congress enact a "rigid ceiling on spending" before approving any new bills. He proposed numerous reductions in "poorly conceived and hastily put together" social programs and promised there would be "very little room for the creation of new programs . . . in 1975 and *no room for the postponement of the reductions and terminations proposed in this budget.*"[6]

During the first several months of 1973, Congress could not fashion a coherent response. Bills to reform the budget process and control impoundments were stalled. The House and Senate passed versions of the spending ceilings Nixon had demanded, but these measures were coupled with impoundment bills that had no chance for passage. Five spending bills were vetoed during 1973, and all five vetoes were sustained. Congress continued its battle over spending priorities, reducing the amount requested by the administration for defense and voting the customary add-ons for domestic programs, ignoring the cuts Nixon had proposed.

Congress remained on the defensive until the Watergate investigations began to take their toll. While neither Nixon nor Congress was a decisive victor in the struggle over actual budget policy, Congress was at a serious disadvantage in the public debate. Nixon vetoed, threatened to veto, and impounded with considerable skill, and in 1973 the Democrats in Congress were uncertain about the eventual electoral repercussions of the spending issue. They had survived the 1972 election quite handily despite Nixon's enormous victory, but there were legitimate fears about 1974 and beyond. By the end of 1973, however, Nixon had suffered a dramatic decline in public standing, which was reflected in the following year's budget. It bore little resemblance to the aggressive document of 1972. Its tone and substance were conciliatory, and it demanded no spending ceilings or program cuts.

Congress survived the Nixon challenge, but its weaknesses had been amply demonstrated. Now legislators saw an opportunity to remedy those weaknesses and actually to extend Congress' authority. Instead of having to match the president's fiscal austerity or be branded irresponsible spenders, Congress could develop and justify alternative budgets. The days of spending ceilings that depended on the president's "good faith" were over.

The Changing Road to Reform

At the height of the battle between Nixon and Congress over the budget, more than 250 bills and resolutions were introduced to revise the budgetary process. The early reform effort was dominated by two initiatives: the plan for internal organization and procedures drawn up by the Joint Study Committee on Budget Control and the proposals for control of impoundments developed by House and Senate committees. Each of these plans was quickly enmeshed in partisan and ideological debates.

The Proposal of the Joint Study Committee

The Joint Study Committee on Budget Control, which Congress had agreed to set up after the debacle of the fiscal 1973 spending ceiling, moved surprisingly quickly and in April 1973 reported a comprehensive package of changes in the budgetary process. The Joint Study Committee's membership was drawn almost exclusively from the Ways and Means, Finance, and House and Senate Appropriations committees, and its report soon came under attack for being too protective of those committees and, perhaps more important, too biased toward spending controls. The Joint Study Committee did succeed, however, in defining the general organizational and procedural directions that Congress would eventually follow.

The Joint Study Committee did not recommend that committee jurisdictions be abolished or restructured, nor, in deference to House sensibilities, did it suggest a return to the joint budget committee that had been set up in the late 1940s. It proposed, instead, separate House and Senate Budget committees that would be responsible for preparing annual congressional budgets to guide but not supplant the normal authorizing and appropriations processes. Their membership would be drawn primarily but not exclusively from the revenue and Appropriations committees, and they would be assisted by a joint professional staff, which would provide budget information and analysis independent of the executive's Office of Management and Budget.

The major procedural innovation proposed by the Joint Study Committee was the setting of annual budget totals by Congress. At the beginning of each session, the authorizing and Appropriations committees would submit their spending recommendations to the Budget committees, which would then report a concurrent resolution setting ceilings on total outlays and budget authority, a revenue floor, and the corresponding level of the public debt. The resolution would, in addition, provide spending subceilings for individual appropriations bills. Congress would have until May 1 to adopt a resolution. If it failed to do so, the president's budget would serve as the ceiling. During floor debate, amendments would be limited by a "rule of consistency": any attempt to increase spending in a given area above the Budget committees' recommendations would have to specify equivalent cuts in other areas or increases in taxes and the public debt. A second concurrent resolution could be reported later in the year, but this provision was intended only for emergencies. The Joint Study Committee assumed that the original spending ceiling and the balance between spending and revenue would be firm, and it included a reconciliation provision whereby adjustments could be forced in congressional spending and tax bills to ensure compliance.

Finally, the Joint Study Committee called for strict controls on future uncontrollable spending. Noting that "backdoor or mandatory spending . . . has been proved in practice to be more difficult to control than spending through the regular appropriations process,"[7] it recommended that any future enactments of permanent appropriations be routed through the Appropriations committees and that new entitlements or other forms of back-door spending (such as contract authority or borrowing authority) be specifically limited by appropriations legislation. Back-door spending would still occur, but it would be much more difficult for authorizing committees to push new uncontrollable spending programs successfully.

The Joint Study Committee was clearly in favor of spending control and even assumed that, since Congress would now be fully capable of restraining spending, impoundment controls would become unnecessary. While the Joint Study Committee voted its report out unanimously, strong opposition soon surfaced, especially among congressional liberals.

The Liberal Reaction. Shortly after the Joint Study Committee issued its final report, the Democratic Study Group (DSG), an organization of liberal House Democrats, issued a detailed attack on virtually all of its recommendations. According to the DSG, the budget-resolution procedure was flawed, the staffing initiative was inadequate, and tax policies were slighted in favor of spending curbs. The DSG warned that membership restrictions for the Budget committees would guarantee domination by conservative Democrats and Republicans from those committees. Once the budget resolution was written, the rule of consistency would make it hard to challenge the Budget committees on the floor. With more than a hint of exaggeration, the DSG concluded that the Joint Study Committee's plan "would lock the congressional budgetary process into a conservative mold for generations to come."[8]

In the Senate, complaints were similar. Walter F. Mondale of Minnesota stated, "Priorities of a budget are fundamentally political questions and should be the product of open debate—not committee action."[9] With many other Democrats, Mondale favored tight congressional controls on executive impoundments but was unenthusiastic about parallel controls on spending.

Liberals in both the House and the Senate feared that conservatives might dominate a new budget process and use the justification of fiscal responsibility to cut spending programs that they disliked. Liberals believed that rigid spending ceilings, adopted early in the session, would provide the perfect vehicle for such cuts. As a result, critics of the Joint Study Committee's approach preferred to abandon comprehensive reform entirely and concentrate exclusively on impoundment controls. If this tactic were unsuccessful, they were prepared to fight for more representative and less powerful Budget committees, more flexible spending ceilings, and less stringent checks on back-door spending.

The Impoundment Connection

With Democrat Sam Ervin of North Carolina directing the effort, the Senate took the lead in responding to the Nixon impoundments. Soon after the 93d Congress convened, Ervin introduced S. 373, an impoundment-control bill; he organized joint hearings of his Judiciary subcommittee and the Government Operations Ad Hoc Subcommittee on Impoundment of Funds.[10] Two months later, S. 373 was reported to the floor.

Ervin's bill required that all impoundments be reported to Congress. The comptroller general would then determine whether an impoundment was for routine managerial purposes, as authorized by law. Routine impoundments would be allowed to stand, but all others would require congressional approval by concurrent resolution, or else they would terminate automatically sixty days after being reported. Congress could also force the immediate freeing of funds within the sixty-day period by concurrent resolution.

The House had meanwhile signaled its commitment to a more modest check. Early in March, the House Democratic leadership had endorsed a proposal introduced by George Mahon, chairman of the Appropriations Committee, which required both the House and the Senate to disapprove objectionable impoundments within sixty days after notification by the president. Unless Congress acted to disapprove, the impoundment would stand. This was the reverse of the Senate procedure, and it was expected that presidential impoundments would fare considerably better under the Mahon bill. In any case, House conferees repeatedly blocked the Senate's attempts to attach its impoundment-control plan to unrelated legislation already in conference.

The House Rules Committee, which also had jurisdiction over the Joint Study Committee's proposals, opened its hearings on impoundment control on March 28. Approximately three months later it reported out H.R. 8480, which differed from both the Mahon and the Senate plans. The Rules Committee's proposal provided for a one-house veto of any presidential impoundment, rather than the two-house or concurrent-resolution plan Mahon had specified. Unlike the Senate-passed measure, however, H.R. 8480 allowed impoundments to stand unless either the House or the Senate passed resolutions disapproving them.*

Republican opposition to impoundment legislation was more intense in the House than in the Senate, and House Democrats were less united than their Senate counterparts. The Republicans therefore launched a concerted effort to block or weaken any impoundment bill or, failing that, to tie it to comprehensive budget-reform legislation. Within the Rules Committee the Republican minority was not successful. Representative John Anderson's request for a rule to allow budget-reform legislation to be added to H.R. 8480 on the floor was rejected by committee Democrats, and he also failed to get

*The House bill also differed from the Senate version in that it contained no exemptions for routine impoundments and provided for referral of impoundment notices to the Appropriations committees rather than allowing direct floor action.

Democrats to agree to a definite timetable for reporting out a separate budget-reform bill. When debate on H.R. 8480 opened July 24, Anderson and minority leader Gerald Ford pressed Rules Committee leaders for a pledge that hearings on budget reform would be held promptly. Richard Bolling of Missouri, the floor manager for H.R. 8480, agreed that hearings would be scheduled on the Joint Study Committee's budget-reform plan, but insisted that impoundment could be treated as a separate issue and should be acted on immediately.

Bolling finally managed to gain House approval of H.R. 8480. Anderson's amendment to replace the one-house veto with the requirement for a concurrent resolution was rejected by one vote, but a Republican-sponsored amendment limiting the impoundment-control provisions of H.R. 8480 to the 1974 fiscal year "in order to keep the pressure on for budgetary reform" was adopted.[11] The obvious divisions among House Democrats, the differences between House and Senate over procedure, and the certainty of a presidential veto blocked further progress on impoundment-control legislation. Anderson's arguments for tying together impoundment controls and budget reform had proved persuasive to the House, and when the Rules Committee finally took up the Joint Study Committee's report in earnest, this linkage was adopted, helping to broaden House support for the eventual budget bill.*

House Action

The Rules Committee opened hearings on budget-reform legislation during mid-July 1973, and additional hearings were held inter-

---

*Joel Havemann suggests that Bolling was responsible for linking impoundment controls and budget reform, and that he did so to gain liberal support for budget reform (*Congress and the Budget* [Bloomington: Indiana University Press, 1978], pp. 30–31). It appears, however, that House Republicans, especially John Anderson, were responsible for this approach. When S. 373 was being considered in the Senate, several Republicans on the Government Operations Committee had argued that congressional budget reform should take precedence over anti-impoundment legislation. Since Senate Democrats were united against this approach and Republicans were split, the argument was not very effective. In the House the situation was quite different. Democrats were divided over the appropriate procedure to be used to control impoundments, and many Democrats also believed that impoundment controls were not a sufficient response to Congress' problems in handling the budget. Given these divisions and the major split with the Senate, House Republicans were in a strong position to push for a comprehensive budget bill. When the one-year impoundment limitation proposed by Republican H. John Heinz of Pennsylvania was adopted, it became quite clear that the Democratic leadership had no choice but to accept the Republican approach. In addition, the linkage lessened the threat of a presidential veto.

mittently through September. Committee markup began in October, and a substitute bill, H.R. 7130, was reported to the House on November 20 and passed on December 5.

While the emphasis of the Joint Study Committee's proposal had been on stronger congressional controls on spending, the Rules Committee defined the objectives of budget reform more broadly. "The dispersion of budget responsibility within Congress," the committee concluded, "has left it unprepared for what are perhaps the two main purposes of the budget process: to manage the economy and to determine public priorities." The committee was adamant, however, that Congress should not try to duplicate the centralization of the executive branch. Budget committees should not be granted "extraordinary power in the making of budget policies." Budget ceilings should not prevent Congress "from expressing its will on spending policy."[12]

The legislation sponsored by the Rules Committee was neutral on the need to limit spending. Congress would not be committed to rigid spending ceilings, as the Joint Study Committeee had advocated. On the contrary, the Rules Committee argued that procedures should not, and in reality could not, keep a majority of Congress from enforcing its spending preferences, even if the result were a violation of spending ceilings.

As presented to the House, H.R. 7130 maintained automatic representation for the Ways and Means and Appropriations committees on the House Budget Committee, but it restricted them to a minority of the seats, apportioned the remainder among the authorizing committees and party leaderships, and required all Budget Committee members to be chosen by their respective party caucuses without regard to seniority.* These provisions were added to allay suspicions that the Budget Committee would be dominated by senior conservatives, a charge that House liberals had leveled against the Joint Study Committee's original reform plan. Moreover, the Rules Committee responded to concerns that the Budget Committee might

---

*A reduction in the Ways and Means and Appropriations committees' representation on the Budget Committee had been discussed when the Rules Committee hearings opened during July. Al Ullman and other House members who had served on the Joint Study Committee had prepared a series of compromises that were presented before the Rules Committee on July 19. These measures included assigning half of the Budget Committee seats to members of authorizing committees, allowing all Budget Committee members to be chosen by normal procedures for assignment to committees, and loosening the restrictions on amendments to budget resolutions offered on the House floor.

develop into a "supercommittee" by limiting service for any member to four years in any ten-year period and by removing restrictions, such as the rule of consistency, on floor amendments to budget resolutions.

In addition, the Rules Committee reshaped the budget-resolution procedure so that there would be at least two budget resolutions each year, one establishing targets or guidelines and another, which would be adopted after Congress completed action on individual spending and revenue bills, affirming or revising the figures contained in the first resolution. Once the fiscal year began, Congress would be authorized to adopt additional resolutions if economic conditions or other relevant circumstances changed. Thus the budget process would be flexible and would preserve Congress' spending options throughout the fiscal year.

In a few respects the recommendations of the Rules Committee and the Joint Study Committee were not too far apart. Both stressed the importance of curbing uncontrollable spending, with H.R. 7130 granting the Appropriations committees greater control over existing as well as future back-door spending programs. The committees agreed that a congressional budget staff was needed, although the Rules Committee called for the creation of a budget office that would serve all committees rather than a joint staff simply for the Budget committees.

Finally, H.R. 7130 incorporated the impoundment-control provisions that the House had adopted in July. The president had to notify Congress of any impoundment action, so that either the House or the Senate could pass a simple resolution of disapproval within sixty days of notification if it objected. If such a resolution were passed, the impoundment would cease immediately.

On the floor, the Rules Committee version of H.R. 7130 survived virtually intact. A Republican move to delete the impoundment-control section was defeated by a vote of 108–295, and the House also rejected, by a vote of 186–221, an amendment to require disapproval of presidential impoundments by concurrent rather than simple resolutions. An effort by Democratic liberals to eliminate the automatic representation of Ways and Means and Appropriations on the House Budget Committee was soundly defeated. After increasing the time for members to study reported budget resolutions before floor action was taken from five to ten days, the House passed H.R. 7130 by a vote of 386–23.

Senate Action

Budget-reform legislation followed a more tortuous course in the Senate. On April 11, 1973, S. 1541, the Congressional Budgetary Procedures Act, was introduced in the Senate. Based on the report of the Joint Study Committee on Budget Control, S. 1541 was referred to the Government Operations Committee, which unanimously reported out a revised version of S. 1541 in November. This bill, in turn, was referred to the Rules and Administration Subcommittee on the Standing Rules of the Senate, which held hearings during January 1974. As numerous objections to S. 1541 were reported by other committees, the subcommittee's chairman, Robert Byrd of West Virginia, convened a congressional staff group to work out a "consensus bill."* A substantially revised version of S. 1541 was finally reported out by the Rules Committee on February 20. For four days in March, floor debate over the new S. 1541 continued, and numerous amendments were introduced. On March 22, the Senate, rejecting all major changes, adopted S. 1541 unanimously, and its provisions were substituted for those of H.R. 7130, which had previously passed the House.

The Government Operations Bill. As reported by the Government Operations Committee on November 20, S. 1541 was similar in some respects to the bill reported by the House Rules Committee one week earlier. When compared to the Joint Study Committee's proposal, both bills eased the requirements for floor amendments to budget resolutions, provided greater discretion to the Appropriations committees under the first budget resolution, and allowed Congress to act on multiple budget resolutions for a single fiscal year. The two measures set the fiscal year to begin on October 1 and end September 30, and provided that a congressional budget office rather than a joint staff would be established to provide all committees, rather than just the Budget committees, with budgetary in-

---

*With few exceptions, the statements, letters, and testimony presented to the Byrd subcommittee called for major changes in the Government Operations Committee bill. Senators Sam Ervin and Charles Percy, the chairman and ranking minority member of the Government Operations Committee, then agreed to have the Byrd subcommittee revise the bill. There were forty-five staff members, representing ten standing Senate committees, four joint committees, the House Appropriations Committee, the Congressional Research Service, and the Office of Senate Legislative Counsel, in Byrd's special group (U.S. Senate, Committee on Rules and Administration, *Report No. 93-688, Congressional Budget Act of 1974* [Washington, D.C.: Government Printing Office, 1974], pp. 2, 3).

formation and analysis. The Government Operations Committee bill eliminated automatic representation of the Finance and Appropriations committees on the Senate Budget Committee, requiring instead that the fifteen-member committee be filled according to regular party procedures.

Unlike the House bill and the measure that finally passed the Senate, however, S. 1541 had a very strong budget-cutting orientation. The Government Operations Committee bill eliminated all forms of back-door spending immediately by requiring that budget authority be provided only in legislation reported by the Appropriations committees. It also made it difficult for Congress to exceed the spending target established in the first budget resolution. Under S. 1541, the spring resolution would contain budget aggregates—total spending, revenue, and the surplus or deficit—and spending subceilings corresponding to Appropriations subcommittee jurisdictions. Although these limits would not be binding—the Appropriations committees would still have discretion over individual spending measures—each appropriations bill would contain a clause that delayed the date of its effectiveness. Once all appropriations had been enacted—the proposed deadline was September 20—the totals for budget authority and outlays would be compared with those in the spring budget resolution. If spending bills fell below the original ceiling, the Appropriations committees would report a bill to make effective the previously enacted appropriations. If the original spending ceiling had been exceeded, however, Congress would first attempt to rescind sufficient spending to bring the totals into line through a ceiling-enforcement bill reported by the Appropriations committees. Only if this procedure failed would Congress be allowed to revise through a second budget resolution the figures on spending, revenues, and surplus or deficit in the first resolution.

The necessity for stronger controls over current and long-term spending was the basis for other recommendations by the Government Operations Committee. Under S. 1541, three-year maximum limits were to be placed on all authorization bills; new spending programs would need prior pilot testing and evaluation. The projected long-term costs of legislation were to be reported by committees, and the Budget committees were to be allowed to review and consider tax expenditures (provisions in the tax code that reduce the "normal" tax liability for an individual or a corporation).

Amending S. 1541. The Senate Rules and Administration Committee originally intended to review only those provisions of S. 1541 that directly affected Senate Rules.[13] Committee chairmen had complained that S. 1541 would infringe on existing committee jurisdictions and prerogatives. The proposed timetable for the budgetary process was criticized as unrealistic, and the recommended procedures were attacked as unworkable.[14] It became apparent quickly that substantial revision was necessary.

As a result, the Byrd subcommittee decided to review S. 1541 in its entirety. The parent Rules and Administration Committee later stated that the objective of this review was to add "a new and comprehensive budgetary framework to the existing decision-making processes, *with minimum disruption to established methods and procedures.*"[15]

The substitute version of S. 1541 reported by the Rules and Administration Committee was quite similar in approach to the budget-reform bill written by the House Rules Committee, especially with regard to the powers of the new Budget committees and the purpose of the budget resolutions. The Rules and Administration Committee limited the jurisdiction of the Budget committees so as not to intrude on existing committee prerogatives, especially those of the Finance and Appropriations committees.[16] As a result, S. 1541 now followed functional categories rather than the jurisdictions of Appropriations subcommittees for the spending subtargets in the first budget resolution. It also mandated a second budget resolution, thus making the figures in the first resolution nonbinding. The provision for delayed effectiveness, the ceiling-enforcement bill, and structured reconciliation process recommended by the Government Operations Committee were dropped in favor of a flexible reconciliation procedure, similar to that in the House bill, which was not "biased" toward spending rescissions.

The Rules and Administration Committee bill also responded to the complaints of spokesmen for authorizing committees by weakening other spending-control provisions contained in the original S. 1541. Controls of back-door spending were substantially loosened. The three-year limit on authorizations was eliminated, as was the requirement for testing and evaluation of new spending programs. Requirements that committees report cost estimates and projections for current and proposed legislation were eased.

69

The Senate adopted the new version of S. 1541 without substantial changes, easily defeating attempts by conservatives to amend it in accordance with the original proposal of the Government Operations Committee. The Senate also rejected liberal-sponsored amendments to make the new budget procedures even looser.

As passed by the Senate, S. 1541 differed somewhat from the House bill with respect to the proposed budget timetable, provisions on back-door spending, and the content of budget resolutions. More important, it did not contain a section on control of impoundments, although the bill contained language that limited the purposes for which presidents could reserve or impound funds. Since the previous House and Senate approaches to the impoundment issue had never been reconciled, this conflict was quite serious. With this important exception, however, the broad outlines of budget reform were clear. Congress would adopt a comprehensive budget to establish its fiscal policy and program priorities. It would not commit itself to a budgetary process predicated on strict spending controls and rigid spending ceilings. Additional budget resolutions could now easily be used, as the Government Operations Committee had feared, to justify the excesses dictated by pressures to spend.

The Congressional Budget and Impoundment Control Act of 1974

The conference committee charged with reconciling the House and Senate versions of budget-reform legislation met in executive session on April 9, 1974, held a public meeting the following day, then did not meet again until June. During the interim, a drafting group composed of congressional staff members put together a compromise bill, which was unanimously approved by seven House and fourteen Senate conferees, who filed their report on June 12. On June 18 the House agreed to the conference report by a vote of 401–6, and three days later the Senate followed with a unanimous vote of 75–0. On June 12, 1974, the Congressional Budget and Impoundment Control Act of 1974 was signed into law. Richard Nixon, who ironically deserved more credit for it than anyone else, hailed it "as the most significant reform of budget procedures since the Congress and this country began."[17] The exaggeration, while understandable, was misleading.

The budget-control provisions worked out during conference were designed to promote flexibility. The conference adopted a detailed budget timetable, but it also agreed to limit the content and effect of budget resolutions and to impose relatively loose controls on back-door spending. It resolved the remaining sticking point by distinguishing two types of impoundments. The one-house veto advocated by the House was applied to temporary impoundments (deferrals), and disapproval by concurrent resolution, pushed by the Senate, was applied to permanent impoundments (rescissions). These provisions were incorporated in Title X of the 1974 budget act.

Organizational Changes

The 1974 budget act established standing House and Senate Budget committees and a Congressional Budget Office (CBO). The Ways and Means and Appropriations committees hold ten seats on the House Budget Committee, and tenure is limited. (The original restriction of two terms for any member within a ten-year period was increased to three terms in 1979.) The Senate Budget Committee has no membership or tenure restrictions. Each committee has its own staff and also receives priority assistance from the Congressional Budget Office, a nonpartisan support staff that supplies budget data and analysis. The primary responsibility of the Budget committees is to report at least two concurrent budget resolutions each year—the nonbinding or target resolution in the spring and the binding resolution in the fall.

Procedures

The congressional budget timetable put into place by the 1974 budget act is based on an October 1–September 30 fiscal year and is divided into four stages. The *first stage* consists of information gathering and analysis for the spring budget resolution. During this period, which runs from November through mid-April, the Budget committees receive materials from the executive branch (the current services and presidential budgets), estimates and recommendations on spending and revenues from other congressional committees, and supporting analysis from the CBO. On or before April 15 they report out the first budget resolution for the fiscal year that will begin on October 1. (See Table 3.1.)

Table 3.1. Procedures in congressional budget process, by stage

Stage	Procedure
I (November 10–April 15)	Information gathering, analysis, preparation and submission of congressional budget by Congressional Budget Office and Budget committees
II (April 15–May 15)	Debate and adoption of congressional budget by both houses; establishment of national spending priorities
III (May 15–September 15)	Enactment of spending bills
IV (September 15–September 25)	Reassessment of spending, revenue, and debt requirements in second budget resolution; enactment of reconciliation bill

SOURCE: U.S. House of Representatives, Committee on the Budget, *Congressional Budget Reform* (Washington, D.C.: Government Printing Office, 1975), p. 16.

The *second stage,* April 15–May 15, is for debate and passage of the first budget resolution. The congressional budget being considered at this point establishes targets for total spending, revenue, the budget surplus or deficit, and the public debt. The spending totals are for outlays and budget authority, and each is broken down into functional categories (defense, income security, health, and so forth) to show congressional priorities. While the functional targets are not binding, the conference report that accompanies the first resolution explains how these allocations are divided among the various spending committees. Congress is required to pass this initial budget by May 15. In order to facilitate subsequent action on spending bills, most authorizations must also be reported by this date. In mid-spring, then, there is a tentative congressional budget that expresses Congress' preferences in regard to spending, fiscal policy, and programs.

From May 15 through September 15, the *third stage,* Congress acts on individual spending and tax bills. Action on all budget and spending authority bills is to be completed by early September. The *fourth and final stage* of the process includes passage of a second budget resolution and any required reconciliation legislation. The second resolution, which is to be adopted by September 15, can affirm or revise totals in the first budget resolution. If Congress' spending or revenue decisions conflict with this second resolution, a reconciliation procedure is available to force committees to report necessary adjustments in spending or revenue bills.

The second resolution allows Congress to reconsider its earlier decisions about budget totals as well as its interim decisions on spending and revenue bills. Unless it is amended by a later budget resolution, the fall budget resolution sets a binding ceiling on spending and a binding floor on revenue. Any legislation that violates these limits would not be in order. Congress retains the option to adopt a new budget resolution if the spending ceiling is threatened, however, and this is a major loophole in the spending-control process.

Interpreting Budget Reform

The budget-control legislation of 1973 and early 1974 brought about significant changes. What began as an effort to strengthen Congress' control over spending and limit the growth of the federal budget gradually broadened to permit Congress to substitute its priorities in regard to fiscal policy and programs for the president's, and to curb the president's discretion over spending. As the nearly unanimous support for the final bill suggests, most groups in Congress could claim at least partial victories. Republicans were able to ease the sting of impoundment controls by linking them to other budget reforms. Conservatives in both parties gained some satisfaction from the requirements for congressional spending and deficit totals. Liberals achieved checks on impoundments and moderated internal controls on spending.

In trying to decide which of these partial victories was most important, we must emphasize what the 1974 budget act did not do. It did not restrict Congress' flexibility in making decisions on spending. Congress would have to set totals and deficits, but it could always raise the totals and the deficits if they seriously restricted Congress' ability to spend. Back-door spending would continue with only modest curbs. The spending prerogatives of authorizing committees would not be seriously threatened.

The 1974 budget act did not transform internal congressional politics, nor was it likely to do so. It did provide Congress with the means to deal with broad budget policy issues and therefore had the potential for altering the balance of influence between the president and Congress. In no sense, however, was it an unambiguous endorsement of the need to control congressional spending. And therein lies the real problem.

The long-term threat to Congress' power of the purse has persisted *because* Congress has such great difficulty in controlling spending. The threat is particularly serious today as a result of the neutrality of the 1974 budget act.[18] Congress must now try to curb spending with a budget process that lacks teeth, and which encourages dependence on the executive branch or on some other form of external control, such as a constitutional formula.

PART II

IMPLEMENTING
BUDGET REFORM

CHAPTER 4

The Budget Committees

The House and Senate Budget committees bear the burden of reconciling different expectations regarding budget reform. They face the difficult task of writing congressional budgets that can be passed on the floor and enforced against relentless pressures to spend. They have to balance demands for overall spending control against the funding requirements of programs that have active supporters inside and outside Congress.

Despite their common jurisdictions and limitations, the Budget committees have had different impacts on the budget process in their parent chambers. The Senate Budget Committee and the Senate budget process have been strongly bipartisan over the years. The budget process in the House has been extremely partisan, and the majority and minority members of the House Budget Committee have traditionally had strong ties to their respective party leaderships. The critical question is whether or not either committee has been able to transcend its limited formal authority and to effect a significant change in congressional spending practices.

Setting the Pattern

Organized shortly after the 1974 budget act was signed into law, the Budget committees spent the remainder of the 93d Congress holding hearings on economic and budget policy issues and preparing for partial implementation of the new budgetary process in 1975. While full implementation was not required until 1976, the House and Senate leaderships agreed that a trial run would provide needed experience in operating under the unfamiliar procedures of the budget-reform law.

The trial run turned into a significant test. Congress adopted two budget resolutions for fiscal 1976, establishing priorities and fiscal policies quite different from those recommended by the Ford administration. The first resolution raised the deficit almost $17 billion above the president's budget, and the second resolution increased the deficit by well over $20 billion. On the spending side, Congress sharply reduced Ford's defense requests while voting substantial add-ons for domestic programs.

The accomplishments of the new process, however, were tempered by serious problems in the House, where the Budget Committee was almost paralyzed by partisan and ideological splits. In the spring the committee first voted 11–13 against reporting out any budget resolution. Committee Republicans, who unanimously refused to support the projected $73 billion deficit, were joined by an unlikely coalition of four Democratic conservatives, who also objected to the large deficit and defense cuts, and one Democratic liberal, who shared neither of these concerns. Finally, two senior Republicans agreed to switch their votes so the House would at least have an opportunity to debate the resolution. Their desire to protect the budget process, however, brought sharp criticism from party conservatives, which probably dissuaded other Budget Committee Republicans from future attempts at cooperation.[1]

Once reported out, the resolution was caught in a crossfire between liberals and conservatives on the floor. First, Democratic conservatives from the Budget Committee tried to reduce spending for social welfare and the deficit. In the beginning they were successful, but the House Democratic leadership then offered a substitute resolution designed to appeal to liberals and moderates in the party. The Democratic strategy was to ignore the Republicans and write a majority-party budget. After the leadership engineered some last-minute vote switches, the substitute passed by a four-vote margin.

In the fall the second resolution for fiscal 1976 was unanimously opposed by Republicans on the Budget Committee, but the shaky Democratic majority was this time able to report it out of committee. During floor debate the Democratic leadership again took control, sponsoring spending increases to gain liberal votes and managing to keep enough moderate Democrats in line to ensure that the resolution passed. The partisan split within the Budget Committee was reinforced on the floor, and the result once again was a barely successful Democratic effort to write a majority-party budget.

A very different pattern emerged in the Senate. Within the Budget Committee, a coalition of southern Democrats and Republicans defeated proposals sponsored by liberal Democrats, including Chairman Edmund Muskie, to cut defense spending and increase domestic spending. The deficit recommended by the Senate Budget Committee turned out to be more than $6 billion under the House figure. The resolution then was supported by all of the Democrats and four of the six Republicans on the committee.

On the Senate floor, Muskie and the Budget Committee's ranking Republican, Henry Bellmon of Oklahoma, successfully argued against all major amendments. Muskie opposed spending increases he had unsuccessfully supported during committee markup and explained his switch as a defense of the budget process:

> I have this perception of the budget process. The committee is made up of 16 members. For months and weeks we worked toward the committee objective of reaching a consensus. . . . If I came to the floor pursuing my priorities, every member of the Budget Committee would come to the floor pursuing his priorities, and we would therefore not have a joint committee consensus. We would simply have some numbers put together by 16 Senators who would then blend into the 100 Senators who are members of this body, all fighting all over again as though there were no budget process to influence the final results.[2]

Bellmon likewise spoke against budget cuts offered by other Republicans: "Much as I would like to see us have a lower deficit, . . . having sat through literally months of deliberations of the Budget Committee . . . [and] looking at the functional breakdown of the figure we have recommended, I cannot agree that making an additional reduction across the board is defensible."[3] Muskie and Bellmon were persuasive: the Senate approved the first budget resolution as reported by the Budget Committee by a bipartisan vote of 69–22.

After a conference committee resolved the differences between the House and the Senate on the first resolution, Muskie and his House counterpart, Brock Adams of Washington, attempted to enforce the spending targets contained in the resolution. Muskie challenged bills on the floor while Adams worked privately with other committees and tried to avoid confrontations. Given the problems within his committee, Adams' conciliatory approach was understandable, but it did result in unfavorable comparisons with what appeared to be a bolder and more powerful Senate Budget Committee.[4] In both cases, however, the targets were enforced successfully.

The first year of the budget process revealed clear weaknesses on the House side—and remarkably persistent ones. Republicans on the House Budget Committee have remained an isolated minority, and the overwhelming majority of House Republicans have opposed budget resolutions year after year. Budgets in the House have been passed by Democrats—but only after almost continuous intervention by the Democratic leadership.

Early developments within the Senate Budget Committee were more fortuitous. Partisanship has been limited within the committee and on the floor. As a result, the budget process has a firmer foundation in the Senate than it enjoys in the House, and the Senate Budget Committee can be more adventuresome in its dealings with other committees.

Committee Decision Making

The wide-ranging differences between the House and Senate Budget committees cannot be easily explained. Undoubtedly the nature of the institution of which each is part has an impact, as do the characteristics of the members and leaders of each committee. The tenure restrictions on members of the House Budget Committee probably reinforce the committee's relative weakness. In 1979 the tenure limit was changed to allow members to serve three terms, but the House has refused to remove the limits entirely. As members of the House Budget Committee cannot base their legislative careers on what amounts to a temporary assignment, their loyalty to the Budget Committee and the importance they accord it are limited. In addition, there are important differences in the decision-making processes of the two committees.

Institutional Constraints

Although the Democrats commanded big majorities in both chambers from 1974 to 1980, their margins in the House were exceptionally large, averaging roughly 2 to 1 for the 94th through the 96th Congresses.[5] The House leadership and Democratic caucus were active and aggressive in attempting to capitalize on their majority and to strengthen party control of the House. In the Senate the party balances have been a bit closer (the Democratic edge from 1974 to 1980 was approximately 3 to 2) and the party leaderships have been less overtly partisan in their approach. In the 97th Congress, beginning in 1981, of course, Republicans control the Senate, but by such a slim margin that a dramatic change in partisan activity in the Senate is unlikely.

Nevertheless, recent voting patterns in the House and in the Senate have not differed greatly. Party votes, which are usually defined as a majority of voting Democrats against a majority of voting Republicans, typically occur for perhaps 40 percent of the votes of record in Congress.[6] Over the past decade, party votes have actually been slightly more frequent in the Senate than in the House.[7] In addition, the level of party voting in the House has varied considerably since 1975.[8] When party votes do occur, the success rates of the majority party in the House and Senate have been quite similar, despite the proportionately larger Democratic majorities in the House. Between 1975 and 1980, House and Senate Democrats won almost 3 of 4 party votes on a yearly average.[9]

The absence of distinctive House and Senate voting patterns extends to the relative strength of ideological blocs. For many years the Senate was considered more liberal than the House, at least on issues other than civil rights. This perception has changed with the shifting party balance in the House and the declining influence of southern Democrats, especially among the leadership of House committees. The "conservative coalition"—the voting alliance of southern Democrats and Republicans that was quite formidable for many years—has become less potent in the House. Since 1975 the coalition has formed on approximately 20 percent of votes of record each session, and it has won about 60 percent of the votes on which it has appeared—a success rate about equal to that in the Senate.[10]

These voting patterns suggest that the House and Senate committees have not operated in widely dissimilar institutional contexts with regard to partisan voting patterns. Party control of the House or Senate is important, but it does not determine the resolution of all legislative issues. Fewer than half of the floor votes in Congress find the party majorities on opposite sides, and when party votes do occur, the majority party is not always assured of victory. The congressional parties lack cohesion, and there are frequently substantial defections from both sides of the aisle on controversial issues. In a situation in which the party lines are not always clearly fixed, highly partisan committees may find legislative success difficult to achieve. Although floor losses may not be too damaging for some committees, the Budget committees *must* pass at least two budget resolutions each year. The House and Senate Budget committees have contrasting approaches to the gathering of necessary support on the floor, in part because of partisan and ideological differences specifically associated with these two committees. With divided party control of Congress in the 97th Congress, these differences will play an increasingly important role.

Committee-Based Factors

From 1975 to 1980, Democratic majorities in the House were proportionately larger than those in the Senate, and these majorities were reflected in the makeup of the House Budget Committee (see Table 4.1). During those years the ratio of Democrats to Republicans on the House Budget Committee was maintained at 17 to 8, making it one of the few House committees (the other major ones being Rules and Appropriations) on which the party balance was not adjusted to reflect Republican gains in the 1978 midterm election. In 1981, despite Republican protests, House Democrats again decided to maintain a disproportionate party majority on the Budget Committee. Since the fixed party balances on Rules and Appropriations strengthen the control of the majority-party leadership, the decision to impose a similar fixed balance on the Budget Committee suggests that it, too, is closely and intentionally tied to the Democratic leadership.

The Senate Budget Committee had a 10–6 ratio between Democrats and Republicans in the 94th and 95th Congresses. At the start of the 96th Congress, in 1979, the committee was enlarged to 20 seats and the division set at 12 to 8. On the Senate Budget Commit-

Table 4.1. Number of northern Democrats, southern Democrats, and Republicans on House and Senate Budget committees, 93d–97th Congresses, 1974–82

Congress	Years	House				Senate			
		Democrats			Republicans	Democrats			Republicans
		Northern	Southern	Total		Northern	Southern	Total	
93d	1974	12	2	14	9	7	2	9	6
94th	1975–76	12	5	17	8	7	3	10	6
95th	1977–78	12	5*	17	8	6	4	10	6
96th	1979–80	14	3*	17	8	8	4	12	8
97th	1981–82	13	5*	18	12	6	4	10	12

NOTE: Breakdowns are based on initial appointments to Budget committees in each Congress.
*Includes James C. Wright, Jr., of Texas, elected Democratic majority leader in 1977. Wright was also on the Budget Committee in 1974, 1975, and 1976, but not as the representative of the Democratic party leadership.

tee, however, southern Democratic representation gradually increased over the years, keeping Republicans from being isolated when they were in the minority (see Table 4.1). In the 96th Congress, for example, Republicans and northern Democrats were exactly balanced at eight seats each after initial assignments were made, with four southern Democrats occupying the pivotal voting position between them. This preponderance of conservatives and moderates is even greater now that there is an absolute Republican majority on the committee.

During 1975 and 1976, a coalition of Republicans and southern Democrats seemed to be developing on the House Budget Committee. As a result, more than one-third of the committee's roll-call votes during this period were decided by one-vote margins.[11] The House Democratic leadership, faced with possible loss of party control on the Budget Committee, strengthened the liberal Democratic contingent and reduced the number of southern conservatives until by the 96th Congress nonsouthern Democrats had taken over an absolute majority of the twenty-five-member Budget Committee. The result was a sharp rise after 1977 of the average party-unity scores of Budget Committee Democrats to a level well above the average for all House Democrats (see Tables 4.2 and 4.3). This partisan dimension has not been greatly altered in the 97th Congress, although southern Democratic representation has been increased.

Since the House Budget Committee was established, its minority members have also demonstrated strong partisanship. Party-unity scores for Budget Committee Republicans are much higher than the House Republican average. Thus both Democrats and Republicans on the House Budget Committee stand out as highly partisan. The voting records of members of the Senate Budget Committee have been less distinctive. There the party-unity scores of Democrats and Republicans have exceeded the averages for their parties, but they have been well below the corresponding levels on the House Budget Committee. The restrained partisanship within the Senate Budget Committee, then, has been paralleled by moderately partisan voting records among its members on issues beyond the purview of the committee. The more extreme partisanship of the House Budget Committee is not an aberration. Its members tend to be committed partisans in their response to other legislative issues.

The House Budget Committee is, as expected, more sharply di-

Table 4.2. Support of party unity and conservative coalition by members of House and Senate Budget committees, 93d–97th Congresses, 1973–82, by party (percent)

Congress	Years	Party unity				Conservative coalition			
		House		Senate		House		Senate	
		Democrats	Republicans	Democrats	Republicans	Democrats	Republicans	Democrats	Republicans
93d	1973–74	72%	85%	76%	68%	27%	91%	19%	71%
94th	1975–76	65	80	72	73	34	82	29	76
95th	1977–78	74	81	64	67	24	86	32	73
96th	1979–80	76	80	68	67	23	81	40	67
97th*	1981–82	74	83	68	73	37	86	43	75

*Based on 1980 voting records.
SOURCE: Compiled from *Congressional Quarterly Almanac*, various years.

Table 4.3. Average support of party unity and conservative coalition in House and Senate, 93d–96th Congresses, 1973–80, by party (percent)

Party	Party unity		Conservative coalition	
	House	Senate	House	Senate
Democrats				
Northern	—	—	23	20
Southern	—	—	62	65
All Democrats	66	66	—	—
Republicans	69	64	74	65

SOURCE: Compiled from *Congressional Quarterly Almanac,* various years.

vided between liberals and conservatives than the Senate Budget Committee, and the disparity was growing well before Republicans gained control of the Senate. As Tables 4.2 and 4.3 indicate, Republicans on the House Budget Committee have more conservative voting records than either House Republicans generally or Senate Budget Committee Republicans. The average scores of Democrats on the House Budget Committee in support of the conservative coalition dropped sharply after 1976 and remained comparable to those of northern House Democrats through 1980.

Republican members of the Senate Budget Committee have exceeded the overall averages of Senate Republicans for support of the conservative coalition. The same has usually been true, although at a much lower level, of course, for Budget Committee Democrats compared to the northern Democratic bloc in the Senate. The ideological distance between Democrats and Republicans on the Senate Budget Committee has generally been less than the overall interparty averages, and the committee has actually been slightly more conservative than the Senate as a whole. Moreover, voting alignments on the Budget Committee have been relatively flexible. On the markup of the first budget resolution for fiscal 1981, for example, only about one-third of the almost 200 motions found a majority of voting Democrats opposing a majority of voting Republicans.[12] Moreover, Democrats won 42 of these interparty splits, while Republicans managed to win 23. A moderate or centrist coalition has been influential in the Senate Budget Committee almost from the beginning, and straight party-line votes have been rare. The two senior Republicans on the Budget Committee, Henry Bellmon

(Oklahoma) and Pete Domenici (New Mexico), were actually on the winning side on a substantial majority of votes between 1975 and 1980.

While Republicans on the Senate Budget Committee were able to influence committee decisions on budget resolutions even when they were in the minority, their counterparts in the House have usually been isolated. Virtually all major votes in the House Budget Committee have found the party majorities on opposite sides—and Republicans on the losing side. With only scattered exceptions, all Budget Committee Republicans have voted against reporting budget resolutions to the floor, have voted against conference reports when they have served as conferees, and have joined most of their fellow Republicans in voting against resolutions on the floor.

This firm Republican stance often works to the advantage of liberal Democrats. For example, in 1979 Democratic liberals attacked the conference committee version of the first budget resolution for fiscal 1980 on the grounds that defense spending was too high and funding for social programs too low. House Republicans were thus placed in the same situation that Budget Committee Republicans had been in for years: should they support a resolution that was more palatable than the likely alternative or continue to reject any responsibility for deficit budgets? This time, five Budget Committee Republicans decided to cooperate with moderate Democrats and support the conference report. Other Republicans voted 3 to 1 against it, despite the fact that their votes could easily have provided the margin for passage, and the resolution was defeated in the House. A version more appealing to liberals was then reported out of conference, and House Democrats managed to put together a majority for passage. When asked why the Republicans had helped the liberal cause and wound up with a resolution even more distasteful to them than the first, Barber Conable of New York, the ranking Republican on Ways and Means and a member of the Budget Committee, explained, "We have been a minority party for a long time, and we have fairly well developed postures. It's much easier to take postures than pragmatic decisions."[13] The same scenario was played out the following spring. This time Budget Committee Republicans took an active role in trying to pass the first budget resolution, but the conference compromise was again rejected when liberal Demo-

87

crats and Republicans voted overwhelmingly against it. The second conference compromise gained even less support among Republicans, but Democrats were able to pass it by a 205–195 vote.

Leadership. From the time it was first organized until the spring of 1980, the Senate Budget Committee had only one chairman— Edmund S. Muskie of Maine. As the Democratic party's vice-presidential nominee in 1968 and a contender for its presidential nomination in 1972, Muskie had a national reputation, and his selection provided the new Budget Committee with immediate visibility and prestige. In giving up his seat on Foreign Relations in order to take over Budget, Muskie signaled his intent to use it as a base for personal leadership and influence in the Senate. And it was his aggressive pursuit of that goal that helped to solidify the committee's standing in the Senate.

Muskie was teamed with Henry Bellmon, who joined the Budget Committee as ranking Republican in 1975. Bellmon's low-key style was an effective complement to Muskie's emotionalism, and his reputation as a sound and thoughtful legislator helped to develop Republican support for the Budget Committee and the budget process. The success that the Senate Budget Committee has achieved, however, must also be attributed to an effective, if anonymous, centrist coalition that has helped the committee to steer a policy course the Senate finds acceptable. Senators Ernest Hollings (South Carolina) and Lawton Chiles (Florida) on the Democratic side and Senators Domenici and Bellmon among the Republicans have served as the core of that coalition since 1975. Because Hollings is now the ranking Democrat and Domenici has moved up to the chairmanship, there is a good chance that this centrist orientation will actually be strengthened.

The House Budget Committee has lacked leadership continuity as well as the kind of bipartisan coalition that the Senate Budget Committee has enjoyed. The first House Budget Committee chairman, Al Ullman (Oregon), was appointed in 1974 and resigned shortly thereafter to take over the chairmanship of Ways and Means. His successor, Brock Adams (Washington), resigned after two years to become secretary of transportation in the Carter administration. Robert Giaimo (Connecticut) took over the Budget Committee in 1977, and after the tenure limits were relaxed, he continued as chairman for the 96th Congress. He retired from Congress in 1980, however, so the Budget Committee found itself with its fourth chairman in only seven years when the 97th Congress convened in 1981.

Neither Giaimo nor Adams was able to develop a working relationship with the Republican leader on the Budget Committee, Delbert Latta (Ohio), that was even remotely similar to the Muskie-Bellmon situation. Latta and most Budget Committee Republicans have been adamant partisans, and it is really irrelevant whether their stance has been due to Democratic rejections of compromise efforts or Republican intransigence. Individual members, such as Democrat Jim Jones (Oklahoma), the new Budget Committee chairman, and Republican Ralph Regula (Ohio), have worked to achieve at least a limited bipartisan consensus within the committee, but these efforts have met with little encouragement from other members or from the party leaders in the House.

The leadership and makeup of the two Budget committees have certainly contributed to their distinctive styles, but the institutional constraints under which they operate have also made a critical difference. The Senate Budget Committee enjoys a high degree of autonomy, as do most Senate committees. The House Budget Committee is under unusual pressure from the parties and their leaderships in the House. Since it is free from tenure limits, the Senate Budget Committee does offer members incentives to protect its cohesion and autonomy, and it certainly provides its chairman and ranking minority member with an influential base in the Senate. These characteristics do not necessarily make it a highly attractive committee for all members (and high turnover rates among past members suggest it is not), but they help the Senate to achieve parity with the House on fiscal matters and thereby serve an important institutional purpose. There are advantages to the Senate in maintaining a strong, if not domineering, Budget Committee, as most Senators recognize.

Quite the reverse seems to be true for the House. The tenure limits that apply to membership in the House Budget Committee do not facilitate continuity and expertise within the committee, nor do they encourage a sense of corporate identity among its members. There appears to be widespread sentiment that the budget process is nothing more than a hindrance to the House, although it may be a necessity for Congress. The budget process makes spending more difficult, and its countervailing benefits—congressional determination of fiscal policy and budget priorities—do not seem to be particularly relevant to House members. The budget process and the House Budget Committee have a rather tenuous and not especially effective existence as institutional necessities and political inconveniences.

Decision Strategies

The prescribed content of the annual budget resolutions was carefully limited to prevent jurisdictional conflicts between the Budget committees and other committees and also to emphasize the macroeconomic purposes of the budget act. The concurrent budget resolutions for each fiscal year contain budget aggregates—the overall levels of spending, revenue, surplus or deficit, and the public debt—and a breakdown of spending into the eighteen functional categories contained in the president's budget. These categories, such as national defense and income security, show spending at a very high level of aggregation. By way of contrast, the Appropriations committees deal with more than 1,200 appropriations accounts in preparing their spending bills.

The aggregates and broad spending categories contained in budget resolutions supposedly permit the Budget committees to deal with macro budgetary issues, such as fiscal policy and policy priorities, without encroaching on other committees' responsibilities for line-item spending. One of the unresolved problems of the new budgetary system, however, is how to maintain or even to define this distinction. The problem arises as the Budget committees explain how they have arrived at the totals contained in their budget resolutions and how they justify them. The committee reports accompanying the resolutions often contain policy assumptions that are subject to challenge by authorizing or Appropriations committees on jurisdictional grounds.

The Budget committees do, of course, consider specific spending and revenue issues in arriving at their recommendations. Within each committee, arguments for cuts or increases in functional categories must often be justified in terms of particular programs. Each committee needs to be able to defend its totals by showing how they can be achieved. Finally, once a resolution has been adopted, the Budget committees must be able to supervise effective "scorekeeping" that shows how funding decisions for specific programs affect the targets.

The Budget committees have attempted to cope with these problems in different ways. The House Budget Committee has followed an essentially line-item procedure from the beginning.[14] The Senate committee has maintained a fairly high level of aggregation in dealing with an immediate fiscal year and focused greater attention on multiyear budgeting and the future implications of current spending decisions. While the House procedure is perhaps better suited to the technical requirements of budget scorekeeping,[15] the Senate committee's approach is more compatible with the policy objectives of the budget process and may be a more effective method of maintaining long-term influence over budget policy.

House Procedures. When Representative Brock Adams served as chairman of the House Budget Committee during 1975–76, he instituted the practice of using a chairman's mark as the starting point for committee markup of budget resolutions. For each of the functional categories, Adams would present the committee with the president's budget request and a chairman's mark or recommendation for that level. When differences between these figures were the result of policy factors rather than estimating methods, Adams was able to explain how the changes he recommended affected specific appropriations accounts. During committee debate, amendments to Adams' marks usually were equally specific. Once the Budget Committee completed a budget resolution, the spending level for all functions could easily be disaggregated, and the policy assumptions behind the resolution would be clear. Since 1979 the mark has been determined by a caucus of Budget Committee Democrats, rather than the chairman.

The insistence on line-item decisions has not been reassuring to other House committees. In 1975 the chairman of the House International Relations Committee complained that the policy judgments the Budget Committee had reported to explain the spending target for international affairs were "premature" and amounted to an "infringement on [the] jurisdiction" of his committee.[16] The chairman of Appropriations cautioned that "the Budget Committee has succumbed in a few instances to the temptation to deal with subjects in its report which are not directly related to its primary objectives and which are being dealt with by other congressional committees."[17]

These criticisms have continued. When the Budget committees managed to include reconciliation instructions, or required legislative savings, in the first budget resolution for fiscal 1981, the House Appropriations Committee promptly and publicly rejected the Budget Committee's instructions on how those savings might be achieved. Moreover, Speaker Thomas P. (Tip) O'Neill at first did his best to sabotage the reconciliation experiment, conveniently ignoring the fact that the House had strongly endorsed reconciliation. O'Neill wondered whether the "Budget Committee [is] going to be the all-powerful committee around here."[18]

Line items have led to other difficulties. Floor amendments to budget resolutions in the House have been numerous, often following the Budget Committee's line-item approach. In 1979 dozens of amendments, some as small as several million dollars, were offered during debate on the spring budget resolution, dragging the House into a long and irrelevant discussion of minor programs. One House veteran denounced the "fast breeder reactor" amendments and insisted on a procedure "whereby those who wish to use the budget process as a means of making political points are limited to making political points on macro issues."[19] The Budget Committee chairman, Robert Giaimo, who complained in 1979 that the House was unfortunately dependent "on the self-restraint of members,"[20] managed the following year to persuade the Rules Committee to limit amendments in order to avoid a repeat of the 1979 embarrassment, but the tension over line items remains.

The other side of this attention to micro issues has been cursory attention to multiyear budgeting. The House Budget Committee finds it so difficult to obtain internal and House-wide agreement on current spending policies that it has little inclination to get into additional controversies over future spending. In 1979, when the Budget committees were instructed to show how balanced budgets might be achieved in future years, the House Budget Committee responded with a perfunctory analysis of current policy projections prepared by its staff. The committee passed up the opportunity to establish a leadership position on long-term spending policy. In 1980, however, the committee finally followed the Senate's lead and included the four years immediately following the current budget, known as "out-years," as part of its spring budget resolution.[21]

The House accepted the multiyear plan, and it is likely that the Budget Committee can institutionalize this practice if it is able to maintain a modest internal consensus. The cooperation of Budget Committee Republicans on the first budget resolution for fiscal 1981 made it much easier to keep the resolution intact on the floor. Continued cooperation, however, is highly uncertain. Moreover, the need for the Senate and House to reach agreement on budgets for the out-years will complicate enormously the task of resolving policy differences in conference.

Because the Budget Committee does not have the same level of program expertise as the spending committees, its commitment to line-item decisions and program details hurts its credibility and its relations with those committees. The multiyear approach can help to draw a clearer line between the macro responsibilities of the Budget Committee and the appropriate jurisdictions of other committees, but until this line is established, the Budget Committee is likely to remain dependent on the House leadership to settle squabbles between committees.

Finally, the Budget Committee remains divided over the appropriate procedure for spending decisions. Budget Committee Republicans have argued for years that a spending total should be decided in advance of decisions on the functional categories. As one Republican member complained, "Until we're willing to deal with aggregates initially, we're . . . merely an adding machine committee."[22] Most Democrats oppose any change in procedure. The Democratic leadership, for example, is concerned that totals would be set so low that spending committees would wind up ignoring the entire process. This admission of weakness underscores the absence of a clear, effective decision strategy that would set the Budget Committee apart from other House committees and let it carve out an area of independent influence.

Senate Procedures. Initially the Senate Budget Committee made no attempt to match the detailed analyses prepared by the House committee, nor did Muskie provide a chairman's mark for each function. As each spending category was discussed, any member could propose numbers. These figures could then be compared with figures in the president's budget, with estimates submitted by other committees, and with estimates of the cost of continuing existing programs, but when changes from these numbers were proposed, whatever the rationale, Muskie and others insisted that the committee finally vote for a number and not for details.

The Senate committee's resistance to line-item analysis has been sharply criticized by House members and especially by members of the House Budget Committee staff. They charge that the Senate committee often does not know how its targets are arrived at, so that the work of the conference committee is complicated immensely. The Senate Budget Committee counters that the House is attempting to make program judgments that are properly the business of other committees.

In 1978, however, the Senate Budget Committee moved to a mission or subfunction format, with heavy emphasis on multiyear budgeting; the committee claimed that this procedure would be more effective for "achieving the broad goals of the Congressional budget process."[23] Each of the major functional categories was broken down into several missions. Spending recommendations were then decided on for a five-year period, and those recommendations were discussed in terms of the future economic and budgetary outlook.

This innovative approach has been continued. During committee markup, each function is discussed on a mission-by-mission basis. The committee staff outlines the major components of each mission, compares the various funding levels available—the president's budget, reestimates of that budget by the Congressional Budget Office, views of authorization and appropriations committees, and estimates contained in current laws—and identifies the policy issues that account for differences in funding levels. The committee then discusses funding levels for a five-year period—the immediately upcoming fiscal year, governed by the budget resolution, and the four out-years. This procedure allows consideration of year-by-year spending *and* the cumulative effect of decisions on current spending.

For each of the missions, any member can offer a set of marks, specifying budget authority and outlays for the five fiscal years, for consideration by the committee. If these numbers are not adopted, alternative numbers are then offered by other committee members. This process continues until the mission's funding level is approved. Unlike the procedure followed by the House Budget Committee, whose majority-party members determine the mark, this procedure allows the minority to participate meaningfully in the writing of the budget resolution, thereby restraining partisanship. And while it does not eliminate the line-item problem entirely—committee members usually defend their "numbers" against alternative funding levels by referring to specific programs—the committee usually stresses that the numbers it adopts do not incorporate binding policy assumptions. Moreover, the emphasis on out-years tends to divert at least some attention from current line items. Because of the out-year estimates, which must frequently be recalculated as the committee proceeds during markup, the staff of the Congressional Budget Office plays a much more active role in Senate Budget Committee proceedings than it does in the House, where the committee staff operates alone during markup.

In 1975 Muskie announced that spending on functional categories would be set before decisions on aggregates. As in the House, Republicans objected. Senators Muskie and Domenici then worked out a compromise that provided that the first round of votes on the functional categories would be tentative and could be revised on second-round votes if the totals were unacceptable. This procedure has eliminated much of the conflict over prior consideration of aggregates; the Senate committee can make cuts or increases in functions already considered and avoid the across-the-board or "meat-ax" cuts that sometimes surface in the House after members have completed consideration of specific functions individually.

House-Senate Differences. To a considerable extent the special-ized approach of the House Budget Committee and the generalist orientation of the Senate Budget Committee reflect traditional dis-tinctions between House and Senate committees. Although the spe-cialization of House members and their appreciation for detail is usually a House strength during the conference committee stage of the legislative process, this conventional advantage does not apply during the budget process. By directing attention to *numbers* and to multiyear budgeting, the Senate Budget Committee has adapted more effectively to the broad objectives of the budget act. It is difficult to make major changes in a single year's budget, but spend-ing policy can be directed over time through a procedure that relates current budget decisions to the future shape and size of the budget. In addition, a multiyear approach allows more informed decisions about the budgetary impact of proposals for new spending or taxes whose short-term effects are negligible but whose long-term impact may be enormous.

Fiscal policy, policy priorities, and budget control were the macro policy areas where congressional control was to be strengthened by the budget act. The Budget committees have a definite leadership responsibility in these areas, but procedures and decision strategies clearly affect the strength of that leadership. In 1979 the Senate Budget Committee was able to deal with pressures for a balanced budget, to show the Senate what the price would be to balance the budget by 1981 or 1982, and to propose a serious plan for doing so. The House Budget Committee effectively ignored the entire matter.

A legitimate if sometimes hazy distinction can be made between macro budgetary issues and substantive policy decisions that the Budget committees must respect. Little is to be gained by continually fighting established committees for pieces of their jurisdiction. The Senate Budget Committee has tried to respect the legitimate prerogatives of other committees as much as possible and to maintain a clear and closely controlled jurisdiction over issues that no other single committee already dominates, a strategy that has worked more effectively than the one followed by the House Budget Committee.

Relations with Other Committees

Once the budget resolutions have been passed, the Budget committees must try to enforce them, often by challenging the spending preferences of other committees. The record of enforcement has been mixed. At times Congress has sustained the Budget committees; on other occasions the discipline of the budget act has been ignored.

The Appropriations Committees

After some initial difficulties, the Senate Budget and Appropriations committees managed to develop an effective working relationship, helped by Appropriations' heavy representation on the Budget Committee. In the 96th Congress, for example, five of the six top-ranking Democrats on the Budget Committee, including Muskie's successor as chairman, Ernest Hollings, were also members of Appropriations, as was Henry Bellmon, the ranking Republican.

In 1975 the Senate Budget Committee attempted to gain jurisdiction over deferrals and rescissions submitted to Congress under Title X of the budget act. The Appropriations Committee claimed exclusive jurisdiction over these matters, but finally settled for joint jurisdiction with the Budget Committee and relevant authorizing committees. Over the next year the two committees frequently tangled over the "crosswalk" procedures used by the Budget Committee to apply functional spending targets to the bills considered by the Appropriations subcommittees. In general, however, the committees have had relatively few serious conflicts. The Budget Committee has avoided explicit judgments on line items, and the Appropriations Committee has agreed to abide by the targets and ceilings in the budget resolutions. Although reconciliation remains a touchy matter, Appropriations has grudgingly accepted the Budget Committee's authority in this area.

The House Budget Committee remains in an ambiguous position with respect to Appropriations. Policy judgments on line items have been a continuing problem, and the Appropriations Committee has probably been even more sensitive to such judgments than necessary. What one does not find in the House, and this is an intriguing failure, is any strong alliance between these two supposed budget-control committees. They have cooperated to a limited extent to tighten controls on back-door spending, but the Appropriations Committee appears now to have taken on some of the advocacy orientation of other spending committees. Appropriations has been curiously nonsupportive of efforts toward reconciliation on the part of the Budget Committee, perhaps because Budget is viewed as a direct competitor. The House Appropriations Committee has probably exhibited more concern over a "super Budget Committee" than has any other committee in Congress, thus weakening efforts to control spending in the House.

The Appropriations committees certainly have not been supplanted by the Budget committees. In the Senate there has at least been accommodation. Because the House has been unable to realize even this limited advantage, the House Budget Committee and the budget process remain vulnerable to challenges by the Appropriations Committee.

The Revenue Committees

The Budget committees have made very little headway in reducing the discretion of the revenue committees of Congress. The Senate Finance Committee and the House Ways and Means Committee are responsible, of course, for the revenue side of the budget and for writing tax legislation. They also handle several large spending programs, notably social security, medicare, and medicaid.

There have been few major disputes involving spending. The major spending programs that the revenue committees deal with are entitlements, most of which increase automatically. Revenues and tax expenditures have been a different matter. There have been repeated battles, predominantly in the Senate, over the authority of the Budget committees to instruct the revenue committees on how to meet a given revenue floor, in particular how to raise additional revenues or distribute tax cuts. The Budget committees contend that these decisions are tied to fiscal policy planning. The revenue committees agree they are bound by the revenue floor in a budget resolution, but they do not accept any other restrictions. The conflict has been going on for several years, and the revenue committees have given up very little ground.

The most dramatic confrontations between these committees involved Muskie and Russell Long of Louisiana, former chairman of the Finance Committee. Their dispute, which began in 1976, first involved the revenue floor in the spring budget resolution for fiscal 1977. The budget resolution set a target revenue level based on a tax cut of more than $15 billion. The report accompanying the resolution explained that this was a net figure that assumed a $17 billion general tax cut for individuals combined with $2 billion in additional revenues from "reforms" in tax expenditures. When the Senate was debating the resolution in April, Muskie responded to a question about these figures by declaring that the "only mandatory number is the revenue total we have included."[24] When the Finance Committee reported its 1,500-page tax bill two months later, it had met the revenue total but had taken no action on the tax-expenditure goals the Budget Committee had set.

Muskie and Bellmon challenged the bill, claiming it was a serious evasion of the budget process. Muskie considered the tax-expenditure issue critical: "No one on the Finance Committee asserts . . . that this bill meets the policy choices that underlie the budget resolution. In fact some Senators seem to think that Congress had nothing particularly in mind at all in adopting the budget."[25] Long countered that he had "not the least bit of resistance" to accepting the revenue target as binding, but he was unwilling to accept instructions on how to meet it:

I submit to the Senator that I do not think any responsible committee—be it Appropriations or Finance or any other—can live with the suggestion that—let us say in a bill for $17 billion in tax cuts—they have no discretion about the $17 billion, any more than the Appropriations Committee could live with the suggestion that the assumptions were that they would spend every dollar of $17 billion in a category without discretion.[26]

The Senate sustained Long's position. Later, Long, with his committee's prerogatives intact, agreed to eliminate some tax expenditures during conference. In 1977 and 1978 Long won other important victories. Against Muskie's objections, he engineered energy tax cuts with delayed effective dates to evade the revenue floor in the fiscal 1978 budget resolution. He also convinced the Senate that tax cuts in future years were not governed by current budget resolutions. With the procedural points settled in his favor, Long was willing to compromise on substantive policy but was adamant about jurisdictional issues.

In the House, the fact that Ways and Means was guaranteed representation on the Budget Committee was expected to minimize these kinds of problems. The record, however, is mixed. Members of Ways and Means probably dissuaded the Budget Committee from attempting to decide substantive tax policies, especially tax-expenditure issues, during the first few years.[27] They appear to have been less effective recently. In 1978 the Budget Committee and the Democratic caucus tried to force Ways and Means to revise the financing system for social security. The Ways and Means Committee finally rejected this instruction. The following year the Ways and Means chairman, Al Ullman, attacked the Budget Committee for issuing instructions on certain tax expenditures. The House supported the Budget Committee, but Ways and Means again refused to take action.

The Senate Finance Committee is something of an anomaly. At a time when strong chairmen and committee loyalties are rare commodities, the Finance Committee under Russell Long provided an important exception. That the Senate Budget Committee had limited success in its battles with Finance was therefore not unexpected. The important point is that these battles usually involved attempts by the Budget Committee to extend its authority, not simply to enforce the budgetary process. The Finance Committee has refused to accept any formal recognition of the Budget Committee's expanded claims although it has recognized that its own discretion is not quite so unlimited as it was before 1974. The relationship between Ways and Means and the Budget Committee is less clear-cut because Ways and Means is no longer the powerful, strongly led committee of the Wilbur Mills era. When the Budget Committee is able to join with the caucus or the Democratic party leadership, it can attempt to pressure Ways and Means, but usually its success is limited. The essential difference here has been that neither committee can be considered to be as independent or influential as its Senate counterpart.

Authorizing Committees

Even though authorizing committees have usually steered away from direct challenges to the budget process, their relations with the Budget committees have at times been strained. In the House, the Armed Services Committee, which has not had heavy representation on the Budget Committee, has been Budget's consistent foe; defense spending is a favorite target of liberal cost cutters. The Armed Services Committee has responded with floor amendments to raise the targets, and while most have been unsuccessful, of late the Budget Committee has begun to respond to Congress' more favorable views on defense spending. Similar challenges from other committees have been less frequent, although the Veterans' Affairs and Agriculture committees have an impressive record of reversing the Budget Committee on the floor.

The fact is, of course, that the House Budget Committee usually has no choice but to accommodate the spending plans of most committees. When House attitudes are negative, as was at one time the case in regard to defense, a committee's request can be cut substantially. More often the cuts are token, and most observers agree that when committees are asked to submit their spending plans to the Budget committees in preparation for the first budget resolution, some cut insurance is included.[28] What the House Budget Committee is really expected to do is provide enough economizing, or at least the appearance of economizing, to avoid embarrassment over the size of the budget. It is not supposed to substitute its judgment for that of other committees or for the whole House.

The Senate Budget Committee has had its share of run-ins with authorizing committees. In 1975 it successfully opposed two author- ization bills on the floor. These victories had minor substantive effects, but they did a great deal to call attention to the Budget Committee and the budget process. In 1977 and 1978 the Budget Committee decided to oppose Agriculture, a move that proved to be a mistake. In 1977 the farm bill exceeded the binding ceiling set by the second budget resolution for fiscal 1978. The Budget Committee recommended that the reconciliation process be used to bring farm spending into conformity with the budget resolution; instead, the Agriculture Committee persuaded the Senate to change the budget resolution and make it conform to the farm bill. The following year Muskie and the Budget Committee proved powerless to block an emergency farm bill reported by the Agriculture Committee. The Senate bypassed its own waiver procedures against the Budget Committee's objections and proceeded to pass the farm bill. The legislation was finally stopped in the House. The Senate Budget Committee has had recurring problems with Agriculture and Veterans' Affairs; as one Senate Republican sums it up, "When it comes to agriculture and veterans, we forget about the budget."[29]

The general pattern of the past several years suggests that the Budget committees have a greater impact on new spending initiatives than on established programs. Since authorizing committees are required to submit their spending plans in advance of the first budget resolution (the "views and estimates" procedure), the Budget committees have an opportunity to raise budgetary objections, hindering, if not entirely foreclosing, serious consideration of such initiatives by authorizing committees. In addition, real obstacles to subsequent committee lobbying for new spending initiatives are created. Given the current mood in Congress, such programs might appear doomed in any case, but this mood was not nearly so pronounced in the past, and the Budget committees deserve much of the credit for promoting restraint.

The task of holding down rates of increase, not to speak of cutting back existing programs, is obviously a much more formidable undertaking. Spending clienteles for these programs are already well organized; authorizing committees are fiercely protective; and most of the spending, especially for nondefense purposes, is uncontrollable, thus necessitating attempts to change existing law in order to achieve savings. In the absence of truly extraordinary sentiments for economy in Congress, the Budget committees cannot be expected to prevail on very many fights with authorizing committees, and in fact, their occasional successes have had only a minor impact on the growth of spending.

During 1980 there were indications that this situation might change. The Budget committees succeeded in including in the first budget resolution reconciliation instructions that required Senate and House committees to report over $9 billion in spending cuts and considerably more in revenue increases to achieve a balanced budget in fiscal 1981. The resolution was an important attempt to put teeth into the budget process, and while the Budget committees conceded that the specifics on meeting budgetary requirements were ultimately the prerogatives of the sixteen House and Senate committees to which the reconciliation language applied, certain entitlements were clearly under attack. But in the end the reconciliation experiment did not meet the Budget committees' expectations, and seemingly endless delays pushed final action on the reconciliation bill to the final days of the lame-duck session, after passage of the second budget resolution. Moreover, the spending cuts and revenue increases finally agreed to by Congress were scaled down substantially. For example, the cost-of-living adjustment for federal civilian and military retirees was not changed from its semiannual to an annual basis, a decision that eliminated a $750 million reduction in spending and retained an adjustment formula that Robert Giaimo, chairman of the House Budget Committee, denounced as producing "the least justifiable expenditures of the federal government."[30]

There were some brighter spots. Because of pressures from reconciliation, the House and Senate committees rewrote the authorization bill for child nutrition and special food programs, eliminating proposed increases and providing some limited savings in the final reconciliation bill. Even more impressive was the Senate Budget Committee's impact on a five-year authorization for higher education. The House Education and Labor Committee had refused to raise interest payments on student loans or to make other cuts to meet reconciliation requirements. During conference, Senate conferees went along with the House, despite strenuous objections and warnings from the Senate Budget Committee. The House then passed the conference report by a vote of 373–16, but in a surprising move, the Senate supported its Budget committee and voted the bill down. The House eventually agreed to the cutbacks, although a

Republican member of the Education and Labor Committee, John Buchanan of Alabama, denounced the "power play" of the Senate Budget Committee and contrasted it to the "measured respect" and "charitable and spirited understanding" between authorizing committees and the Budget Committee in the House. Buchanan complained that "it was almost as if the authorizing committee had to ask permission of the Budget Committee to set education policy," and bewailed "the caveat that we represent our people conditioned upon the blessing of the Senate Budget Committee."[31]

Buchanan was not the only conservative to find fiscal restraint uncomfortable when it was applied to popular programs. The move to maintain the semiannual increases in federal pensions was led by one of the House's most outspoken conservatives, Robert Bauman of Maryland, and Republicans supported, by a vote of 105–41, instructions to House conferees on the reconciliation bill to insist that the semiannual adjustments be retained. In the Senate, when the Governmental Affairs Committee reported out only a one-year adjustment in the formula, the Budget Committee's chairman, Ernest Hollings, argued that reconciliation instructions dictated a permanent change. His attempt to overrule the Government Affairs Committee, however, was rejected by the Senate, and all but one of the Republicans on the Budget Committee, including Domenici, deserted Hollings on this savings issue.

The loss of congressional will on federal retirement benefits is not an isolated example; it demonstrates that even staunch fiscal conservatives may find it very difficult to vote for cuts in major entitlements or other spending programs that have organized support or widespread public backing. The rhetoric of the opposition party is not always a good guide to what the party will do once it commands a majority, and Republicans on the Senate Budget Committee may not find it politically feasible to deliver the budget cuts they have promised. They may also find that their Republican colleagues on the authorizing committees have become protectors of the spending committees' prerogatives.

The Impact of the Budget Committees

The contrasts between the Senate and House Budget committees are often striking. The Senate committee is, by most accounts, independent, influential, and effectively integrated into the Senate's decision-making process. It has come reasonably close to the requirement set down by the Government Operations Committee in 1973 that the budget process "must be nonpartisan."[32] The House Budget Committee is far from impotent, but it is not an independent committee or, on its own, an especially influential one. Perhaps because the House Budget Committee has been unable to articulate clearly the institutional stakes involved, the House appears to have little regard for the macro policy issues that define the budget process.

Although the Senate Budget Committee appears more powerful than its House counterpart, it has not achieved authoritative control of spending or other budget policy issues. Both committees are, in truth, adding-machine committees that take the demands of spending committees and impose as much restraint on them as the current congressional mood allows. Neither Budget committee has the charge or the authority to act as sole interpreter of Congress' preferences in regard to spending. Even the Senate Budget Committee must recognize that it has powerful competitors when it comes to spending.

The Budget committees deserve great credit for implementing a complicated and demanding budget process. The House and Senate rarely violate the procedures and often meet the deadlines mandated by the budget process; each year, sometimes after exhausting debate, the required budget resolutions are finally passed. The content of these resolutions provides another criterion for evaluating the impact of the Budget committees. When the congressional budgets are examined, it is possible to judge what the committees have accomplished in the way of spending control and priorities. It is also possible to see just how much difference a strong, bipartisan Budget committee has made in the Senate in contrast to its weaker counterpart in the House.

CHAPTER 5

Congressional Budget Policy

The concurrent budget resolutions adopted by Congress each year are the heart of its budget process, expressing congressional decisions on fiscal policy by defining the balance between total spending and revenue. The breakdown of total spending by functional categories represents congressional priorities. The spending target in the spring budget resolution and the spending ceiling in the fall resolution are Congress' procedures to control spending.

Under the budget act, Congress must pass at least two of these budget resolutions each year. The first resolution, whose deadline is May 15, sets spending and revenue targets to guide subsequent congressional action on spending bills and tax legislation. The second budget resolution, whose deadline is September 15, is supposedly *the congressional budget* for the fiscal year that begins October 1, and once it has been passed, Congress cannot enact legislation that will breach its spending ceiling or revenue floor.

One provision of the budget act, however, allows Congress to "adopt a concurrent resolution on the budget which revises the concurrent resolution on the budget . . . most recently agreed to."[1] The "final" budget resolution is therefore far from final. Indeed, Congress has frequently enacted third budget resolutions to accommodate discretionary and nondiscretionary increases in spending.

The possibility of third budget resolutions obviously weakens the concept of a firm congressional budget. The most serious problem relates to control of spending, but there are problems with fiscal policy and priorities as well. As long as Congress has the option of raising its spending ceilings, it can escape the need to impose real discipline on its spending choices—and that is precisely what has occurred. Over the past several years there have been important differences between House and Senate budget policies, especially over spending for defense and social welfare and the rate of overall budget growth. Each year the House-Senate conflicts over the first and second budget resolutions have been serious and protracted, but they have had only limited impact on congressional spending policy. The budget resolution procedure has been sufficiently flexible to obviate the need for definitive congressional budgets.

House Budget Policy

The House of Representatives has found it hard to reach agreement on budget policy, primarily because of the sharp partisan division over deficits and fiscal policy. These debates on fiscal policy are not the result of differences between committees. The arguments between Democrats and Republicans in the House Budget Committee are replayed on the House floor when Republicans, unable to reduce spending totals and deficits recommended by the Budget Committee to what they consider tolerable levels, have offered official substitute resolutions. While none has been adopted, the votes in recent years have been fairly close, reflecting the growing uneasiness among Democrats over deficit spending.

The House also has been divided over defense spending—with predictable results. Democrats on the Budget Committee engage in annual warfare over how deeply to cut the president's defense budget requests. The recommended cuts are too large to satisfy pro-defense Democrats and Republicans and too small to please House liberals. When the budget resolutions are debated, defense proponents try to raise the defense targets and liberals propose steeper cuts, frequently coupling them with transfers of funds to social welfare programs. But as concern over deficits has grown in the House, support for defense spending has also increased, making it much more difficult for liberals to attack defense spending successfully and increasing pressure on social welfare spending.

Floor debates over spending within the functional categories often make up in symbolic intensity what they lack in practical effect. Spending estimates for many programs are imprecise; as a result, the numbers debated with such fervor are often much less important in terms of what will actually be spent than are short-term changes in economic conditions or other factors that Congress cannot control. It is not that the numbers are irrelevant, but rather that House members tend to exaggerate the impact of many floor amendments. Frequently the debates over budget policy in the House turn out to be much more programmatic than the authors of the budget act anticipated or thought desirable. Instead of debating broad budget policy, the House often wastes time discussing issues that are more carefully considered at other stages of the legislative process.

Policy Conflicts and Amendments

A congressional committee's success in defending its proposals during floor consideration is a measure of its influence. The Budget Committee must therefore defeat floor amendments as well as secure final passage of budget resolutions. The House Budget Committee has had a mixed record with regard to floor amendments. On occasion Democratic party and Budget Committee leaders have orchestrated the amending process in order to secure passage of budget resolutions. At other times the amending process has been uncontrolled.

Fiscal Stimulus. The first two budgets adopted by Congress—for fiscal years 1976 and 1977—contained very large deficits designed to provide economic stimulus and promote economic recovery. The first concurrent resolution for fiscal year 1976 provided for a deficit of $68.8 billion as "appropriate in the light of economic conditions and all other relevant factors."[2] The following year Congress set the deficit at $50.8 billion. Both deficits were well above the levels recommended by the Ford administration, but substantial deficits were considered unavoidable and were in fact justified on economic grounds. The issue was just how substantial those deficits should be.

House conservatives were appalled at the size of the proposed deficit in the first budget resolution reported for fiscal year 1976. Phil M. Landrum, a senior southern Democrat who had been selected from the Ways and Means Committee to serve on the Budget Committee, offered a floor amendment to reduce the recommended deficit by approximately 10 percent; it was approved by a vote of 227–180. The House Democratic leadership then mounted a strenuous effort to reverse the House's action in order to prevent the wholesale loss of liberal support for the budget resolution. After easily defeating two Republican proposals—one to balance the budget and a second to reduce the deficit below the level provided by the Landrum amendment—majority leader Thomas P. (Tip) O'Neill finally secured House approval of a substitute amendment that incorporated a deficit reduction of $3 billion through unspecified tax reforms rather than spending cuts and also rejected the Budget Committee's recommendations for caps on retirement-income programs. O'Neill was just able to hold together a Democratic majority, and the budget resolution was passed by a vote of 200–196.

In the fall O'Neill again went after liberal support, arranging for the Budget Committee's second resolution to be amended to provide additional job and education programs. Republican substitutes similar to those offered in the spring were overwhelmingly rejected, and the House approved the amended version of the second resolution by a vote of 225–191. When the conference version was considered on December 12, 1975, however, the margin for passage was only two votes.

This first-year strategy on the part of the Democratic leadership benefited from the obvious reluctance of moderate Democrats to sabotage in its infancy a reform that had been so widely acclaimed. Since failure would also have conceded leadership in budget policy to a Republican president, the Democratic drive to preserve an independent congressional budget process had an obviously partisan dimension. But the size of the fiscal 1976 deficit clearly was troubling to many Democrats.

Decisions on the fiscal 1977 budget were much easier, in part because of a fortuitous shortfall in spending that reduced the deficit by almost $8 billion for fiscal 1976, allowing Congress to stay well within its established spending limits. The Budget Committee's first and second resolutions came through floor debate relatively unscathed. The House adopted two amendments that raised the spending target for veterans' benefits but turned back attempts to change the balance between defense and social welfare spending. Once again Republican-sponsored amendments to balance the budget and reduce the deficit were easily defeated. The first resolution for fiscal 1977 was approved 221–155; the second, which contained primarily spending reestimates, was passed by a similar margin without amendments.

Flexibility or Confusion. These easy successes proved transitory.

Early in 1977 the heavily Democratic 95th Congress had a new Democratic president, who requested changes in the already approved budget for fiscal 1977. He also presented recommendations for the fiscal 1978 resolutions being prepared by the Budget committees. The results were confusion over the 1977 budget, House rejection of the first resolution for 1978, and questions about the independence of the congressional budget process.

The Carter administration's economic stimulus plan for the 1977 fiscal year included increases in spending and reductions in taxes—primarily through a $50 tax rebate to individuals. Congress reacted positively to the Carter spending proposals, and in early March both Houses adopted a third budget resolution for fiscal 1977, raising the spending ceiling, lowering the revenue floor, and increasing the deficit set forth in the second resolution. At first glance the new resolution seemed to demonstrate the flexibility of the budget procedure, but some members expressed reservations. A senior southern Democrat warned his colleagues, "If we make light of the congressional budget and turn it from a far-sighted economic program into a quarterly economic update—I think we will regret it."[3]

In April the president suddenly withdrew a large part of his stimulus package, including the suggested tax rebates, and the Budget committees had to revise the third budget resolution. This necessity added to the problems of the House Budget Committee, which was already having difficulties with defense spending. Although Carter's revisions in the Ford administration's budget for fiscal 1978 had included a reduction in defense spending, the House Budget Committee voted to recommend additional cuts. During markup, both the new Democratic majority leader, Jim Wright of Texas, and Republican Marjorie Holt of Maryland offered amendments raising the defense spending target in line with the Carter budget. These amendments were defeated. The defense issue, however, precipitated a chaotic floor fight, during which the administration lobbied for increases in defense spending. The House agreed to raise the defense spending target—but then approved spending increases in other programs. As a result, the amended resolution was unacceptable to both liberals and conservatives and was rejected by a vote of 84–320.

Following this debacle, the Budget Committee and the new Democratic leadership attempted to regain control of the budget process. The committee fashioned a compromise resolution, raising its original recommendation for defense spending slightly and including a portion of the other funding increases that had passed on the floor. Majority leader Wright asked his Democratic colleagues to take action to avoid further embarrassment: "I . . . earnestly plead for you to vote to sustain the committee and redeem the commitment of the House to make this budget process work. If a budget resolution should not be adopted . . . Congress itself would be the victim of a self-imposed paralysis."[4] This time a series of pro-defense amendments was defeated, including the one the House had approved during the first debate. The only successful amendment was an increase in spending for veterans' benefits. Finally the resolution was passed by a vote of 213–179.

House Democrats complained about the administration's lobbying efforts and intervention. Speaker O'Neill suggested a lack of understanding, stating, "It is unfortunate the Secretary of Defense made an end-around play, not knowing the procedures of Congress."[5] Budget Committee chairman Giaimo was less conciliatory: "This is the United States Congress where the Democratic majority is going to write the legislation. It is not the Georgia legislature. . . . You don't just call up from downtown and send word from the Secretary of Defense to Armed Services Committee members and others and say 'Write a budget resolution.'"[6] But the White House was not the major problem. The Budget Committee was sharply split, and thus vulnerable to challenges by authorizing committees. For example, on the second resolution for fiscal 1978, floor amendments raised outlays and the deficit by approximately $1 billion over the Budget Committee's recommendations. Once more spending for veterans was increased, and the Agriculture Committee succeeded in having the ceiling on agriculture spending raised.

The 96th Congress. During 1979 and early 1980 the budget process in the House became increasingly fractious. In 1979 the number of floor amendments to the first budget resolution for fiscal 1980 got entirely out of hand. In the fall a split over the defense budget threatened passage of the second resolution. The House decided to limit floor amendments in 1980, thus solving one problem, but the decision to prepare a balanced budget and to increase defense spending once again threatened to destroy the budget process in the House.

110

The "balanced budget" that the House adopted for fiscal 1981 was, for many Democrats, a political necessity. Over the years, Republican substitute budget resolutions had attracted growing support (see Table 5.1). For example, the balanced-budget proposals offered by Republican conservative John Rousselot gained nearly 200 votes in 1979 (for the 1980 budget) and again in 1980 (for the 1981 budget). Republicans on the Budget Committee had come up with their alternative budgets each year, and Democrats had been hard-pressed to defeat them on the floor. In 1979 Speaker O'Neill

Table 5.1. House votes on Republican-sponsored substitute budget resolutions, fiscal years 1976–81

Amendments and fiscal year	Budget resolution	Vote (yes–no)
Balanced-budget amendments[a]		
1976	First	94–311
	Second	127–283
1977	First	105–272
	Second	111–264
1978	First	131–271
	Second	169–230
1979	First	170–226
	Second	153–235
1980	First	186–214
	Second	181–224
1981	First	191–218
Deficit-reduction amendments[b]		
1976	First	159–248
	Second	159–257
1977	First	145–230
1978	First, initial round	150–250
	First, second round	150–240
1979	First	197–203
	Second	201–206
1980	First	
	Latta "official" substitute	191–228
	Holt-Regula substitute	198–218
	Second	187–230
1981	First	175–242

[a]Sponsored by John Rousselot of California.
[b]Sponsored by Republicans on the Budget Committee.
SOURCE: Compiled from *Congressional Quarterly Weekly Report,* various years.

set up a special task force to coordinate Democratic efforts to defeat the Republican budget plan. The leader of the task force, Norman Mineta of the Budget Committee, exhorted his fellow Democrats to stick together: "The bottom line is, Do you want a budget written by the Democratic majority or a budget written by the Republican minority?"[7] The Republican substitutes were finally rejected, but the House then turned around and adopted an across-the-board spending cut of 0.5 percent, which had been rejected by the Budget Committee and was opposed by the House Democratic leadership.

The balanced-budget issue became more troublesome for Democrats as the 1980 election neared. The chairmen of the House and Senate Budget committees, the Democratic congressional leadership, and the Carter administration agreed in March 1980 to attempt to balance the budget for fiscal 1981, and the House Budget Committee approved its first-ever surplus budget on March 20. This time Budget Committee Republicans voted for the resolution, but six liberal Democrats opposed it and promised to take their fight to the floor. With amendments limited, a token Republican effort to cut spending and taxes was rejected, as were several liberal attempts to increase social welfare spending.

The House continued, however, to have trouble with defense. The Budget Committee leadership won approval for its defense spending target, but only after promising to increase defense spending in conference with the Senate, a pledge that mollified the Armed Services Committee, which had narrowly been defeated on a pro-defense amendment the year before.

Even as the fiscal 1981 resolution was passed, apprehension over the fate of the balanced budget was growing. The apparent balance was extremely precarious, depending on unlikely economic conditions as well as unprecedented restraint on spending in Congress. Nevertheless, the fiscal 1981 budget was something of a highlight for the Budget Committee. It had managed to achieve a limited bipartisan consensus, to fight off liberal and conservative floor amendments, to include a multiyear plan covering fiscal years 1982 and 1983, and to persuade the House to accept instructions on reconciliation for its spending committees. Within a short time, however, the situation reverted to normal. The Democratic leadership in the House helped to defeat the compromise in the first conference on the fiscal 1981 budget, supported the Appropriations Committee in a reconciliation fight with the Budget Committee, and made it clear that the silent demise of the balanced budget would not be greatly mourned. As always, neither the House nor the Budget Committee could stick to a consistent policy line.

Voting Patterns

The results of these policy disputes are typically narrow margins for passage and, in several instances, rejected resolutions (see Tables 5.2 and 5.3). Since Republicans provide little or no support for budget resolutions, liberal Democrats can press for domestic spending increases on the floor. When the House turns down compromises worked out by conference committees, liberals are usually able to win at least symbolic increases for social welfare programs.

In the absence of a bipartisan or even majority-party consensus, the House has to struggle to keep the budget process from collaps-

Table 5.2. House votes on Budget Committee reports, concurrent budget resolutions, 1975–80, by party

Calendar year	Resolution	Fiscal year	Democrats		Republicans (yes–no)	Total (yes–no)
			Northern (yes–no)	Southern (yes–no)		
1975	First	1976	151–33	46–35	3–128	200–196
	Second	1976	162–31	52–36	11–124	225–191
1976	First	1977	159–20	49–24	13–111	221–155
	Second	1977	154–16	61–22	12–113	227–151
1977	Third	1977	176–15	49–35	14–119	239–169
	Third revised	1977	—	—	—	—
	First	1978*	50–132	32–53	2–135	84–320
	First	1978	142–39	64–19	7–121	213–179
	Second	1978	139–32	56–27	4–129	199–188
1978	First	1979	152–25	46–36	3–136	201–197
	Second	1979	154–25	61–17	2–136	217–178
1979	First	1980*	147–33	64–17	9–134	220–184
	Second	1980	135–42	53–25	4–146	192–213
	Second	1980	157–25	55–27	0–154	212–206
1980	First	1981*	128–54	75–8	22–131	225–193
	Second	1981	133–33	68–12	2–146	203–191

*Also incorporates revisions of the most recent budget resolution for the preceding fiscal year. Senate and conference versions followed this same procedure, combining the third resolution for the ongoing fiscal year with the spring budget resolution for the next fiscal year.

SOURCE: Compiled from *Congressional Quarterly Weekly Report,* various years.

Table 5.3. House votes on conference committee reports, concurrent budget resolutions, 1975–80, by party

Calendar year	Resolution	Fiscal year	Democrats Northern (yes–no)	Southern (yes–no)	Republicans (yes–no)	Total (yes–no)
1975	First	1976	164–28	61–27	5–138	230–193
	Second	1976	147–21	39–40	3–126	189–187
1976	First	1977	161–21	53–24	10–125	224–170
	Second	1977	156–17	57–19	21–107	234–143
1977	Third	1977	172–16	46–35	8–122	226–173
	Third revised	1977	—	—	—	—
	First	1978	122–53	70–17	29–107	221–177
	Second	1978	148–33	63–22	4–132	215–187
1978	First	1979	134–47	65–18	2–133	201–198
	Second	1979	158–22	60–17	7–123	225–162
1979	First	1980	50–130	58–22	36–108	144–260
	First	1980	103–70	71–10	28–116	202–196
	Second	1980	146–26	59–19	0–145	205–190
1980	First	1981	30–133	67–13	44–96	141–242
	First	1981	122–45	73–10	10–140	205–195
	Second	1981	Voice vote			

SOURCE: Compiled from *Congressional Quarterly Weekly Report,* various years.

ing. The hardy perennials—defense, social welfare, and deficits— are refought virtually from scratch each year. Coalitions shift as budget resolutions are tailored to gain majority support, and Democrats on the Budget Committee are dependent on the House Democratic leadership to manage this coalition building. If the incipient moves toward bipartisanship on the Budget Committee achieve some permanence, the committee might be able to develop a stable base of support in the House for a long-term budget strategy. The more likely event, however, is a return to all-out opposition among Republicans, especially as the first balanced budget has proved to be nothing of the sort, and sharper attacks by Democratic liberals.

Senate Budget Policy

The Senate Budget Committee has led a less precarious existence than its House counterpart, although it, too, has had to defend its resolutions against more and more amendments each year. As in the House, some of these amendments have been sponsored by Budget

Committee members who have sought to win on the floor what they have been unable to accomplish within the committee, while others have been pushed by spending committees dissatisfied with the funds they have been allocated. Although the Senate Budget Committee has not been able to defeat all amendments, it has managed to defuse the deficit and defense controversies that have been so prevalent in the House. Because the Senate Budget Committee has forged a strong bipartisan coalition, it has generally managed to focus attention on long-term budget-control strategies.

Amendments

During its first two years of operation, the Budget Committee managed to pass all of its resolutions handily. The first resolution for fiscal 1976 was reported out of committee by a 13–2 vote, and Muskie and Bellmon proceeded to defend the resolution against both liberal and conservative proposals on the floor. When James Buckley, elected on the Conservative ticket in New York and assigned to the Budget Committee, proposed a cut of more than $30 billion in the deficit, committee Republicans joined Muskie in characterizing the proposal as unrealistic and unwise. The Buckley amendment was voted down, 21–69. Even when Republican Robert Dole of the Budget Committee proposed a more modest cut of only $2.2 billion, Bellmon opposed it, and it was rejected, 33–62. When Democrat Walter Mondale, also a member of the committee, proposed doubling the funding for economic recovery programs to $9 billion, Muskie, who had supported that funding level during committee markup, led the opposition and succeeded in defeating the Mondale amendment. The only amendment offered by a senator not on the Budget Committee was conservative Republican Jesse Helms's balanced-budget substitute, and it was defeated by a vote of 9–75. The first budget resolution was then passed by a 69–23 vote. During consideration of the second resolution, Edward Kennedy proposed to raise the revenue floor by eliminating tax "loopholes," but this proposal was turned down by a 21–76 vote. No other amendments were offered, and the second budget resolution was easily approved.

The following year several spending committees attempted to revise the first budget resolution. Alan Cranston of California, a Budget Committee member and third-ranking Democrat on the Veterans' Affairs Committee, attempted to increase the spending target for the veterans' benefits and services function. Russell Long, chairman of the Finance Committee, proposed changes in the health and income security categories for programs under his committee's jurisdiction. Birch Bayh, of the Judiciary Committee, sought to raise the spending target for the law-enforcement function, and another Democrat, Walter Huddleston of the Agriculture Committee, attempted to increase the agriculture funding level. They were all defeated, as were liberal attempts to cut the defense budget and conservative attempts to cut the deficit. The first resolution for fiscal 1977 was approved, 62–22. There were no roll-call amendments on the second resolution, which passed by a vote of 55–23.

The Budget Committee's impressive record came to an abrupt halt in 1977. During debate on the first resolution for fiscal 1978, the chairmen of the Banking, Housing and Urban Affairs, and Veterans' Affairs committees successfully pushed for increased funding for programs handled by their committees. In the fall the Budget Committee took on the Agriculture Committee and lost. As part of its second budget resolution for fiscal 1978, the Budget Committee recommended a $5.6 billion ceiling for agriculture and included a reconciliation provision instructing the Agriculture Committee to reduce spending to that level. Herman Talmadge of Georgia, chairman of the Agriculture Committee, responded by offering an amendment to raise the ceiling by $700 million and thus make the reconciliation provision moot.

Bellmon and a majority of Budget Committee members deserted Muskie, and the Senate approved the Talmadge amendment. During the debate, Muskie argued once again against piecemeal Senate consideration of add-ons:

> If we could . . . let the Senate go to [sic] the budget function by function and exercise its own judgment on each function, and then at the end add up the total and if it is too high, cut back—that is another way of doing it. However, I suspect that if we were to do that, we would convert the Senate budget process into a Christmas tree operation of the kind that we have seen so often with respect to tax bills, and that is a dangerous business.[8]

Muskie also was unsuccessful in opposing an amendment to the revenue floor to accommodate tuition tax credits, although he did win disapproval of general tax cuts and spending reductions.

While numerous amendments were offered to the first and second budget resolutions for fiscal 1979, none followed the pattern of spending committee challenges—and none was adopted. All but one of the fourteen roll calls on fiscal 1979 budget amendments involved proposed cuts in spending or taxes. The exception was an amendment by John Tower of Texas, ranking minority member on the Armed Services Committee, to increase defense spending.

Similarly, most of the amendments offered during debate on the fiscal 1980 first budget resolution also called for spending or tax cuts. Only one of these amendments, a minor cut targeted at government travel and filmmaking expenses, was approved. Other amendments called for spending increases. Edward Kennedy, chairman of the Judiciary Committee, attempted to increase funding for the Law Enforcement Assistance Administration, but his amendment was defeated by a vote of 38–46. Howard Metzenbaum of Ohio, a Democratic member of the Budget Committee, successfully pushed for an increase in funding levels for nutrition programs authorized under the Older Americans Act, legislation that had been sponsored by the Labor and Human Resources Committee, of which Metzenbaum was also a member. The other major proposal adopted against Budget Committee opposition was also offered by a member of the Budget Committee: Democrat Lawton Chiles of Florida succeeded in eliminating a portion of the "savings" the Budget Committee had assumed could be made in the social security program.

Although the Senate showed no inclination to change the defense spending target recommended by the Budget Committee, it did engage in a heated debate on a line-item issue. Democrat Donald Riegle of Michigan had led a successful fight in the Budget Committee to delete funds requested by the Defense Department to purchase four U.S.-built destroyers that had been ordered by the shah of Iran and then canceled by the new Iranian government. When John Stennis of Mississippi, chairman of the Armed Services Committee, indicated that he would simply drop other items in order to fund the destroyer purchases, Riegle tried to force further cuts in the defense appropriation on the Senate floor. Muskie and others argued that Riegle's attempt to impose line-item restrictions on the Armed Services Committee was inappropriate, and the Riegle amendment was defeated by a vote of 26–62.

The second budget resolution for fiscal 1980 was an important

117

victory for the Budget Committee. Before floor action, Muskie reached an agreement with the Appropriations Committee on how cuts would be made in pending bills, and the Budget Committee then easily defeated the Agriculture and Veterans' Affairs committees on direct floor tests as they sought to evade reconciliation instructions for spending cuts. Although the Senate then proceeded to add some $40 billion in budget authority for defense above the levels recommended by the Budget Committee for fiscal years 1980–82, it did turn back all other challenges to the Budget Committee's plan.

The fiscal 1981 budget resolution reported the following spring found the Budget Committee fighting off almost two dozen amendments, many similar to the minor variety the House Budget Committee had been plagued with the year before. Liberal attempts to transfer funds from defense to social welfare were easily defeated, as was a Republican call for major spending and tax cuts. The only amendment to survive was a proposal to restore a portion of the $1.7 billion that the Budget Committee had cut from the state revenue-sharing program.

In the fall the Budget Committee was unable to maintain its revenue recommendations against sentiments for tax cuts. Despite Bellmon's efforts, most Republicans supported a tax-cut amendment sponsored by William Roth of Delaware. With Democrats split, the amendment was adopted and incorporated into the Senate version of the second budget resolution. Since most conferees now admitted that any attempt to balance the budget in fiscal 1981 was futile, the House-Senate conference added a substantial tax cut in the second resolution.

The Senate Budget Committee has had disputes with spending committees, but most of these quarrels have not been protracted. The Budget Committee's floor strategy has been fairly successful in discouraging add-ons, just as it has generally been able to hold the line against both piecemeal and across-the-board spending cuts. In addition, it has made a determined effort to avoid the line-item approach that has caused so much trouble in the House. (Even in its fabled confrontation with the Senate Armed Services Committee in 1975, when Muskie enforced the defense spending target against a defense authorization bill, the Budget Committee was careful to limit its objections to overall spending. And since the original Senate authorization was lower than the House bill, Muskie's challenge had the effect of upholding the Senate's position.) In the Senate, a relatively peaceful relationship has been established between the Budget Committee and the spending committees, markedly strengthening the Budget Committee's hand during floor debate. Whether that peace can be maintained if the Budget Committee aggressively pursues spending cuts in the 97th Congress is another matter.

Voting Patterns

Unlike the House, the Senate has usually demonstrated bipartisan support for budget resolutions (see Tables 5.4 and 5.5). Democratic support for both Budget Committee and conference versions has been consistently high, usually extending across the ideological spectrum. Northern and southern Democrats have generally provided heavy majorities for passage, and Republican support has averaged around 50 percent, a striking contrast to the almost unanimous Republican opposition in the House.

Not all Republicans, however, agreed with Bellmon's strategy of cooperation on the Budget Committee. Some conservatives criticized the bipartisan approach, and Domenici, who ranked below

Table 5.4. Senate votes on Budget Committee reports, concurrent budget resolutions, 1975–80, by party

Calendar year	Resolution	Fiscal year	Democrats		Republicans (yes–no)	Total (yes–no)
			Northern (yes–no)	Southern (yes–no)		
1975	First	1976	36–1	14–3	19–18	69–22
	Second	1976	41–0	9–8	19–15	69–23
1976	First	1977	32–4	13–2	17–16	62–22
	Second	1977	27–3	14–2	14–18	55–23
1977	Third	1977	40–0	15–3	17–17	72–20
	Third revised	1977	—	—	—	—
	First	1978	36–3	5–11	15–17	56–31
	Second	1978	33–4	13–4	17–13	63–21
1978	First	1979	35–4	13–4	16–19	64–27
	Second	1979	30–3	12–3	14–12	56–18
1979	First	1980	29–4	15–1	20–15	64–20
	Second	1980	28–12	17–2	17–22	62–36
1980	First	1981	31–5	18–1	19–22	68–28
	Second	1981	21–14	12–7	15–25	48–46

SOURCE: Compiled from *Congressional Quarterly Weekly Report,* various years.

Table 5.5. Senate votes on conference committee reports, concurrent budget resolutions, 1975–80, by party

Calendar year	Resolution	Fiscal year	Democrats Northern (yes–no)	Southern (yes–no)	Republicans (yes–no)	Total (yes–no)
1975	First	1976	Voice vote			
	Second	1976	40–1	13–3	21–15	74–19
1976	First	1977	34–6	15–3	16–20	65–29
	Second	1977	34–2	17–1	15–17	66–20
1977	Third	1977	Voice vote			
	Third revised	1977	—	—	—	—
	First	1978	29–4	8–7	17–12	54–23
	Second	1978	36–4	13–4	19–13	68–21
1978	First	1979	Voice vote			
	Second	1979	28–2	8–1	11–4	47–7
1979	First	1980	Rejected by House			
	First	1980	31–3	17–1	24–13	72–17
	Second	1980	26–9	13–5	26–13	65–27
1980	First	1981	Rejected by House			
	First	1981	28–4	16–1	17–21	61–26
	Second	1981	24–11	12–7	14–20	50–38

SOURCE: Compiled from *Congressional Quarterly Weekly Report,* various years.

Bellmon on the Budget Committee, was particularly assertive in pushing for Republican alternative budgets. Now that Domenici has become chairman, the potential for greater partisanship certainly exists. Moreover, even if Domenici manages to build an effective conservative-moderate coalition on his committee and in the Senate, he will face a House Budget Committee controlled by Democrats and responsive to the Democratic leadership.

The Senate Budget Committee has managed to institutionalize the budget process in the Senate and to gain acceptance for multiyear budgeting, reconciliation, and other procedures that strengthen the process. It has also directed a fairly consistent approach to budget policy over the years, with emphasis on increases for defense and restraint in spending. These policy initiatives have found widespread acceptance in the Senate, but they have resulted in sharp disagreements with the House that will doubtlessly become more severe as Senate Republicans press for greater and greater restraint in spending. The budget process may be, as Domenici concedes, a "minor disciplinary mechanism," but he also argues that without it, Congress "will have to expect worse."[9] To an increasing extent the Republican majority in the Senate may be committed to maintaining and strengthening a process whose demise would not be greatly mourned by many Senate and House Democrats.

House-Senate Policy Differences

The House and Senate have been on opposite sides of numerous budget policy questions. For years they disagreed sharply over the level of defense spending and the resulting balance between defense and social welfare spending, with the Senate considerably more supportive than the House of increases in the defense budget. In addition, there have been important if less publicized conflicts over spending control, economic forecasting, and long-term budgeting. Each fiscal year has been marked as well by specific policy controversies over such matters as public works jobs, tuition tax credits, and general revenue sharing. This last category has usually been handled through compromise or by ambiguity in conference reports. When Senate and House conferees have supported competing programs, they have often settled on a funding figure and left the House and Senate to make the final decisions about alternative policies. The recurring problems with budget priorities and spending control, however, have been more difficult to resolve. And while the Senate has finally prevailed on defense, the House has done rather well on spending.

Budget Priorities: Defense and Social Welfare

Every time House and Senate conferees attempt to reconcile the budget resolutions passed by the separate chambers, they face the delicate problem of balancing defense and social welfare spending. The House Budget Committee substantially cut the amounts requested for the defense budget during the Ford administration, settled for more modest cuts the next few years, and has lately become more supportive of defense; the House as a whole, after some difficult floor fights, has generally gone along. On social welfare spending, the House Budget Committee has been much less willing than its Senate counterpart to limit future growth. Neither Budget committee, it should be understood, has advocated substantial cuts in major social welfare programs. Rather, the differences have involved the degree of incremental growth and the accommodation of new program initiatives.

The defense–social welfare argument tends to be fought in terms of two functional categories—the 050 function (national defense) and the 500 function (education, training, employment, and social services). Included in the latter category are the various federal programs for elementary, secondary, and higher education; job training and public service jobs programs; and the supportive and protective services that are provided for the disadvantaged, the disabled, and children. House-Senate conflicts over these categories tend to center on budget authority as well as outlays, as both sides attempt to influence long-term spending. In the first concurrent budget resolution for fiscal year 1979, the Senate provided budget authority for defense of $129.8 billion, $2.4 billion above the level supported by the House (see Table 5.6). The House approved budget authority of $34.1 billion for the education, training, employment, and social services category, $2.5 billion above the Senate figure. During conference, House Democrats waged a long and emotional battle to cut the defense budget and to protect the House funding level for the 500 function. When House conferees finally agreed to cut the 500 function by $1.1 billion in return for a defense cut by the

Table 5.6. Amounts by which Senate and House differed on budget authority and outlays voted for defense and social welfare, first budget resolutions, fiscal years 1976–81 (in billions of dollars)

Fiscal year	Excess voted by Senate over House on defense (function 050)		Excess voted by House over Senate on social welfare (function 500)[a]	
	Budget authority	Outlays	Budget authority	Outlays
1976	$ 0.5	$1.0	$ −1.7	$1.0
1977	1.0	0.3	2.2	1.8
1978	3.2	1.7	−4.4[b]	0.8
1979	2.4	0.9	2.5	0.2
1980	3.1	0.8	3.2	1.4
1981	12.6	7.8	4.4	2.7

[a]Includes education, training, employment, and social services.

[b]This figure is largely the result of an accounting change. The Senate included $4 billion in forward funding of public service job programs. This inclusion was agreed to in conference.

SOURCE: House and Senate Budget Committee reports, 1975–80.

Senate of an equivalent amount, three Democratic liberals refused to sign the conference report and attempted, unsuccessfully, to defeat the proposed resolution on the House floor.

The problem arose again during conferences on the fiscal 1980 and 1981 budgets. The Senate and House versions of the first 1980 budget resolution differed by $3.1 billion in budget authority for defense and $3.2 billion in budget authority for the 500 function. Senate conferees agreed to a $1.2 billion defense reduction in exchange for a $1.8 billion reduction in the House funding level for function 500 programs. House liberals denounced this compromise and, assisted by the usual Republican opposition to all budget resolutions, succeeded in having the House reject it. When House and Senate conferees met again, the House proposed a further cut of $200 million in defense and a $300 million increase in function 500 budget authority over the original conference report. The Senate finally agreed to a $350 million increase but insisted there would be no further reductions in defense. While not entirely pleased, House liberals decided to accept this accommodation.

In the fall House liberals helped to defeat the Budget Committee's second budget resolution for fiscal 1980, the first time a second resolution had been rejected. The reasons for rejection were unclear, as the House had just voted down an amendment to raise defense spending to the level supported by President Carter and the Senate. A week later the House turned around and approved a second resolution that was hardly distinguishable from the one it had voted down. The conference with the Senate lasted more than three weeks, with defense and social welfare again splitting the conferees. House conferees agreed near the outset to raise their levels of outlays and budget authority for defense substantially, though still below Senate figures. In return, they finally persuaded Senators to accept a compromise on function 500 that came close to the House-passed figure.

The spring of 1980 found the House and Senate once more divided over defense spending. In late May the House rejected the conference report on the first fiscal 1981 resolution, with liberals leading the attack on a budget they said was not "truly balanced" between defense and domestic spending.[10] Having rejected the resolution, the House immediately and confusingly instructed the Budget Committee conferees to insist on the same defense figures in the second round of negotiations. The House's actions were, as far as Chairman Giaimo was concerned, "ridiculous."[11] The conference made only minor changes in the level of defense spending and agreed to modest increases in budget authority for a variety of domestic programs. By the time the conference was completed, few members of Congress still believed there was a serious chance of balancing the fiscal 1981 budget.

In the past the House and Senate have been far apart on defense. The original fiscal 1981 differences were in fact dramatic, with the budget authority differential at over $12 billion and the outlay gap nearly $8 billion. By the time the second resolution was debated, the House was willing to accept defense spending levels nearly as high as those adopted by the Senate. At least for the short term, it appears that the Senate-House differences on defense will be relatively narrow, but they will certainly not disappear.

When the defense issue is linked to education and job funding, it becomes much more difficult for House Democrats to reach a consensus. There has obviously been a pro-defense shift in the House, but House Democrats face the unenviable task of responding to increased demands for defense, to persistent pressures for increases for domestic programs, and to criticisms that Congress cannot restrain overall spending. And the weak position of the House Budget Committee prevents it from providing the firm and steady leadership needed to resolve these problems.

In terms of budget priorities, the House and Senate will continue to have problems. The defense budget is likely to remain a source of conflict, and Democratic liberals, especially in the House, may be able to use the issue of defense versus social welfare to keep the budget process in a precarious state well into the future.

Spending Control

The differences between the Senate's efforts to control spending and those of the House are likely to grow in importance. The Senate Budget Committee has strongly supported the strengthening of initiatives to control spending—planning for balanced budgets, the use of reconciliation to enforce spending limits, the incorporation of controls on federal loan and credit activities in budget resolutions, and procedures that will make it more difficult for Congress to evade the spending ceilings in budget resolutions. In its report on the spring budget resolution for fiscal 1981, the Senate Budget Committee provided a plan showing the Senate how outlays could be re- [FIND THIS] duced to 21 percent of GNP and advocated serious consideration of proposals to limit increases in entitlements. [12]

The Budget committees' emphasis on controlling spending shows up in the budget aggregates they recommend and the House and Senate adopt. Precise comparisons of recommended outlays are difficult, as the Budget committees often estimate program costs differently. What appear to be differentials in outlays may simply reflect differences in estimating rather than of policy. Still, a comparison of total outlays for the past several years shows modest but consistent differences between the Budget committees and between the House and Senate. The spring budget resolutions reported by the Senate Budget Committee have usually been below those reported by the House Budget Committee with respect to total outlays (see Table 5.7). The same holds true for budget resolutions passed by the Senate and those passed by the House. For the fiscal period 1976–81, the differential separating the Budget committees is slightly more than $11 billion; the differential between the House and Senate is about $2 billion less. Conference versions of the budget resolutions have put total outlays roughly midway between the House and Senate figures.

Despite its support for higher levels of defense spending, the Senate Budget Committee has been a strong budget-cutting force, a fact that becomes even clearer when budget authority, which affects future spending, is examined. In its spring budget resolutions the Senate Budget Committee has recommended levels of total budget authority that, with the exception of fiscal 1977, are well below those reported by the House Budget Committee (see Table 5.8). The cumulative difference for fiscal years 1976–81 is over $25 billion. The House-Senate difference is almost $20 billion. In this instance, the House's higher figures have prevailed. The House-Senate conferences have set budget authority levels even above those passed by the House, a fact that suggests that in order to keep current outlays down, the Senate must accede to House pressures on future spending.

The Senate Budget Committee and the Senate are not in any sense radical budget cutters, but spending pressures appear to be much stronger in the House. It may well be, moreover, that the Senate Budget Committee could recommend even lower levels of budget

Table 5.7. Total outlays recommended by House and Senate Budget committees, voted by House and Senate, and final conference committee decisions, first concurrent budget resolutions, fiscal years 1976–81 (in billions of dollars)

	1976	1977	1978	1979	1980	1981	Total, 1976–81
House Budget Committee	$368.2	$413.6	$464.3	$501.3	$532.7	$611.8	$2,891.9
Senate Budget Committee	365.0	412.6	458.8	498.9	532.4	612.9	2,880.6
House	368.2	415.4	464.5	500.9	529.9	611.8	2,890.7
Senate	365.0	412.6	459.2	498.9	532.6	613.1	2,881.4
Conference committee	367.0	413.3	460.9	498.8	532.0	613.6	2,885.6

SOURCE: House and Senate Budget Committee reports, 1975–80.

Table 5.8. Total budget authority recommended by House and Senate Budget committees, voted by House and Senate, and final conference committee decisions, first concurrent budget resolutions, fiscal years 1976–81 (in billions of dollars)

	1976	1977	1978	1979	1980	1981	Total, 1976–81
House Budget Committee	$395.6	$452.3	$502.0	$568.1	$608.4	$694.6	$3,221.0
Senate Budget Committee	388.6	454.9	497.4	566.1	600.6	687.9	3,195.5
House	395.9	454.1	502.3	569.5	605.1	694.6	3,221.5
Senate	388.6	454.9	504.6	566.1	600.3	688.2	3,202.7
Conference committee	395.8	454.2	503.4	568.8	604.4	697.2	3,223.8

SOURCE: House and Senate Budget Committee reports, 1975–80.

growth than it does were there any serious prospect that the House would go along. In defending the revised conference report on the first budget resolution for fiscal 1981, Chairman Hollings explained the Senate's predicament:

> If we go back to conference, the level of spending called for in this budget will indeed be revised—up, not down—that is, if we can get any agreement at all . . . we have seen the lay of the land in the other body. . . . [We] must know what the realistic results will be if the House gets yet another crack at providing more for this group and more for that one—more countercyclical this and more antirecessionary that.[13]

The Senate Budget Committee believes that the budget process does impose some restraint and therefore cannot be allowed to fail. If it does, spending would be even more difficult to control. At the same time, the limits of the restraint must be recognized. In terms of outlays, for example, actual spending since fiscal 1976 has exceeded the cumulative total of even the House spring budget resolutions. The budget authority picture is even stronger evidence of the remarkable persistence of spending pressures. For fiscal years 1976–80, *enacted* budget authority exceeded the spring budget targets by over $70 billion and Senate Budget Committee recommendations by over $90 billion.

Influencing Budget Policy

Congressional budgets, like other legislation, are exercises in compromise. The Senate and its Budget committee have agreed on larger budget shares for defense within the context of limited overall budget growth. In negotiating with the House, they have enjoyed some success on defense spending, but the House has been able to get much of the nondefense spending it wants as well. The relative weakness of the House Budget Committee contributes to the lack of spending discipline in the House and, ironically, puts additional pressure on Senate conferees to give their House counterparts spending levels they can defend back on the floor of the House.

In addition, budget resolutions *do not* impose fixed limits on spending. The ceilings can always be raised, and they frequently are. In the absence of fixed limits, Congress can avoid the really unpleasant choices between spending programs. As one House liberal admitted, passage of the second resolution for 1981 was made easier by the "widespread assumption that there will be a third budget resolution giving people another chance to come back and fight another round."[14] Moreover, spending advocates can hold the budget process hostage any time those choices are forced upon them. The budget process is just not capable of handling the diverse pressures of spending control, priorities, and fiscal policy, as long as totals are never fixed and the actual failure of the process would simply make it easier for Congress to spend.

During the postelection session in 1980, Hollings took the floor to defend his Budget committee's "five-year tradition of responsible and well-constructed budgeting," declaring that the budget was not "hemorrhaging" and that the budget process was not "a sham and a fraud and a charade."[15] If Hollings sounded a bit desperate, we can understand why. Despite the budget process and the Budget committees, congressional spending had not been tamed.

CHAPTER 6

The Congressional Budget Bureaucracy

Before 1974 Congress relied heavily on the executive branch for budgetary data and analysis. As a result, Congress was susceptible to manipulation by the president and executive branch agencies, and the independence of the congressional budgetary process was suspect. Accordingly, the 1974 budget act created the Congressional Budget Office (CBO) to provide Congress with "objective" budgetary information. In addition, separate staffs were authorized for each of the newly established Budget committees. Congress now has its own large (more than 350 staff members), expensive (almost $20 million annually), and at least mildly controversial budget bureaucracy, which gives it direct access to sources of budgetary data and analysis rivaling those of the executive branch. The president's sources of information are no longer overwhelmingly superior, and Congress can take and support an independent position on budget policy.

Despite the overall success of the congressional budget bureaucracy, the CBO's size and cost, its director's flair for publicity, and the resources it devotes to policy analysis rather than to conventional budget analysis have been attacked. Critics have also charged that in advising Congress on alternative fiscal policy strategies and, to a lesser extent, programs, the CBO has shown a bias in favor of spending to stimulate the economy and activist federal policies. Now that Republicans are in the majority in the Senate, this criticism will be taken much more seriously.

How Things Have Changed

Shortly after President Carter proudly announced his "lean and austere" budget for fiscal 1980, the CBO reported that the administration's numbers were suspect because the economic assumptions behind the budget were too optimistic. The CBO claimed that spending was underestimated, revenue overestimated, and the predicted deficit too low. After examining Carter's "prudent and responsible" 1981 budget, the CBO again reported that spending and the deficit would be higher than he had predicted. These CBO reports were accepted as routine. Several years earlier, full-scale congressional review of presidential budgets was a dramatic innovation.

While each of the Budget committees has a large staff that helps draw up the annual budget resolutions and provides support for other committee activities, the CBO is the primary source of budget information for Congress. It is responsible for supplying Congress with various types of budget numbers—estimated spending for existing agencies and programs in the current and future years, estimated costs of legislation reported by House and Senate committees ("bill costing"), and comparisons of congressional taxing and spending decisions with overall budget targets ("scorekeeping"). In 1979, at the request of the Budget committees, the CBO added an inflation analysis unit to provide estimates of the inflationary impact of major legislative proposals.

In addition, the CBO prepares annual reports on budget issues, including fiscal policy options and budget priorities. It is authorized to assist the Budget committees and other committees with commissioned reports on economic and other policy issues. Unlike the clearly defined functions related to budget estimates, these policy-analysis activities provide the CBO with considerable discretion about organizational purpose and jurisdiction.

How far this discretion should extend has yet to be fully resolved, but the initial choice of Alice Rivlin as director of the CBO was a definite victory for those who, like Muskie, saw an aggressive and wide-ranging CBO as part and parcel of an effective budgetary process.[1] Rivlin, who had served as assistant secretary of health, education, and welfare for planning and evaluation during the Johnson administration and later moved on to the Brookings Institution,

131

was a controversial choice for the CBO post. The House Budget Committee originally supported Philip S. Hughes, an assistant comptroller general in the General Accounting Office, for director. Because House members expected the CBO to emulate the low profile and policy neutrality of other congressional staff organizations, Hughes's background was more reassuring than Rivlin's, which suggested a predisposition toward policy advocacy and toward government activism and planning. It was not until Brock Adams became chairman of the House Budget Committee, early in 1975, that Muskie was finally able to gain approval of Rivlin, and the early reservations about her political philosophy have not yet been completely erased. House members continue to complain that the CBO is more oriented toward the Senate, that it reflects an uneasy balance between policy analysis and budget analysis, and that its impartiality is sometimes questionable. While complaints about Rivlin's competence are rare even among the CBO's critics, there is concern over the direction the CBO has taken under her leadership. And although Rivlin was recently appointed to a second four-year term, the Senate Budget Committee's new Republican leaders are likely to curb her discretion over CBO's role and work.

The CBO's reputation outside Congress has become quite formidable, and the basic budget information it provides is very highly regarded. According to some observers, the "CBO is now considered the best source of budget numbers in Washington."[2] By working closely with outside consultants and economic forecasters, the CBO has sought to strengthen its credibility in the private sector. In addition, Rivlin has managed to attract substantial media coverage for herself and the CBO. She has been available to the press, has testified frequently at congressional hearings, and has called press conferences to release major CBO reports. While some members of Congress find this continuous publicity inappropriate for a congressional staff institution, it has helped the CBO to achieve unusual prominence among these institutions. Adam Benjamin, Jr., chairman of the House Appropriations Subcommittee on the Legislative Branch, complained to Rivlin during the CBO's fiscal 1980 appropriations hearings; "Most of your reports are made public, and if there has been any criticism of your agency by the Congress, perhaps they felt with some degree of reservation that you were sharing too much or having too much of the limelight."[3]

Even though the Budget committees and Congress do not formally respond to the president's January budget proposals for several months, the CBO can provide immediate responses to the executive branch's economic assumptions, program costs, and policy justifications. Thus the president and his advisers are forced to explain discrepancies and defend their figures while the budget is in the public eye. Where once the president's monopoly over budget numbers gave him a decided advantage over Congress, the CBO has made the competition considerably more equal.

Independence from Whom?

When Muskie presented the final version of the 1974 budget act to the Senate, he explained that the proposed Congressional Budget Office would help Congress to make "independent decisions on budget policies" by providing it "with the kind of information and analysis it needs to work on an equal footing with the executive branch."[4] Muskie's emphasis on congressional-executive relations was deliberate. Many members of Congress suspected, for example, that the president's program preferences sometimes affected the cost projections issued by the Office of Management and Budget (OMB). When a president did not like a program Congress was considering, his case could easily be buttressed by OMB's inflated cost projections. Presidential budgets also showed an interesting pattern of underestimated expenditures and overestimated revenues.

If congressional independence could be compromised by overreliance on presidential budget numbers, however, the program costs estimated by congressional committees were similarly suspect. It was not unusual for committees to underestimate spending for their favored programs by emphasizing low initial costs and ignoring escalating long-term costs. And like the president, committees tended to use the most favorable economic and policy assumptions when they were forced to calculate program costs for future years.

The CBO's primary role has been to provide Congress with analyses and alternatives to presidential budgets. But just as the OMB keeps executive agencies honest about the costs and future needs of their programs, the CBO's estimates of the costs of proposed legislation and projections of the future costs of spending bills serve as a check on congressional committees. Indeed, the CBO and OMB have cooperated almost from the beginning in trying to improve their budget estimates. James L. Blum, who heads the Budget Analysis Division within the CBO, recently reported that his staff was "in daily contact with the OMB staff discussing the accuracy of the different budget estimates, what lies behind [those] . . . prepared by the Administration or . . . developed independently within the CBO."[5]

Although they are often obscured by the publicity accorded to confrontations between the president and Congress, the relations between most executive agencies and the congressional committees that authorize their programs are characterized by a high degree of cooperation and support. Since the clientele served by agencies forms many of the constituency groups that elect members of Congress, the interests of bureaucrats, legislators, and constituents coalesce around expanded programs and more funding. The budgetary implications of these shared interests are obvious, and congressional committees as well as executive agencies may find that manipulation of budget numbers is a useful strategy. By supplying objective information, the CBO reduces Congress' reliance on committees or members whose advocacy role should not be ignored.

An interesting example of this function surfaced during Senate Budget Committee markup of the first fiscal 1980 budget resolution. Senator Domenici proposed that the budget authority for pollution-control programs administered by the Environmental Protection Agency (EPA) be cut by $1 billion below the 1980 funding level recommended by the Senate's Environment and Public Works Committee. When Domenici argued that the EPA's construction grant program for waste-water treatment plants was already grossly undercommitted, he was heatedly challenged by Muskie, the second-ranking Democrat on Environment and Public Works and a leading supporter of the EPA program. Muskie contended that Domenici's proposed cut would severely damage the program and produced a letter from the EPA supporting his contention that funding cuts would adversely affect numerous local communities. Lawton Chiles entered the debate, asking the CBO whether it had any information. A CBO staff member responded by reading a statement refuting the EPA's analysis and implicitly supporting Domenici.

Muskie's long-standing fondness for the CBO did not prevent him from losing his temper at this point and yelling at the rather forlorn-looking CBO representative. Under these somewhat tense circumstances, Domenici's motion was approved by a vote of 9–7, with only two senators, Democrats Hollings and Chiles, crossing party lines. At Muskie's urging, the committee later reversed itself and voted more modest cuts than Domenici had proposed. The CBO analysis, however, was used again when the Senate Appropriations Committee considered the EPA's funding legislation.

While the CBO's intervention in this case was unusual, it illustrates the important role the CBO can play in protecting Congress against internal as well as external manipulation. Recognizing the necessity of having credible estimates, committees now usually cooperate with the CBO in projecting program costs.[6] And even the executive branch has recognized that unsubstantiated numbers can and will be challenged. When President Carter's welfare-reform package was being drawn up in 1977, for example, HEW sought the CBO's advice on designing a model to estimate program costs.[7]

Budget Analysis and Policy Analysis

The organizational structure and allocation of resources within the CBO are a rough reflection of the balance between its budget analysis and policy analysis functions. Bill costing, scorekeeping, and budget estimates and projections, all part of the budget analysis function, account for virtually all of the work of the Budget Analysis and Tax Analysis divisions. In addition, some of the economic forecasting activities and the new inflation-impact assessments provided by the Fiscal Analysis Division are directly related to budget analysis.

The CBO's policy analysis function, which involves examining the budgetary implications of various alternative approaches to federal programs, is conducted by three divisions with broad jurisdictions: Natural Resources and Commerce, Human Resources and Community Development, and National Security and International Affairs. The Office of Intergovernmental Relations, which handles the CBO's relations with other federal agencies, state and local governments, and private groups, also conducts policy studies.

The two functions account for approximately equal shares of CBO's funding and resources; recent estimates place about 40 percent of the CBO's budget in policy analysis, 40 percent in budget analysis, and the remainder in general management and administration. This allocation has remained fairly stable since 1976, when additional personnel were shifted to the Budget Analysis Division.[8]

Budget Analysis

Because direct access to timely and accurate estimates of program costs becomes critical as budgetary pressures grow in severity, providing such information is the major contribution that the CBO makes to congressional decision making. Thus members of Congress are no longer dependent on the executive branch, with its possible biases, or on congressional committees, which have their own biases. When estimates of the costs of current and proposed programs vary among the CBO, OMB, and congressional committees, the CBO's numbers are likely to prevail. While costs are not the only criterion on which policy decisions are based, the CBO's budget analysis services have given Congress a definite institutional boost.

Bill Costing and Inflation Impact. The CBO now does cost estimates for almost 90 percent of the bills reported by congressional committees, roughly double the rate several years ago.[9] This activity includes five-year estimates for all authorizing legislation, for bills providing new budget authority, and for new or increased tax-expenditure legislation. As a result, Congress is now able to consider the budgetary implications of virtually all pending legislation. The CBO's estimates are routinely used by the OMB and other executive agencies as well because the CBO is the only organization that does bill costing on such a comprehensive basis.

The precise effect of bill costing on particular pieces of legislation cannot be determined, but the CBO's numbers often have a decided impact. For example, early in 1978, the CBO prepared cost estimates on several welfare-reform plans, including a comprehensive program submitted by the Carter administration. According to the CBO, the Carter proposal greatly underestimated long-term costs. In 1982, the CBO estimated, the Carter welfare-reform package would add $17 billion to the costs of maintaining existing programs, almost double the amount of net additional costs estimated by the administration. The CBO's analysis differed from HEW's in several respects—economic assumptions, potential participation rates under the proposed program, and predictions about jobs programs and tax policies in effect by 1982. The major difference, however, was that the CBO did not accept the administration's estimates of future savings from the phasing out of existing programs to offset partially the costs of a replacement program.[10]

The CBO went further, estimating the costs of alternative plans. A more liberal program sponsored by a House Welfare Reform subcommittee was estimated to be even more costly than the Carter program. More modest proposals were then submitted by the Republican leadership in the Senate and by Al Ullman, chairman of the House Ways and Means Committee. The CBO provided relevant comparisons, allowing Congress to make more informed judgments about the budgetary impact of these competing plans. As was noted at the time, the CBO's real contribution was "less to provide Congress with precise numbers than to provide a comparison of costs, a range within which it can judge and make decisions."[11] The CBO's role as intermediary between the president and Congress is particularly important in cases such as this, when cost estimates are seriously at variance.

Even though the CBO tends to receive the most attention when it undercuts administration positions, it sometimes plays a supportive role. In the drawn-out struggle between the Carter administration and congressional supporters of domestic sugar producers during 1978 and 1979, the CBO's numbers supported the White House. Frank Church, chairman of the Senate Foreign Relations Committee, held up ratification of the International Sugar Agreement in order to force consideration of legislation that would raise prices through the imposition of import fees and quotas. The CBO's analysis of the Church–de la Garza bill showed that sugar prices would be boosted well above the ceiling claimed by Church's staff, and the administration was able to use the pricing factor to defend its more limited program for increased price supports. Finally, on November 1, 1979, Church agreed to schedule committee consideration of the International Sugar Agreement in return for administration pledges to raise domestic price supports. At times, of course, the CBO's reinforcement may have little effect. When the House considered expanded programs to assist higher education programs in 1979, both the CBO and the Carter administration reported that the costs

137

contained in the House bill were substantially underestimated. The House, however, dismissed the CBO's figures as guesswork, ignored the administration's position, and passed the legislation.

The CBO's support role has been enhanced by the addition of inflation-impact analysis to the decision-making process. Unlike bill costing, inflation-impact statements will be made selectively. Current estimates are that perhaps 100 bills per session will require this type of analysis,[12] including highly controversial legislation for agricultural price supports, national health insurance, the containment of health costs, and minimum wages.

Bill costing and inflation-impact analysis are complicated technical exercises that do not ordinarily yield definitive numbers and whose accuracy is sometimes hard to evaluate. They do allow Congress to consider objective numbers, however, and to have access to a range of fiscal considerations. While this service does not guarantee better policy decisions, it at least ensures the inclusion of important information in the legislative process.

Scorekeeping. The periodic scorekeeping reports issued by the CBO are used by the Budget and Appropriations committees to monitor the spending and revenue levels Congress has set in budget resolutions. The scorekeeping reports cover the actions that Congress has taken on spending and revenue legislation, the status and potential impact of pending budget legislation, and the relationship between these matters and Congress' original budget targets. Scorekeeping allows Congress to enforce or revise its original budget. And if Congress usually seems inclined to revise upward, at least it cannot profess ignorance about the overall effects of its decisions on spending and revenue bills.

At the CBO's suggestion, the Budget committees have moved to strengthen the discipline that is associated with scorekeeping. The first concurrent budget resolution for fiscal 1981 contained reconciliation provisions requiring spending committees to report specified cuts. In addition, final passage of legislation that permitted expenditures above the amounts allocated in the first budget resolution was prohibited before the second budget resolution was passed. These initiatives were designed to counter the upward spending drift that has traditionally occurred between the first and second resolutions. Once the second resolution is passed, scorekeeping is necessary to keep binding revenue and spending levels from being breached. Any legislation that breaks those levels is out of order; such legislation can be passed only if Congress adopts additional budget resolutions that revise the spending ceiling or revenue floor.

The CBO has developed an accurate scorekeeping system. Initially there were problems with "crosswalk" procedures used to convert the functional categories used in budget resolutions to appropriations accounts handled by the spending committees. The CBO developed a fully automated scorekeeping system that has replaced the system used by the House Appropriations Committee. During the fiscal year the CBO supplies numerous comprehensive and special scorekeeping reports, including daily ones on current budget levels when Congress is in session.

Multiyear Projections. Each fiscal year the CBO gives Congress five-year projections of the implications of current budget policy for spending and revenues. These projections are normally used as a baseline against which to assess future budget options and to give Congress some idea about the flexibility of future-year budgets. Current policy projections are an essential part of multiyear budgeting, which has thus far been used mainly by the Senate. For several years the Senate Budget Committee has included the upcoming fiscal year and the next four out-years in its budget resolution reports. The House Budget Committee adopted a similar format for the fiscal 1981 budget.

The CBO has argued very strongly for a multiyear budgeting format.[13] Rivlin has testified that this would be a more effective way to control spending and set priorities than the current year-to-year approach.[14] She has also suggested that it would be preferable to statutory or constitutional spending limits, a view that parallels the Senate Budget Committee's defense of multiyear budgeting during Muskie's tenure as chairman.

Budget Estimates. When Congress debates its budget resolutions, the numbers that finally emerge are treated with more deference than they deserve. The CBO continues to have problems with its basic budget estimates, a shortcoming it shares with its counterpart in the executive branch. In fiscal 1976 and 1977, both the CBO and the OMB overestimated spending, and recently they have made even larger errors in the opposite direction—substantial underestimates both for single programs and for the entire budget. These imprecisions are a serious and growing problem, as they undercut congressional budget resolutions. Future-year projections are subject to severe limitations as well, so that Congress is stuck with changeable budget numbers whether it budgets on an annual or a multiyear basis.

In an effort to raise the accuracy of its budget estimates, the CBO has sought assistance from private forecasters and expanded its monitoring of spending by executive agencies. Its stated goal is to estimate total outlays within a 1 percent margin of error six months before the start of a fiscal year.[15] Even if the CBO achieved this goal, however, the same margin of error would not apply to individual programs. Moreover, Congress would still face the prospect of multibillion-dollar under- or overestimates.

Despite these limitations, members of Congress treat the CBO's numbers as highly credible, at least compared to those supplied by the executive branch. What this means, in practice, is that the CBO's budget estimates tend to be less inaccurate, rather than exact. Whatever its causes, this lack of accuracy can undermine spending discipline. For example, it is usually too late and too difficult for Congress to make changes to protect its original budget totals when underestimates finally become apparent. Moreover, if those original totals required selected cuts in spending, which then disappeared in a flood of unanticipated increases for other programs, it becomes harder to get agreement on future cuts.

Policy Analysis

Under the budget act, the CBO has a broad authorization to examine fiscal and other policy issues in order to inform Congress about alternative budget policies. The CBO's policy analysis activities include its annual reports on budget policy options, responses to specific requests by the Budget and other committees, and self-initiated reports that it prepares in anticipation of congressional needs. Despite the CBO's repeated insistence that it makes no recommendations, many members of Congress disagree about the objectivity and dispensability of policy analysis, especially the CBO's analyses of fiscal policy.

Fiscal Policy Analysis. A major objective of the budget act was to enable Congress to determine fiscal policy. As a result, the CBO has been quite active in supplying Congress with information about various fiscal policy strategies. During its early years, when a Democratic Congress was facing a Republican president, the CBO's information and analyses were used by the Democratic congressional leadership to justify more activist federal stabilization policies and larger deficits than those proposed by the executive branch. As concern over continued deficits and inflation has mounted over the past few years, however, the attractiveness of this fiscal strategy has declined, and criticism of the CBO has increased. Congressional conservatives, for example, argue that the staff of the CBO embodies a virtually uniform strain of economic thinking, namely, a Keynesian orientation, which necessarily affects the fiscal policy analysis provided by the CBO. Critics outside Congress bring similar charges, claiming that in analyzing alternative policies the CBO makes economic assumptions and uses time periods in such a way that activist stabilization policies appear to be much more attractive than they really are.[16]

The CBO has also been caught up in the current controversy over cutting taxes instead of spending to stimulate the economy. Past CBO analyses have stressed that government spending has a greater short-term impact on the economy than an equivalent tax cut, since a portion of the money not paid in taxes goes into private savings and is not immediately spent. Lately the CBO has acknowledged that its forecasting models may underestimate the long-term advantages of tax cuts, but proponents of tax cuts remain dissatisfied with what they believe is a consistent CBO bias in favor of spending.

While suggesting that lower deficits and spending cuts are extremely expensive ways to fight inflation, the CBO tends to look favorably on greater federal intervention in the economy. For example, the CBO believes inflation might be attacked through programs to combat structural unemployment; a federal incomes policy, including an expanded federal role in determination of wages and prices; and federal efforts to increase output.[17] Such an approach is not, of course, demonstrably incorrect, but it is based on forecasting models and economic assumptions that are chosen by CBO analysts. While the CBO does issue technical papers that explain the limitations of these forecasting models, members of Congress are less likely to search out the uncertainties than to look for a definite fiscal strategy. Thus the CBO's disclaimers about its estimates of the rates of economic growth, unemployment, and inflation associated with a specific fiscal approach may be overlooked.

Its critics see the CBO's shortcomings as fundamental: its assumptions and models are biased against spending and tax cuts and toward maintenance of a large federal sector, and it encourages Congress to adjust fiscal policies continually by emphasizing short-term stabilization policies. Among congressional conservatives, the CBO's fiscal policy analysis is simply a justification for increased spending and continued deficits. According to a senior Republican on the Senate Budget Committee, "Many of us don't pay any attention to them [CBO] anymore. I have a lot of respect for Alice Rivlin, but her people are just not neutral [on economic policy]."[18]

The CBO admits that economic forecasting is often inexact. William J. Beeman, who heads the CBO's Fiscal Analysis Division, has stated that some of its critics may be at least partly right: "We can all agree that it is very important for policy analysts to emphasize uncertainty and to report longer-run effects. I would also agree that among the hundreds of macroeconomic estimates we have made, there have been instances when we were not sufficiently attentive to this issue. . . . The impression that such shortcomings are a general practice or perhaps even a policy at CBO . . . is contrary to fact." However, Beeman states, "A case can be made that continued emphasis on uncertainty is not always consistent with the requirements of the budget process, [since members of Congress must make decisions and] expect CBO to come forward with the best point estimates and judgment we can muster."[19]

The CBO's problems are not unique; in fact, the economic difficulties of recent years cast a rather dismal light on attempts to advise on economic policy generally. The CBO, however, is associated with a particular fiscal approach in the minds of some legislators. The truth of their belief may be arguable, but Congress will probably broaden its contacts with other sources of economic analysis and advice to defuse the controversy and to lessen the CBO's potential influence.

Program Analysis. The CBO's analyses of federal programs provide Congress with information about alternative approaches, especially their budgetary effects. From the beginning members of Congress have been concerned over policy advocacy by the CBO and possible duplication of efforts by other congressional agencies that also do policy analysis. In 1977 the CBO worked out a notification system with the Congressional Research Service, the Office of

Technology Assessment, and the General Accounting Office to reduce duplication, and this system has been reasonably effective, but the issue of policy advocacy has not faded. Since it would seem unnecessary to do policy analysis if it did not in some way affect the policy debates in Congress, there is no reason to expect the issue to disappear.

The policy analysis provided by the CBO has had a mixed reception. The CBO's annual reports on budget options have been a major disappointment. The first of these reports, issued in 1976, was a 400-page compendium that even CBO staff members considered superficial and useless.[20] The following year the CBO issued a much shorter report, supplemented by some two dozen separate issue papers designed to provide in-depth analyses of budget policies. The emphasis on issue papers has continued, but they appear to have had very little influence on markups or debates on budget resolutions in either chamber.

Within the broader legislative process, however, the CBO's work has received somewhat greater attention. Its studies of the food stamp program, urban policy, the financing of social security, and the Carter energy program have been well publicized. The CBO has provided Congress with a variety of additional studies on energy, policies on health insurance and health costs, and federal regulatory policy. The Senate Budget Committee remains the single biggest source of requests for policy analyses; other committees make comparatively limited use of the CBO's services.[21]

Congress is better equipped to assess the cost estimates and justifications of policy contained in executive branch proposals as a result of the CBO's policy analysis. On President Carter's legislation mandating containment of hospital costs, for example, the CBO's analysts concluded that while the administration's original estimates of savings were too high, neither the hospital industry's voluntary program nor attempts to promote competition in the hospital industry could match its cost-cutting effectiveness.[22] The House nevertheless rejected the controversial cost-containment bill in November 1979, as high inflation continued to eat away at its savings justification. A CBO analysis that undercut the executive branch's position dealt with the Department of Transportation's rules for making the existing public transit system accessible to the disabled. According to the CBO, the addition of lifts and elevators to the bus and rail system, recommended by the department, would cost $6.8 billion over a thirty-year period and would accommodate only 7 percent of the severely disabled population—at a cost of approximately $38 per trip. This plan was almost ten times as expensive as door-to-door service, which it was estimated could serve more than one-fourth of the disabled population at a cost of $4.4 billion over the same period of time.[23] The argument that Congress should force a change in the department's plan drew immediate fire from lobbies for the handicapped, including the American Coalition of Citizens with Disabilities, but at least Congress finally had to confront the cost implications of its legislation.

Policy analysis can also help Congress to evaluate committee proposals. Late in 1979 the CBO analyzed and compared the windfall-profits tax for the gas and oil industry passed by the House to the bill being worked out by the Senate Finance Committee. In this instance Congress was left with a classic trade-off. The Senate bill, according to the CBO, would give the government $130 billion less in revenues over a ten-year period but would increase domestic production by 8 percent during that period.[24]

Perhaps the most widely used analysis that the CBO has issued was its February 1980 report on budget-cutting options.[25] Prepared at the request of House Budget Committee members, the report identified and reviewed some seventy-five options for reducing spending and raising revenues. The spending cuts were grouped into several categories, ranging from reasonably painless management efficiencies to unquestionably painful reversals of past policy decisions. As the Budget committees initiated efforts to balance the fiscal 1981 budget, the CBO's report was an important reference for congressional and even executive officials. It also helped to counter some of the charges that the CBO favored spending.

The issue, however, is not the usefulness of policy analysis or the quality of the CBO's work, which is considered to be quite good.[26] Rather it is whether there is a need for major and separate divisions within the CBO to analyze policy. According to Rivlin, policy analysis is not much in demand by the House Budget Committee: "I think we have had an excellent relationship with the House Committee with respect to all our budget analysis and costing and estimating functions. They rely on us very heavily. . . . The Senate Committee, however, is more oriented toward program analysis, and we do more analytical studies for the Senate Committee than we do for the House Committee."[27]

The differences between the committees show up in other ways. While the CBO's staff members provide direct assistance during the Senate Budget Committee's markup sessions, they do not play an active role during House markup. In addition, the staff of the Senate Budget Committee appears to work more closely with the CBO, and to evaluate its performance more positively, than does its counterpart staff in the House.[28]

Since formal oversight of the CBO by the Budget committees has been virtually nonexistent, Rivlin's assessments cannot be gauged with any precision.[29] It does appear that Democrats on the Budget committees have been generally satisfied with the CBO's work and willing to accept the equal priorities accorded to budget analysis and policy analysis. Certainly neither committee has expressed any great concern over the costs associated with these activities. Now that Republicans are in charge of the Senate Budget Committee, this situation may change. In 1975, when Rivlin sought approval to expand the CBO staff to 259 positions, the House Appropriations Subcommittee on the Legislative Branch responded by limiting the CBO to 193, although it rejected proposals to eliminate the policy analysis divisions. The skepticism concerning policy analysis within CBO remains, however, as subcommittee chairman Adam Benjamin reminded Rivlin at the CBO's budget hearings in 1979: "Somewhere along the line somebody is going to have to make the decision as to what priorities are. I still see a struggle as to whether you want to do policy or budget analysis, and it seems to me that those who grew up [sic] in the 1974 law did not envision a $13 million agency at that time."[30] Benjamin was questioning not only the appropriate functions of the CBO, but also the costs, a question that is going to become even more important given the economic policies of the new administration.

The House members who drew up the 1974 budget act thought that a budget office of perhaps seventy-five to one hundred persons would be adequate.[31] It was only at Senate insistence that separate committee staffs were authorized. Even by congressional standards—outlays by the legislative branch increased from $335 million in fiscal 1970 to approximately $1.3 billion ten years later—the subsequent growth of the CBO and the Budget committees' staffs has been impressive.

Since fiscal 1976 the CBO's budget has climbed from less than $5 million to over $14 million for fiscal 1982, well above the rates of increase for most congressional staff agencies over the same period. While the current limit of 218 permanent positions (see Figure 6.1) is considerably below the 259 that Rivlin requested several years ago, the comparison is somewhat misleading, as the number of staff members does not include persons outside the government hired as consultants or paid under contracts. The CBO's contracts for studies and surveys are now running at about $1 million annually.

The staffs of the Budget committees are also quite large. The Senate Budget Committee had the fifth largest staff of all Senate

Figure 6.1. Organization of Congressional Budget Office and allocation of positions, by division

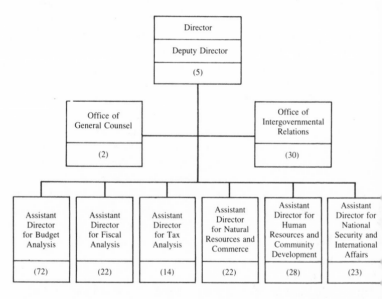

SOURCE: U.S. House of Representatives, Subcommittee on Legislative Branch Appropriations, Committee on Appropriations, *Hearings, Legislative Branch Appropriation for 1981* (Washington, D.C.: Government Printing Office, 1980), pp. 144, 160.

committees in 1979. Of its more than ninety employees, most were professional staff members. The House Budget Committee's staff of seventy-five in 1979 placed it in the middle range among standing committees of the House.[32] Putting together the actual operating budgets of the Budget committees is difficult, as a variety of funding sources are used to meet committee expenses. Recent data support an estimate of at least $2.5 million annually for the staffing costs of each Budget committee.[33]

Since members of Congress rarely attack their own committee budgets, the CBO receives what little heat there is over staffing costs. Some duplication between the CBO and the Budget committees' staffs is probably inevitable and certainly does not appear to bother members of either Budget committee. The CBO's policy analysis activities, however, overlap with those of other congressional staff agencies, such as the General Accounting Office, the Congressional Research Service, and the Office of Technology Assessment, which together have more than 6,500 permanent positions and a combined budget of over $250 million. Clearly the congressional budget bureaucracy is large and costly, a finding that is perhaps ironic, given the fiscal discipline that defenders of the budget process exhort others to demonstrate.

CHAPTER 7

Managing the Budget

In theory, when Congress passes its second budget resolution, it establishes the size and composition of the budget for the fiscal year. Subsequent actions to reduce spending through presidential impoundments or to increase it through supplemental appropriations have become routine, however, making the very idea of a "final" budget suspect. These impoundments and supplemental appropriations, although initiated by the executive branch, are responses to circumstances that presumably have developed after regular appropriations have been made, and they involve Congress directly.[1]

Title X of the 1974 Congressional Budget and Impoundment Control Act established congressional controls over presidential impoundments.[2] The authors of the budget act did not specifically limit the use of supplemental appropriations in the belief that the annual spending ceilings and coordinated budgetary decision making mandated by the act would force Congress to integrate requests for supplemental funds "into the overall picture."[3] They hoped that Congress' participation in budget management would promote flexibility and fiscal discipline while protecting its spending policies and priorities.

Unfortunately, these hopes proved to be far too optimistic. Congressional controls on presidential impoundments have been effective. Presidents now find it extremely difficult to prevent funds from being spent when they have policy disagreements with Congress. Indeed, there is some evidence that presidents have lost discretionary authority to stop even clearly unnecessary spending.[4] The record on supplemental appropriations, however, suggests that Congress has been more concerned with protecting favored spending programs than with strengthening its control of the budget. Congress'

148

reluctance to allow spending cuts through impoundments is matched by its reluctance to deny supplemental funding, which has become an even more serious problem because of the expansion of the uncontrollable portion of the budget.

The current high levels of mandatory spending make it difficult to limit supplemental funding and to stay within ceilings, especially when the president's ability to restrict other types of spending is contingent on Congress' approval. Unless Congress demonstrates that it can stay within its own spending limits—not just check presidential impoundments—however, it will reinforce doubts about its ability to manage the budget responsibly.

Impoundment

Richard Fenno's description of House members on the 1972 election trail suggests the political explosiveness of fiscal issues during the Nixon administration: "One-half the Representatives I was with blasted the House for being so spineless that it gave away its power of the purse to the President. The other half blasted the House for being so spineless in exercising its power of the purse that the President had been forced to act."[5] Faced with possible electoral sanctions for opposing the president's efforts to control spending or a perceived loss of institutional power if they went along, members of the House were sharply divided. Since only one-third of the Senate faced reelection, most of its members could assess institutional prerogatives from a more disinterested perspective. For both chambers, however, Nixon's proposed 1972 spending ceiling was not nearly so serious a challenge as his use of and justification for impoundment, which, the executive branch declared, rested on a firm foundation of historical precedent, statutory authority, and constitutional interpretation. Thus the administration believed that the president had broad discretion to decide whether to spend funds that Congress had appropriated. After years of acrimony and dozens of court cases, Congress finally—with Title X of the 1974 budget act—established statutory checks on presidential impoundments.

Background

The claim that Richard Nixon was simply the latest president to impound appropriated funds had some validity. Presidential impoundments can be traced back to the Jefferson administration and were used with varying frequency by the Roosevelt, Truman, Eisenhower, Kennedy, and Johnson administrations. During the depression, for example, Roosevelt treated the figures given in spending bills as ceilings and impounded funds whose expenditure he considered excessive or unnecessary. Once World War II began, he used his war powers to halt domestic projects that Congress had funded against his wishes. Congress complained loudly and often but was unable to agree on an effective response to executive impoundment.

Harry Truman, Dwight Eisenhower, and John Kennedy used impoundments to block weapons systems and defense spending. Lyndon Johnson did the same, and also extended his impoundments to domestic programs. With Vietnam spending fueling inflationary pressures, Johnson ordered selective cuts in agriculture, education, housing, and highway construction.[6] The Johnson impoundments were temporary and not aimed at domestic programs opposed by the administration. The impoundments were justified as a means of limiting overall spending and fighting inflation; they were not enacted simply to accomplish routine managerial objectives within the affected programs. This distinction was one that would reemerge with Johnson's successor.

The Nixon administration also defended executive impoundments on statutory grounds. The Antideficiency Acts of 1905 and 1906, for example, authorized the president to withhold appropriated funds in order to establish reserves. Under amendments passed in 1950, this authorization was extended "to provide for contingencies, or to effect savings whenever savings are made possible by or through changes in requirements, greater efficiency of operations, or *other developments subsequent to the date on which such appropriation was made available*."[7] According to Nixon spokesmen, the "other developments" clause constituted a broad grant of authority, allowing the president to impound funds in order to fight inflation or even to effect program reductions he proposed but Congress failed to act on. Neither the Full Employment Act of 1946 nor the Economic Stabilization Act of 1971 authorized impoundments, but they provided a mandate for presidential economic management that, the Nixon administration argued, logically encompassed spending reductions designed to fight inflation and thereby gave validity to impoundments.

Although these and other statutory claims were imaginative, they were tenuous. The legislative history behind the 1950 antideficiency amendments, for example, showed that legislators had rejected use of the reserve authority to settle policy disputes between the president and Congress.[8] The Nixon Justice Department, in an opinion by William Rehnquist, then assistant attorney general, advised that even the statutory debt limit could not be used as authority to cut spending except in unusual cases. Rehnquist also dismissed the argument of inherent executive power, declaring that "it seems an anomalous proposition that because the executive branch is bound to execute the laws, it is free to decline to execute them."[9]

These various defenses, even those most lacking in merit, were advanced with a certainty and confrontational style that infuriated Nixon's opponents in Congress. Moreover, the Nixon impoundments were far larger than those of his predecessors, amounting, according to one estimate, to almost 20 percent of controllable expenditures;[10] they were aimed at domestic programs opposed by the president, and by and large they were intended to be permanent. When Congress overrode the president's vetoes, as it did with the Federal Water Pollution Control Act Amendments of 1972, the administration announced that it would impound half of the $18 billion that had been allotted for fiscal years 1973 through 1975. Several argicultural programs, including programs to preserve wetlands for waterfowl and to fund water and sewer systems in rural areas, as well as the rural environmental assistance program, were unilaterally terminated. Funds for housing, transportation, and welfare programs were also impounded. Between 1969 and 1973 tens of billions of dollars appropriated for more than 100 programs were impounded. By these actions Nixon clearly intended to implement his own budget rather than the spending laws that Congress enacted.[11] The impoundment dispute involved basic questions about who would determine budget policy and priorities.

The Courts and Congress

The Nixon impoundments generated numerous court suits as well as legislative efforts to check the president's spending powers. Although the administration won few cases, the question of the constitutionality of impoundment was not resolved. The only case that the Supreme Court ruled on—*Train v. City of New York,* which dealt with the impoundment of funds to control water pollution—

was not decided until 1975. The ruling was narrow, holding only that the administration was required to allot funds to the states, although the Court's opinion did suggest that attempts to circumvent the intent of Congress through impoundment would be suspect.[12]

The lower courts rejected the inflation-fighting defense as a justification for refusing to spend appropriated funds; such statutes as the Antideficiency Act were held not to represent roving commissions to cripple or terminate programs; and impoundments to implement the president's budget were overturned with the admonition that his budget was simply a proposal, not a fait accompli. The courts also ruled that the intent of Congress was not to be measured solely by the presence of mandatory language in a statute. According to these rulings, the president's exercise of discretion on spending had to be consistent with the general policy provisions and aims of legislation.[13] The president could not just eliminate programs he decided were without merit or set arbitrary spending limits for others.

The impoundment issue could not be handled effectively through the judicial process. Decisions of lower courts did not constitute rejection of any and all impoundments, and the case-by-case approach was so slow that the administration could substantially delay spending regardless of the final decision. The courts also found it difficult to force the actual spending of funds, making further delay or evasions possible. As the legal system inched along, therefore, Congress attempted to resolve the problem its own way.

In 1973 the House and Senate passed separate versions of impoundment-control legislation. House and Senate conferees were unable to resolve their dispute over procedures, and in the face of the president's certain veto, impoundment-control legislation was stalled for over a year. In 1974 impoundment-control and budget-reform provisions were linked for practical as well as for political reasons. The linkage brought together liberals who opposed budget reform and fiscal conservatives opposed to impoundment controls. In addition, legislators recognized that the provisions were genuinely complementary. As the House Rules Committee stated, budget reform without impoundment checks "would leave Congress in a weak and ineffective position. No matter how prudently Congress discharges its appropriations responsibility, legislative decisions have no meaning if they can be unilaterally abrogated by executive impoundments."[14]

The impoundment compromise—Title X of the 1974 budget act—defined two types of impoundments and established procedures to deal with each. Rescissions are impoundment actions that cancel existing budget authority. If the president determines that part or all of the budget authority for a program or agency is not needed, he must notify Congress by special message of the amount, justification, and estimated impact of the proposed rescission. If Congress fails to adopt a rescission bill within forty-five days, the president is required to release the funds proposed for rescission.

Deferrals are actions to withhold or delay the obligation of funds during a fiscal year. Again the president must notify Congress by special message of the amount, justification, and impact. In the case of a deferral request, however, the impoundment stands unless either the House or the Senate disapproves it. There is no time limit on when this one-house veto can be exercised, but once it is cast, funds must be released immediately.

The executive branch must therefore report *all* impoundments to Congress, and the General Accounting Office (GAO), which decides whether impoundments have been properly classified as deferrals or rescissions, is authorized to monitor executive actions and, if necessary, to bring suit in federal court to enforce compliance. The GAO is also responsible for reporting to Congress any impoundment actions that have not been submitted for review.

Title X was a sweeping response, but it did not state whether the president could impound funds for fiscal policy or other policy considerations. Senate spokesmen, notably Edmund Muskie, contended that the president could not impound for policy reasons, but House members argued that the president could legitimately impound funds on that basis. A GAO opinion issued December 4, 1974, upheld the position of the House, and the Ford administration used it as the basis for an unexpectedly large number of impoundments for reasons of policy.[15] Congress also neglected to settle the matter of committee jurisdiction over requests for deferrals and rescissions. The Appropriations committees successfully sought the bulk of jurisdictional responsibility, but Congress reserved limited review for the Budget and other standing committees.

Impact: The Ford Administration

Richard Nixon resigned shortly after signing the budget-reform act, leaving the Ford administration to provide the first test of the

new impoundment procedures. President Ford continued the aggressive use of policy-based impoundments until the last months of his
administration. Over two and a half years, Ford reported 480 impoundment actions to Congress—150 rescissions and 330 deferrals.
Almost 90 percent of the rescissions were policy-based, while
roughly two-thirds of the deferrals were routine managerial actions.[16]

Congress responded by refusing to enact most of the requested
rescissions and by disapproving many deferrals as well. In fiscal
years 1975 and 1976, less than 10 percent of approximately $7
billion in rescissions was approved by Congress, which also rejected
over $9 billion in deferrals during fiscal 1975 and almost $400
million in fiscal 1976.[17]

Although Congress was willing to accept most routine impoundments, it insisted on maintaining its spending preferences. During
September and October 1974, President Ford requested $637.7 mil-
lion in rescissions, most of which—$540 million—was accounted
for by the Department of Agriculture's rural electrification loan
program and rural conservation service program. Congress had

Table 7.1. Initial rescissions requested by president and granted by Congress for fiscal
year 1975 and previous years, by executive department or agency

Executive department or agency	Rescissions requested by president	Rescissions granted by Congress[a]
Department of Agriculture		
Rural Electrification Administration loans	$455,635,000	$ 0
Agricultural conservation program (REAP)	85,000,000	0
Forest Service roads and trails	61,611,000	61,611,000
Department of the Interior		
Bureau of Land Management roads and trails	4,891,000	4,891,000
National Park Service road construction	10,461,000	10,461,000
Appalachian Regional Development Commission		
Airport development	40,000,000	40,000,000
Department of Housing and Urban Development		
College housing	16,371,284	16,371,284
All departments and agencies	$673,969,284[b]	$133,334,284[c]

[a]HR 17505, enacted December 10, 1974.
[b]Includes estimated unused contract authority of $237,000.
[c]Includes estimated unused contract authority of $200,000.
SOURCE: *Congressional Quarterly Almanac, 1974,* p. 140.

154

funded these programs against presidential opposition for years, and it insisted on maintaining them in its first use of rescission procedures, even though it did agree to noncontroversial cuts in budget authority for a few minor programs (see Table 7.1).

The second time Congress considered rescission requests, it again maintained its domestic spending priorities, particularly those associated with social welfare programs (see Table 7.2). The House and Senate agreed to rescind $183.2 million in defense appropriations despite opposition by both Appropriations committees. After

Table 7.2. Additional rescissions requested by president and granted by Congress for fiscal year 1975 and previous years, by executive department or agency

Executive department or agency	Rescissions requested by president	Rescissions granted by Congress
Department of Agriculture	$ 36,133,940	$ 7,856,470
Department of Defense	278,800,000	183,200,000
Department of Housing and Urban Development	264,117,000	0
Department of Health, Education, and Welfare	284,719,332	0
Department of State	2,100,000	2,100,000
Department of Justice	16,000,000	9,400,000
Department of Commerce	18,550,000	14,250,000
Department of the Treasury	24,000,000	1,530,000
Executive Office of the President	5,000,000	5,000,000
All departments and agencies	$ 929,420,272	$223,336,470
General Services Administration, spending limitations	20,022,900	20,022,900
Total	$ 949,443,172	$243,359,370[a]
Department of Agriculture	$ 191,700,000	$ 10,000,000
Department of Defense	955,000	955,000
Consumer Product Safety Commission	1,709,000	500,000
Department of Labor	12,000,000	0
Department of Health, Education, and Welfare	924,030,250	0
Department of Commerce	129,999,704	4,999,704
All departments and agencies	$1,260,393,954	$ 16,454,704[b]

[a]HR 3260, enacted March 26, 1975.
[b]HR 4075, enacted March 26, 1975.
SOURCE: *Congressional Quarterly Almanac, 1975*, p. 872.

the Appropriations committees reported out rescission bills that did not eliminate almost \$123 million in funds for the F-111 fighter plane as the president had requested, floor amendments were adopted to cancel the funding. An attempt to gain corresponding reductions in a variety of social programs, however, was soundly defeated. Congress also rejected a subsequent request to rescind the funds for programs to train health personnel.

Disputes also arose over technical procedures and Congress' intent. The GAO reclassified several early deferrals as rescissions, pointing out that deferrals would effectively cancel spending under the affected programs. There were frequent complaints in Congress that impoundment reports were late and that the rescission procedure was being abused by the administration. When budget authority for a program expired at the end of a fiscal year, Congress could not force the executive branch to obligate funds within the forty-five days of continuous session mandated for consideration of rescission legislation. In fact, the continuous-session requirement made it possible to extend this period substantially.[18] In Ford's case, members of Congress charged that this loophole was being exploited to subvert congressional spending policies.[19]

Reaction was especially negative when impoundments were directed against congressional add-ons—appropriations in excess of the president's recommendations. Even Republicans complained. Senator Ted Stevens of Alaska, a member of the Appropriations Committee, pointed out that rescissions were following a disturbing pattern: "I do not think this has been thought out. It is like other rescission areas. It is amazing. In Interior, wherever there are congressional add-ons, there are automatic rescissions, just like the automatic impoundments. Everything that was added on by the Congress was impounded. Now almost everything that is added by the Congress is rescinded. You just have a new mechanism for delay."[20]

During fiscal year 1976, as the aggressive impoundment strategy continued, congressional resistance hardened. Of the \$3.6 billion in rescissions proposed by the president for fiscal 1976 and the transition quarter, all but \$138 million was rejected by the Congress. None of the approved rescissions affected HEW, HUD, or the Agricultural Department. Moreover, Congress disapproved about two dozen deferrals, totaling some \$390 million. Activity slowed the following year because of the presidential campaign, but shortly before leaving office, Ford submitted major rescissions in defense spending for the building and conversion of navy ships which Congress approved, along with minor cuts in other programs.[21]

President Ford tried to use impoundments as item vetoes on spending bills, just as his predecessor had done. While Congress rejected most of these impoundments, Ford was often able to delay spending and, more important, to maintain pressure on Congress to hold down spending. This success suggests that the president is not powerless in the face of impoundment-control procedures. Indeed, by providing statutory legitimacy for presidential impoundments, the budget law has made it possible at times for a president to put Congress on the defensive. Clear ideological differences between the White House and Congress are likely to bring about replays of the Ford strategy, with rescissions used to resurrect policy fights the president loses during the appropriations process. Congress can ultimately force spending, but impoundments will extend the fight for institutional advantage that characterizes the earlier stages of the budgetary process.

The Carter Administration

When the 1976 election produced a Democratic president and Congress, many people expected the impoundment battles of the Nixon-Ford years to disappear. On the deferral side, there was, in fact, considerable harmony. The House and Senate did not reject a single Carter deferral during fiscal 1977. Over the following three fiscal years there were only isolated disapproval resolutions, affecting less than $65 million of the almost $20 billion that the administration deferred from obligation. Most of these deferrals were routine actions scattered throughout the executive branch. Indeed, the deferral process now seems noncontroversial. Rescission procedures are another matter. During Carter's first two years in office, some interesting questions about impoundment were revived in the course of battles over the B-1 bomber, Minuteman III missiles, and water-resource projects.

The battle over the B-1 bomber went on through the last six months of 1977 and involved both funding already approved in the 1977 budget and proposed appropriations for 1978. On June 28, 1977, the House turned down an attempt to delete funding for production of B-1s from the 1978 defense appropriation bill by a vote of

178–243. But on July 18 the Senate voted 59–36 to eliminate the B-1 funding from the 1978 budget. The House remained closely divided, but finally, on September 8, the House voted 202–199 to remove future funding for B-1 production. Proponents of the B-1 were successful only in retaining modest research funding for 1978.

The 1977 defense appropriations bill, passed while Ford was president, had included funding for three B-1 bombers. Two days after the House had indicated its intention to maintain B-1 funding in fiscal 1978, Carter announced that he would take steps to cancel production of the bomber, a weapons system that he had attacked as wasteful and unnecessary during the campaign, and the following week the Pentagon canceled contracts with Rockwell International for three B-1s. On July 20, almost two weeks after production contracts were canceled, the president proposed rescission of $462 million for B-1 production in fiscal 1977. By attaching the B-1 rescission to a supplemental defense appropriation for fiscal 1978, the Senate managed to keep the issue open. During December the House rejected the rescission, but it finally reversed its position the following February.

Supporters of the B-1 charged that the president had violated the spirit of the budget act by terminating the production program before Congress approved rescission legislation. They also argued that Carter had violated provisions in a fiscal 1977 supplemental appropriation barring the use of funds provided in that legislation to terminate programs before final approval by Congress.[22] The actual cancellation was important, as everyone acknowledged that once production lines had been shut down, a decision to reopen them would escalate the already high costs of the B-1 program. If Congress eventually refused to go along with the rescission, it would then have to provide additional funding.

According to the Defense Department and OMB, however, it made no sense to propose a rescission while continuing to obligate funds. Immediate cancellation would result in savings if Congress approved the rescission, and in any case, production could be reopened if Congress insisted. Indeed, that is what happened with the Minuteman III missile program. Carter announced termination of production on July 11, 1977, and sent a rescission proposal to Congress on July 26. The forty-five-day deadline expired on October 14, at which time funds were made available for obligation.[23]

The water-projects controversy did not result in formal impoundment actions, but it did direct attention once again to delays and terminations of contracts. In the revisions of the fiscal 1978 budget Carter sent to Congress in February 1977, he announced a tentative decision to eliminate 19 ongoing water projects and promised a final review of 300 additional projects by April 15. The administration did not propose rescissions in fiscal 1977 funding, and both the secretary of the interior and the director of OMB promised that no attempt would be made to impound funds.[24] Congress was informed, however, that no future construction contracts would be awarded for projects recommended for de-authorization. Contracting would end in advance of congressional action, just as it had done on the B-1 and Minuteman III programs.

Congressional supporters of the water projects found this policy unacceptable. Lloyd Meeds of Washington, Democratic chairman of the House Interior Committee's Subcommittee on Water Power and Resources, charged that termination of contracts before de-authorization was "every bit as objectionable as impoundment."[25] In the Senate, Muskie, whose state of Maine had a major project on Carter's first "hit list," also brought up the impoundment analogy. He strongly supported legislation that prevented the administration from holding back funding for the construction of water projects during fiscal 1977, and which also disapproved in advance any deferrals for specific projects and stated that Congress would deny any requests for rescissions affecting those projects. While the legal effect of the deferral and rescission provisions was nonexistent, they were, Muskie said, an advance warning of congressional opposition.[26]

The battle then shifted to the Appropriations committees. Both Congress and the administration gave some ground on individual projects in the fiscal 1978 public works appropriations bill, but Congress opposed Carter's attempts to tighten executive control over spending for water projects. The impasse deepened when Carter maintained that projects for which funding had been eliminated in the fiscal 1978 compromise were permanently terminated. The House and Senate argued otherwise and sought to resurrect several such projects in the fiscal 1979 appropriations bill. Carter vetoed that bill on October 5, 1978, and his veto was sustained. Although the 1978 truce was later reinstated, the termination issue was never fully resolved.

Carter's overall record on actual rescissions was reasonably successful: most of the fiscal 1977 requests were approved; Congress agreed to almost half of the $1.3 billion in rescission proposals in fiscal 1978; and almost 80 percent of the more than $900 million in rescission requests for fiscal 1979 were finally enacted.[27]

The following year, Congress was forced to rescind over $3 billion in 1980 budget authority in order to stay within the spending ceiling set by its third budget resolution. Therefore, Carter's rescission proposals, which totaled less than $1.5 billion, were, with only scattered exceptions, met or greatly exceeded by congressional cuts. Congress' actions, however, were less frugal than they appeared, for this third budget resolution, passed during June 1980, had increased the budget authority ceiling by $20 billion and the outlay ceiling by $25 billion over those set by the second resolution. There was concern, however, that even these increases would not be sufficient to cover forthcoming supplemental appropriations, and Congress required the Appropriations committees to report the necessary rescissions of budget authority and outlays as part of the supplemental appropriations.

A major development during the Carter administration was the cancellation of programs in advance of congressional review by termination or curtailment of contracts. Congress has been unable to fashion a satisfactory response to this type of initiative, which gives the executive branch an advantage in determining the final decision. At the same time, Congress has been unwilling to exempt routine impoundments from the reporting requirements of Title X or otherwise to allow the president and OMB greater flexibility in day-to-day management of the budget.[28] Although the rescission actions on the 1980 budget showed that substantial immediate cuts were possible (at least under duress and if Congress initiated them), Congress is still not likely to approve major impoundments it considers to be based on policy. More important, Congress has shown little inclination to broaden the president's authority to impound funds. Indeed, Republican efforts to extend this authority on behalf of the incoming Reagan administration were rejected during the postelection congressional session in 1980, and the House Democratic leadership appears absolutely determined to resist similar attempts in the future.

Supplemental Appropriations

The impoundment controls now in effect prevent the president from unilaterally cutting spending and protect the integrity of the congressional budgetary process through legislative review and potential rejection of proposed cuts in spending. A different type of problem is posed by unanticipated increases in spending during a fiscal year. Just as impoundments can distort priorities and policy preferences, the need for supplemental funding can force changes in congressional budgets, making it much more difficult to control spending.[29]

Background

When additional funding is required for agencies or programs after regular appropriations have been enacted, the president submits requests for supplemental appropriations to Congress. The conventional justification for these requests is urgency—an unanticipated or emergency situation creates needs that must be met immediately. In reality, supplemental bills have been used routinely for years to make up for deliberate underappropriations, to fund newly enacted programs, and to accommodate increases in entitlement programs resulting from inflation or other factors. President Carter's economic stimulus program was another example of how supplementals can be used. The $20 billion in supplemental funding contained in that legislation was justified on grounds of fiscal policy.[30]

In the decade before 1974, Congress passed an average of four supplemental spending bills per year, increasing spending from less than $300 million in fiscal 1964 to almost $22 billion in fiscal 1966. The average supplemental funding over the ten-year period was approximately $10 billion per year.[31] Much of the supplemental funding during this period was for the Vietnam war (see Table 7.3). Beginning in fiscal 1970, however, substantial increases in non-Vietnam funding appeared. From 1970 to 1974, supplemental appropriations totaled nearly $53 billion, or almost 5 percent of total outlays. Therefore, when the budget-reform effort began in 1973, supplemental appropriations were contributing substantially to the fragmentation of the budgetary process and to the weakening of spending controls.

Table 7.3. Total supplemental appropriations authorized by Congress and supplemental appropriations unconnected with the Vietnam war, fiscal years 1964–74 (in billions of dollars)

Fiscal year	Total supplemental appropriations	Non-Vietnam supplemental appropriations
1964	$ 0.3	$ 0.3
1965	5.6	4.9
1966	21.9	8.8
1967	19.4	7.2
1968	8.2	4.5
1969	5.8	4.6
1970	6.3	6.3
1971	10.0	10.0
1972	11.6	11.6
1973	11.4	11.4
1974	13.7	13.7

SOURCE: Adapted from Louis Fisher, "Supplemental Appropriations, Fiscal Years 1964–1978," paper presented to the 1979 meeting of the Midwest Political Science Association, Chicago, April 20, 1979, pp. 28–30.

These problems are not new, however. When congressional budgeting suffered one of its periodic failures during the 1880s and 1890s, there was a symptomatic increase in the granting of deficiency (or supplemental) appropriations.[32] Agencies would deliberately spend their appropriated funds before the end of a fiscal year and then return to Congress for additional funding. Congress usually acceded to these "coercive deficiencies," although some critics, such as James A. Garfield, charged collusion rather than coercion: "One of the vicious party devices too often resorted to for avoiding responsibility for extravagance in appropriations is to cut down the annual bills below the actual amount necessary to carry on the government, announce to the country that a greater reduction has been made in the interest of economy, and after the elections are over, make up the necessary amount by deficiency bills."[33] In order to regulate agencies' spending practices, antideficiency legislation was adopted in 1905 and broadened in 1906, and the executive branch later established apportionment of funds to agencies.

After World War II, Congress again wrestled with the budgetary problems posed by deficiency appropriations. The House Appropriations Committee, for example, reestablished a deficiency subcommittee in 1959 in an attempt to tighten controls over requests for supplemental funds. Coordinated review was fiercely resisted, however, and after several years the regular subcommittees regained jurisdiction over supplemental appropriations.[34]

In 1966 the Joint Committee on the Organization of Congress recommended greater strictness in the use of supplemental appropriations. Declaring that "fiscal responsibility is best exercised by the regular process of appropriating through annual bills,"[35] the committee suggested that the routine use of supplementals was contributing to the erosion of congressional fiscal controls. Appropriation bills were rarely passed before the fiscal year began, and once they were enacted, supplemental requests pushed spending still higher. With back-door spending also increasing rapidly, control over spending was becoming more and more elusive.

The 1974 budget act did not directly restrict the use of supplementals, but it did provide a timetable and spending-ceiling procedure that promised a more orderly and coordinated approach to spending decisions. The spring deadline for authorizing legislation, for example, would allow Congress to anticipate funding requirements more accurately. The spring and fall budget resolutions would introduce coherence to spending and revenue decisions, and the binding spending ceiling in the fall budget resolution would serve as a brake on supplemental funding. Unless overall spending was under the ceiling, Congress could not pass supplemental appropriations without first adopting a new budget resolution. According to the *Washington Post*, these new procedures ensured that supplementals would no longer be used to cover up spending:

> It will be a good deal less comfortable to play the old game in which Congress loudly cuts a department's budget and then quietly restores part of the money in a supplemental appropriation bill. Under the law now in effect, any supplemental that exceeds the budget limit will be out of order unless Congress is prepared to raise the budget total first. Congress can still increase appropriations whenever it chooses. But it will have to declare explicitly the changes that it is making in a fiscal policy that is no longer the President's alone.[36]

Continuing Problems

Contrary to expectations, the record since 1974 suggests that supplementals remain a serious obstacle to Congress' efforts to con-

Table 7.4. Supplemental appropriations authorized by Congress, fiscal years, 1975–80 (in billions of dollars)

Fiscal year	Supplemental appropriations
1975	$29.6
1976	22.3
1977	36.3*
1978	16.1
1979	14.0
1980	16.9

*In addition to this figure, $13.1 billion in supplemental funding was required by a technical change in the handling of the long-term costs associated with housing contracts; actual funding was not increased.

trol spending. In part, this difficulty is reflected in the budgetary impact of recent supplementals (see Table 7.4). For fiscal years 1975–80, more than two dozen supplemental bills were passed, resulting in budgetary increases that averaged more than $20 billion annually. The Budget committees routinely provide a cushion in the second budget resolution to accommodate anticipated supplementals, such as the costs of annual federal pay increases. In considering regular appropriations bills, the Appropriations committees allow similar margins to meet supplemental requests. Each year at least one large spring supplemental is anticipated, but problems arise when these advance estimates are too low.

The spending-control problem therefore does not stem from the use or even the magnitude of supplemental funding. Rather, it has to do with the relationship between supplemental appropriations and the second budget resolution for each fiscal year. If the supposedly binding ceiling in the second budget resolution must always be raised in order to accommodate the following spring's supplemental requests, the discipline of the budget process disappears. In 1975, 1976, and 1978, shortfalls in spending and a sufficient cushion for supplementals permitted Congress to enact large supplementals without raising the spending ceiling. In fiscal 1977, a third budget resolution and accompanying $20 billion supplemental were justified on grounds of fiscal policy. In fiscal 1979 and again in fiscal 1980, however, Congress had to raise its budget ceilings to make room for supplemental appropriations. In both instances, unanticipated increases in uncontrollable spending, particularly entitlement programs with indexed benefits, threatened the spending ceilings and necessitated nondiscretionary supplemental funding.

The fiscal 1979 supplemental is instructive. Both the House and Senate Appropriations committees warned that mandatory spending increases were overwhelming savings in the discretionary portion of the budget. The issue of entitlements coupled to escalator clauses received the greatest attention. The committees pointed out that all major entitlement programs—various retirement and social welfare programs such as social security, food stamps, veterans' pensions, aid to the disabled, and school lunch and child nutrition programs— had built-in adjustments for increases in price indexes. These entitlements, moreover, accounted for about 55 percent of total annual budget outlays (compared to 40 percent in 1969) and for 75 percent of all uncontrollables (compared to 64 percent in 1969).[37] The squeeze on the 1979 spending ceiling occurred when entitlements increased more rapidly than expected, necessitating both the raising of the ceiling and an expanded supplemental to cover nondiscretionary spending increases for which appropriations were required.

Faced with an increasingly fragmented approach to spending, the Senate Budget Committee successfully fought to include in the conference report on the second budget resolution for fiscal 1980 language stating the "sense of Congress" that there would be no third budget resolution for that year. If congressional committees did not voluntarily sponsor the necessary spending cuts to preserve the second budget resolution's spending ceiling, the allowance for supplementals (roughly $11 billion) would have to be reduced accordingly.

The language not only was nonbinding but also provided an exception for "national or international developments beyond the power of Congress to control."[38] Muskie nevertheless argued that it would put Congress on notice that unless spending cuts were made, "the effect on the spring supplemental will be to crowd out important programs that . . . have a high priority."[39] In trying to use supplemental appropriations as a trade-off for other spending, the Senate Budget Committee was attempting to force Congress to take its spending ceilings seriously, something that seemed possible given Congress' apparent commitment to keep the 1980 deficit below $30 billion. By the following spring, however, the pressures to spend had grown so strong that no serious effort was made to prevent a third resolution or to protect the deficit level, which eventually approached $60 billion.

An examination of supplemental appropriations over the past few years reveals spending-control problems that weaken the budget process. Despite the budget timetable, authorizations are frequently late, so that the Appropriations committees have difficulty taking into account legislative changes that may affect regular appropriations bills, which in any case are sliding further and further past the September deadline. With supplemental funding levels hard to estimate and the decision-making period being extended ever further into the fiscal year, coordination of spending decisions with each other and with revenue decisions becomes more and more difficult. Finally, with uncontrollable spending dominating the budget and reducing the discretion over supplemental funding, the possibilities of effective discipline are minimal. The impact of automatic spending on budget ceilings and supplementals is serious, yet Congress has refused to limit automatic increases in entitlements and thereby to strengthen its control of actual spending.

Congress has also been reluctant to forgo even discretionary supplementals in order to protect its own budgets. In contrast to the assertiveness it displays on impoundments, Congress responds rather meekly to supplemental requests that are sent up by the president. The fiscal 1979 supplemental, explained the House Appropriations Committee, was "reported out at the insistence of the Office of Management and Budget and the President."[40] The Senate Appropriations Committee complained about all the supplemental requests it had received and said it was "obvious that the President and the OMB must impose tighter fiscal management controls over the executive agencies."[41]

One congressional expert has concluded there is "broad agreement that the President could be the most influential force in diminishing supplementals by simply not sending them up to Congress." Otherwise, he predicts, Congress will exercise little independence, for while "legislators could summon the courage to say 'No,' . . . it is politically difficult to oppose a presidential request that is supposedly made on an emergency basis."[42]

If this assessment is correct, the effort to control spending is in serious trouble. By its own actions on entitlements and escalator clauses, Congress has actually reduced the portion of the budget it

:an effectively control on a year-to-year basis. By refusing to set
;trict standards for consideration of supplemental appropriations,
Congress allows the executive branch to gain routine approval for
:ven discretionary supplemental requests, doing little to enhance its
·eputation for fiscal austerity.

Controlling Spending

Impoundment and supplemental appropriations show a contradic-
tory congressional approach toward budget control. On the impoundment side, Congress tends to treat its decisions on spending as
sacred. The attitude is defensive: the typical rhetoric suggests that
basic institutional prerogatives are at stake, and Congress' decisions
on spending are said to have been carefully considered and to be part
of a coherent plan.

Where supplemental appropriations are at issue, Congress accepts
and indeed encourages limits on its ability to say no. Executive
requests are routinely approved at a time when mandatory spending
has an enormous budgetary impact primarily because Congress continues to insist on protected status for favored programs.

If Congress is serious about controlling spending, it will have to
resolve these contradictions. Somewhat greater discretion will have
to be accorded presidents as they use routine impoundments to rein
in free-spending executive agencies. At the same time, Congress
must broaden its own discretion over annual budget decisions by
restricting mandatory spending. Unless Congress does so, it will
face mounting problems in staying within its budget ceilings and
enforcing coordination on budget decision making.

PART III

CONGRESSIONAL
BUDGET REFORM

CHAPTER 8

The Liberal Agenda

Congressional liberals were fearful at first that budget reform was no more than a thinly disguised conservative plot to cut the federal budget. As spending control was deemphasized, however, liberals began to see the possible benefits of the new budget process—an opportunity to "reorder priorities," to set independent congressional fiscal policy, to change the course of tax policy. Each of these processes was a major undertaking, and together they depended greatly on Congress' ability to provide policy leadership and to tackle issues with high political costs.

The liberal agenda and its accompanying assumptions about Congress provide an interesting perspective on the policy record of budget reform. To liberals, not only is that record probably not very reassuring, but the future also must seem rather bleak, for it looks as if attention once again will focus on spending control. And this time liberals are not likely to succeed in neutralizing budget-control measures; their numbers have been reduced and their ideas are no longer fashionable.

Budget Priorities

The term "priorities," with its suggestion of a deliberate and rational approach, is attractive to liberals. Moreover, it gives the perennial debates over defense and social welfare a useful symbol. The assumptions that underlie a heavy emphasis on priority setting are reasonably clear, if not well realized, as Congress works its way through the budget. Within a given level of available resources, decisions must be made about allocations. Earlier agreements about priorities shape these allocations, so that competing claims are measured against each other every year and within the context of broader debate about what government should do and how much it should spend to do it.

The budget act requires Congress to set budget totals. By dividing spending among the functional budget categories, it also enables Congress to make formal statements about priorities, something Congress sought when reform was being debated. Indeed, Senator Alan Cranston, a liberal Democrat from California, suggested that "budget reform by itself can play an important role in upgrading the capability of Congress" by directly involving legislators in "determining national economic policy and national priorities." Representative Jonathan Bingham, a New York City Democrat, explained that the new process would "allow meaningful debates on national priorities at the beginning of each Congress."[1]

Since Congress had already engineered a massive "welfare shift" in the budget, the potential significance of procedural change was greatly exaggerated. Indeed, the steady expansion of uncontrollable spending had narrowed annual budget margins, making it difficult to estimate spending accurately, much less to manage priorities with great precision.

Congress has, in fact, treated the priorities issue very gingerly. Despite the urgings of many Republicans that spending totals be set in advance of functional allocations, the House and Senate Budget committees have from the beginning proceeded through the budget function by function before arriving at a grand total. Within the committees and even on the floor, attempts to link increases or decreases in one function to offsetting changes in another are discouraged. There seems to be conscious effort to minimize direct either-or choices.

Each year there is a ritual battle over the defense budget and spending for social welfare, which essentially defines congressional priority setting. Over the past couple of years, Congress has had to confront increasingly difficult choices as it seeks to control spending; the result may be greater explicit attention to budget priorities. The immediate results on defense, however, are not likely to provide much cheer for congressional liberals.

The Prereform Welfare Shift

While year-to-year budget margins are usually small, even marginal decisions can, over time, produce important alterations in the shape as well as the size of the budget. Between the mid-1950s and mid-1970s, for example, Congress presided over radical growth in the federal budget as a whole, a decline in the defense share, and steady growth in the allocations for social welfare. Congress managed this shift during both Republican and Democratic administrations, and without official pronouncements about budget priorities.

Between fiscal 1955 and fiscal 1975, the defense share of the federal budget declined from well over 50 percent to approximately 25 percent. The portion allocated to payments for individuals (primarily income security and income assistance programs) rose during this same period from less than 20 percent of total outlays to just under 50 percent. Grants to states and localities, which roughly tripled as a proportion of total outlays between 1955 and 1975, provided additional funding for assistance programs. The relative priorities for defense and social welfare were—at least in budgetary terms—reversed.

This reversal was accomplished in two ways. Real growth in defense outlays was halted. In constant dollars, defense spending in 1975 was more than 10 percent below the 1955 level. From the mid-1950s to the mid-1960s, real defense spending remained stable; then during the Vietnam war, it increased substantially, reaching its peak in 1968. Subsequently, however, real defense spending declined sharply, dropping by about 25 percent between 1970 and 1975.[2]

Congress accomplished the other part of the defense–social welfare reversal by reserving the bulk of real budget growth for benefit programs. Between 1955 and 1975, payments for individuals went up by almost $100 billion in constant dollars; this increase represented about 80 percent of the real growth in the *entire* federal budget for the period. The welfare shift, then, was financed through real budgetary growth combined with static defense spending, with the latter being partially masked by increases in absolute dollars.

Postreform Priorities

Liberals in Congress expected the shift to welfare to continue, if perhaps at a slower pace, with the formal congressional debates on priorities. Post-Vietnam antagonisms toward the military and the post-Nixon weakening of the presidency strengthened the position of defense critics, who seemed to have public opinion on their side, at least for a time.[3]

Moreover, with most of the social welfare budget protected by its uncontrollable status, the bulk of controllable spending was in defense—over two-thirds of the 1976 defense budget was technically controllable, and perhaps as much as 10 percent could be adjusted without radical policy changes.[4] As far as defense was concerned, liberals finally seemed to have means, motive, and opportunity.

Since 1975 the defense budget has changed, although not in the way liberals expected. The decade-long decline in real defense spending had ended by 1977, and by 1980 both Congress and the Carter administration had come to agree that substantial rates of real growth would be maintained through at least the mid-1980s. And now the new administration and the Republican-controlled Senate support even higher increases for defense. The emphasis on defense, coinciding with growing fiscal austerity in Congress, tightens the squeeze on the rest of the budget. Since Congress clearly can no longer do everything it would like to do in the way of spending, it may finally have to face choices among priorities.

During the Ford administration, the defense–social welfare debate had an obvious and important partisan dimension as well as an institutional dimension. The majority of congressional Democrats were not inclined to agree with a conservative Republican president's budget policies, and they were also intent on proving that Congress could generate positive alternatives. In his fiscal 1977 budget, Ford designated a large boost in defense spending as "one of the highest priorities for our government."[5] His next budget and future-year planning levels emphasized a "continuation of this real growth trend."[6] Ford also recommended low spending totals and reduced growth in outlays for social welfare.

Congress followed a different course, but there were signs of at least partial agreement. Defense appropriations for fiscal 1977, for example, were well below Ford's requests, but even the substantial reductions that year were relatively modest in comparison with cuts in previous years. The gap between the Ford administration's proposals for the defense budget and the spending levels in Congress' budget resolutions narrowed over a three-year period (see Table 8.1). The shifting mood in Congress was signaled by the Senate Budget Committee, which, in reporting the second budget resolution for fiscal 1977, placed "substantial growth . . . for national defense" at the top of its priority list.[7]

If Congress was responding to Ford's lead on defense, it was not on social welfare. Of the four budget functions that make up "human resources" spending, only one—education, employment, training, and social services (function 500)—has an appreciable degree of year-to-year controllability. (The other three categories are income security, health, and veterans' benefits and services.) Here Ford's spending requests were raised substantially and consistently by Congress (see Table 8.1). The congressional add-ons for this function were much larger—absolutely and proportionately—than the corresponding cuts in defense or, for that matter, the congressional changes in most functions. For the three years shown, outlay levels for function 500 in the fall budget resolutions averaged about $6 billion per year over the Ford budgets. Actual expenditures, despite a large shortfall in 1976, averaged more than $5 billion over original administration estimates.

Congress was able to accommodate growth in defense and in social welfare by approving budget totals larger than those Ford proposed. Congressional budget resolutions from 1976 to 1978 set outlay ceilings that averaged more than $20 billion per year above the Ford administration's budgets.[8] Budget authority increases were similar in scale. So long as spending totals were reasonably flexible and higher congressional budgets could be defended on fiscal policy grounds, Congress could avoid or at least postpone uncomfortable choices among programs.

The Carter presidency, however, coincided with economic and foreign policy challenges that made such difficult choices seemingly inevitable. Congress was under attack for its failure to keep spending under control. There was a growing consensus that the imbalance between the military capabilities of the United States and those of the Soviet Union required larger defense budgets. Although Carter's budgets were initially more expansive and less defense-oriented

Table 8.1. Outlays and budget authority requested by President Ford for defense and social welfare, recommended by first and second congressional budget resolutions, and actual amounts, fiscal years 1976–78 (in billions of dollars)

	Fiscal year	Presidential request		First Congressional resolution		Second Congressional resolution		Actual amounts	
		Defense	Function 500*	Defense	Function 500*	Defense	Function 500*	Defense	Function 500*
Outlays	1976	$ 94.0	$14.6	$ 90.7	$19.8	$ 91.9	$21.3	$ 89.4	$18.7
Budget authority		107.7	13.7	100.7	19.0	101.0	20.9	103.8	21.2
Outlays	1977	101.1	16.6	100.8	23.0	100.6	22.2	97.5	21.0
Budget authority		114.9	15.9	112.5	24.6	112.1	24.0	110.4	30.4
Outlays	1978	112.3	19.4	111.0	27.2	110.1	26.3	105.2	26.5
Budget authority		122.9	18.0	118.5	26.8	116.4	26.4	117.9	22.4

*Includes education, training, employment, and social services.
SOURCE: *Budget of the United States Government*, various years; House and Senate Budget Committee reports, various years.

than Ford's, they soon became more and more similar to Ford's. Congressional budgets were being reshaped in much the same way, creating severe tensions in Congress.

Carter's first term can be divided into two distinct periods. Shortly after taking office, Carter revised Ford's fiscal 1978 budget, raising total outlays by almost $20 billion and making small reductions in defense spending. The following year, Carter called for "prudent real growth in our defense capabilities . . . considerably more moderate than those proposed . . . by the previous administration."[9]

The 1980 budget was a different story. Although a real growth level of 3 percent was requested for defense, total budget outlays showed virtually no real growth. In order to bring the deficit below its self-imposed target of $30 billion, the administration even recommended limited cuts in social welfare spending. After a bruising fight in the House and rejection of an initial conference version of the spring budget resolution, Congress adopted spending targets that were quite close to Carter's, despite the dissatisfaction of House liberals. In the Senate, however, Carter was pressed to raise his defense budget even higher and to agree in advance to comparable future-year increases. Carter resisted until December 1979, when in an unusual move he previewed his 1981 defense budget, announcing that he would call for a real growth rate of approximately 4.5 percent through the mid-1980s. When the 1981 budget was presented to Congress in January, the emphasis was on defense.

At the same time that the president was shifting his position, Congress was altering its own policy choices. In its second budget resolution for fiscal 1979, Congress established a ceiling for defense outlays $5.4 billion under the president's request—a difference later erased by supplementals and other increases. In the second resolution for 1980, Congress voted for *higher* defense levels than Carter had initially proposed, and the third resolution provided still additional increases. This remarkable turnaround did not come about easily. Disagreement between the two houses over defense contributed to a delay that pushed adoption of the fall resolution two months beyond the statutory deadline. Moreover, the stage was set for continuing battles; the Senate had revised its original budget targets for 1981 and 1982, adding more than $42 billion in defense budget authority and raising the defense budget share to over 25 percent, its highest level since 1975.

Congress faced a second and even more complicated dilemma, however, in the management of the 1980 budget. In the fall, outlays had to be raised by almost $16 billion over the figure indicated in the first resolution, partly because of defense increases but to an even greater extent because of automatic, inflation-adjusted increases in entitlement programs. Outlays for income security, for example, were estimated at $179.1 billion in the president's January budget, at $183.3 billion in the spring resolution, and at $190.0 billion in the fall resolution. In order to keep within what members considered a politically acceptable deficit target ($30 billion—the same figure the president had trumpeted earlier), Congress had to cut some programs below the rate of inflation, and the predictable result was a prolonged dispute over outlays for function 500 programs. Here the difference between the House and Senate figures was less than $1 billion, but Robert Giaimo, chairman of the House Budget Committee, saw it as symbolic of "deep philosophical differences" between the two chambers.[10] Even with cutbacks in function 500 and other discretionary outlays, however, Congress had no assurance that its budget would survive a new round of growth in uncontrollables, and indeed it did not. Several months later Congress revised its 1980 budget again, raising outlays this time by an additional $25 billion and abandoning its earlier deficit target. The final deficit for 1980 was over $59 billion, more than double the original projection.

Trends in Priorities

Determining the budget priorities for the 1980s will present serious challenges to Congress and an increasingly severe test of the budget process. Congress has reversed itself on defense. As Table 8.2 indicates, projected outlays show defense receiving an increasing share of the budget. (To put the Carter and congressional switches in perspective, the Ford budgets for 1976–78 requested an average defense share of 26 percent. The budget policies of the Reagan administration are, of course, weighted even more heavily toward defense.)

Assuming that Congress continues to raise the defense allocation, the rest of the budget will have to be adjusted if spending is to be controlled. For example, the income security function, which accounted for 21.9 percent of spending in 1970, had increased to over 33 percent in 1980, and is projected at just under 36 percent in

Table 8.2. Shares of federal budget outlays allocated to defense and human resources, fiscal years 1955–83 (projected) (percent)

Fiscal year	Defense	Human resources
1955	58.1%	21.3%
1960	49.0	27.7
1965	40.1	29.9
1970	40.0	37.3
1975	26.2	51.7
1976	24.4	54.0
1977	24.2	53.6
1978	23.3	52.2
1979	23.8	52.6
1980	23.4	52.3
Carter[a]	23.7	53.3
Third budget resolution	23.7	52.1
1981		
Carter[b]	23.7	54.6
First budget resolution	25.0	54.1
Second budget resolution	25.1	58.5
1982		
Carter[c]	24.9	52.6
Reagan[d]	27.1	52.4
Congress[e]	27.1	52.5
1983		
Carter[c]	25.7	52.7
Reagan[d]	30.9	53.4
Congress[e]	30.5	53.2

[a]Based on the January budget submitted for fiscal 1980.
[b]Based on the January budget submitted for fiscal 1981.
[c]Based on the January budget submitted for fiscal 1982.
[d]Based on the fiscal 1982 budget revisions submitted in March 1981.
[e]These figures reflect spending estimates contained in the first budget resolution for fiscal 1982.

1981. The health function, which represented 6.6 percent of spending in 1970, is projected at 10 percent in 1981. As a result, total spending for human resources will present Congress with serious control problems over the next several years.

The apparent top spending priority, then, is still human resources, as their budget share will continue to dominate the budget for the foreseeable future. In a sense, however, the figures may be misleading. The bulk of spending for human resources is automatic, a response to demographic factors and economic conditions, not to debates on priorities. Unless Congress is willing to reexamine past decisions about eligibility requirements and benefit levels, its budget-cutting energies will have to concentrate on the shrinking controllable portion of the budget.

Even though human resources will no doubt have a considerably larger share of the budget in 1984 than they did in 1974, current liberal rhetoric, especially in the House, suggests quite the opposite. The liberals' current discontent, however, may be the inevitable result of their past success. By ensuring automatic spending for social welfare, liberals have left themselves with little to do. Major new programs are virtually impossible because of constraints on spending, and benefit levels for existing programs are indexed. Attacks on the defense budget are, at least for the time being, token efforts. The federal budget is, more than ever, a social welfare document, but present-day liberals apparently get precious little satisfaction from it.

There is some genuine cause for concern, moreover, if not for the reasons liberals typically offer. Today Congress cannot deal with priorities as effectively as it did in the prereform period, because of the protected status of much of the budget. Programs do not compete on an equal basis. Either-or choices are limited, even if Congress would be willing to make them.

The 1974 pronouncements concerning budget priorities can be fairly characterized as essentially rhetorical and at least partly misleading. For two decades Congress had made very clear choices about budget priorities, and the result was a radical transformation in the federal budget. The claim that Congress had been excluded from the debate on priorities was simply wrong. Further, since 1974 Congress has not demonstrated any great enthusiasm for making direct choices on priorities. The procedures used by the Budget committees intentionally avoid such choices, and the overwhelming rejection of proposals to transfer funds from one budget function to another, so that the gain of one is the other's loss, indicates that Congress prefers to deal with each function separately. Such an approach, however, does suggest that the term "budget priorities" is overworked and misunderstood.

Fiscal Policy

Perhaps the most widely heralded achievement of the 1974 budget reformers was the procedure by which fiscal policy decisions were made the responsibility of Congress. Representative Richard Bolling, Democrat of Missouri, declared that the "foremost responsibility of Congress must be the determination of macro-economic budget policy," which would be reflected in congressional budget resolutions that set "overall budget aggregates."[11] The annual budget resolutions would be the means of establishing spending and revenue totals and specifying "the surplus or deficit . . . appropriate in light of economic conditions and all other relevant factors." The "economic assumptions and objectives" contained in congressional budget resolutions would be explained by the Budget committees.[12]

This latest assertion of congressional authority was greeted by a great deal of enthusiasm. The Senate Budget Committee held hearings on fiscal policy and the budget as soon as it was organized. During February 1975 it scheduled a series of macroeconomic "seminars" for committee members. Panels composed of representatives of the private sector and government economists met with senators to discuss budget policy choices, the relationship between fiscal and monetary policy, and the workings of the economy. A good deal of congressional self-congratulation took place during these meetings. One refreshing contrast was provided by Senator Joseph R. Biden, Jr., Democrat of Delaware, who recounted an earlier discussion with his father. When Biden proudly told his family that the Banking Committee was providing "the most intensive seminar course I have ever had in my life," his father replied, "Son, do you not think that is a hell of a place to start to learn?"[13]

The Democratic leadership in Congress, buoyed by the massive party majority brought in by the 1974 midterm election, was eager to formulate alternative economic policies and to try to wrest control over economic policy from the Ford administration. The more euphoric Democrats had visions of a "veto-proof Congress" that would cut the presidency down to size and demonstrate the feasibility of congressional government. It was a difficult time to begin, however. The record of economic forecasts in 1973 and 1974 was abysmal. Just as Congress was ready to join the Keynesian consensus, the economics profession discovered that the expected trade-offs between inflation and unemployment were disappearing. Oil and commodity prices were rising, and future levels were impossible to predict. Then in the fall of 1974 the Ford administration identified inflation as the most serious economic problem facing the nation and announced that its budgetary response would be fiscal restraint.

This policy probably would have created sharp divisions among congressional Democrats over spending control and balanced budgets. As it was, although divisions did occur, notably in the House, they were eased by a sharp turnaround in economic policy. As Muskie recounted, when the Budget Committee had first met in August 1974, "the paramount problem appeared to be inflation," and the most popular remedy for it was "fiscal restraint—large cuts in Federal spending and a balanced budget for fiscal 1976."[14] By November the unemployment rate was 6.5 percent, the highest level since 1961, and there were fears that it might climb to over 8 percent during 1975. Even though inflation remained high (consumer prices rose 12 percent during 1974), the immediate concern was with recession and unemployment.

Over the next several months the Ford administration and Congress argued about the appropriate response. Agreement that a budget deficit was inevitable was almost unanimous, but the size that deficit should be and its composition created conflicts. Initially Congress was tentative in asserting a distinctive policy approach, allowing Ford to enforce a degree of restraint on spending. When the Carter administration took over, Congress was considerably bolder about its fiscal policy capability, but continued deficits and increasing inflation have sapped much of that confidence. At a time when restraint and balanced budgets are tests of institutional virtue, Congress appears less convinced of its ability to lead the way in economic policy.

Raising the Deficit

In early December 1974 several prominent economists testified before the Senate Budget Committee that deficits as high as $25 to $35 billion might be needed during fiscal 1976. The 1976 budget that President Ford sent to Congress shortly thereafter recommended $349.4 billion in spending and a deficit of $51.9 billion. Ford proposed $16 billion in temporary tax cuts linked to an equivalent reduction in domestic spending. During congressional hearings on the Ford budget, Joseph Pechman of the Brookings Institution stated that the $50 billion fiscal stimulus was seriously inadequate, but he congratulated the administration for the "candor and honesty" of its budget documents, which, he claimed, marked the first time that any administration, Republican or Democratic, had given Congress "a set of estimates that are not only consistent, but seem to be a fair appraisal of what the President's program is likely to produce."[15]

Before long, however, congressional sensitivity to the deficit issue was leading to charges that administration budget figures were being manipulated. In April 1975, OMB reestimates of the president's budget raised the deficit to $60 billion. Later that month, as Congress prepared to debate its first-ever budget resolution, the president issued a statement challenging Congress to match the $60 billion deficit figure. Muskie fumed that the president was trying "to gain some political advantage over the Congress" by using a deficit figure that he and his advisers knew was "not an honest number." *Voodoo* Bellmon, who, like many other congressional Republicans, was afraid of backlash from his constituents if he supported a deficit budget resolution, agreed that the number was "phony," adding that the "educational process" the Senate had recently been through showed the Budget Committee's deficit policy to be the only realistic approach.[16] To ease senators' concerns, the Budget Committee's report pointed out that revenue losses from the recession accounted for most of the deficit, clearly making it "a recession deficit, not a spending deficit."[17]

The Senate Budget Committee won quick approval for its $365 billion outlay target and $67.2 billion deficit. In the House the going was much rougher, as Republicans refused to vote for a $70 billion deficit and Democratic liberals pressed for more jobs programs and even higher spending, but the House finally adopted a resolution containing the $70 billion deficit level. The House-Senate conference then agreed to a $68.8 billion compromise on the deficit and a $367 billion spending target.

In adopting the second budget resolution for 1976 in December, Congress voted to raise the outlay ceiling almost $8 billion over the figure set by the first resolution and to increase the deficit to over $74 billion. What the Senate Budget Committee termed the "moderately stimulative fiscal policy" of the first resolution was deemed a success.[18] "The course of the economy [had been] turned around," the House Budget Committee said, "from the most serious recession of the post-war era."[19] If Congress was pleased with the result, it was still reluctant to embrace the approach wholeheartedly. The Senate Budget Committee claimed that with adjustments for administration underestimates, the congressional budget was "very close to what the President advocated when he 'drew the line' at a $60.0 billion deficit."[20]

Identifying a clear winner in the fiscal 1976 episode is difficult.

None of Ford's spending vetoes, including that of a massive jobs bill, was overridden, but Congress rejected Ford's attempt to place restrictions on the food stamp program and ignored his proposals to impose similar restraints on other uncontrollable spending programs. The administration suggested that despite these defeats, its steady pressure for restraint had worked.[21] The final spending figures for 1976, however, are inconclusive. An unanticipated spending short-fall reduced outlays more than $8 billion below the congressional ceiling, and the deficit turned out to be $66.4 billion, almost half-way between the Ford commitment and the congressional budget.

The struggle for institutional advantage continued during prelimi-naries for the 1977 budget. In October 1975 Ford had called on Congress to enact a $28 billion tax cut, but he had linked it to a $395 billion spending ceiling for fiscal 1977. When Congress simply extended the 1975 tax reductions into 1976, Ford vetoed the legisla-tion. In a quick compromise worked out during December, Ford agreed to an extension in exchange for a largely symbolic congres-sional pledge to consider equivalent reductions in outlays in the 1977 budget. The leaders of the Budget committees, however, re-mained upset about what they viewed as continuing attempts by the administration to subvert the new budget process.

As signs of economic recovery began to appear, the House and Senate became more confident about their ability to handle deficits. The first congressional resolution for fiscal 1977 added nearly $20 billion in outlays and almost $8 billion of deficit to the Ford budget. Once again the Senate Budget Committee was quick to emphasize that conflicting estimates accounted for much of the difference. With comparable estimates, the committee maintained, the proposed deficits were only about $1 billion apart.[22] The real differences, however, were quite a bit deeper. Congress, rejecting substantial permanent tax cuts, instead continued to rely on spending to stimu-late the economy. It also continued to ignore Ford's proposed cuts in domestic programs. James T. Lynn, director of the OMB, called the congressional budget "appalling" and refused to recommend that Republicans in the House and Senate vote for it.[23] The second res-olution adopted by Congress in the fall was virtually a carbon copy of the first.

Congress vs. Carter

When the 95th Congress met in January 1977, economic recovery seemed to be lagging, and the spending shortfall in fiscal 1976 was being looked at as the possible cause. With Democrats still firmly in control of Congress and a Democrat now in the White House, the lure of additional fiscal stimulus was irresistible. On January 31 President Carter sent a two-year $31.2 billion stimulus package to Congress. For fiscal 1977, which had started four months earlier, Carter called for almost $16 billion in new stimulus, most of it in the form of tax rebates. Congress, in an attempt to demonstrate its continuing independence, proceeded to raise spending for jobs programs and increase the size of the stimulus. Congress' third budget resolution for fiscal 1977 raised the outlay ceiling, lowered the revenue floor, and brought the deficit to almost $70 billion, an increase of about $20 billion over the deficit figure in the second resolution.

Many members of Congress had begun to fear that too much was being attempted—that quarterly updates in economic policy were unwise and certainly beyond the capability of Congress. This argument was strengthened when the administration abruptly changed its assessment of the recovery and withdrew the tax-rebate plan. Congress was then forced to revise its third resolution amid embarrassed complaints about institutional independence. In any event, spending during fiscal 1977 fell well below the congressional budget, and the deficit of $45 billion was much closer to Ford's original budget proposal of $43 billion than to the $52.6 billion in the final budget resolution. Even with Democratic control of the executive branch, the implementation of Democratic fiscal policy proved frustrating.

This pattern was repeated the next year. Carter revised Ford's 1978 budget, increasing outlays by $20 billion and the deficit by more than $10 billion. Congress, confident that it was safe from the fiscal attacks of the Ford years, proceeded to increase the deficit target to just under $65 billion, almost $18 billion more than the figure in the Ford budget. In its second resolution, Congress lowered the deficit slightly in response to revised spending estimates, but even these estimates proved inaccurate. The actual deficit for 1978 nearly matched Ford's original projection.

Carter's second year in office coincided with what Alice Rivlin,

director of the Congressional Budget Office, called "the most difficult moment for economic policy makers since the beginning of the
budget process in 1974." Inflation was "accelerating," noted Rivlin,
just when the economic recovery was showing "signs of running out
of steam."[24] Carter's 1979 budget reflected this junction. It promised
"a balanced budget in the future if the . . . economy continues its
recovery,"[25] and it held real spending growth to its lowest level since
1973. It also recommended a large tax cut, however, and a $60
billion deficit. Abner Mikva, a House Democrat from Illinois,
pointed to the parallel dilemma that Congress faced in trying to
control spending and deficits: "The spending total in Carter's budget
leaves some chores . . . undone, but realistically there is no way they
can be done. This year is almost a test of our capacity to run
government."[26]

Congress' first budget resolution for 1979 incorporated a change
in the administration's fiscal plan. The Budget committees were
worried about the inflationary impact of another large deficit and
also about the problem of defending that deficit three years into an
economic recovery. Muskie and Giaimo met with Carter and agreed
to delay the tax cut, thereby reducing its impact during the fiscal
year and lowering the deficit. Over the next few months, fiscal
concerns mounted. National health insurance, welfare reform, and
urban aid all fell victim to congressional worries about the budget.
In the fall, Congress prepared for the midterm election by again
lowering the deficit, this time to under $40 billion. While most of
the reduction was accounted for by reestimates of spending, there
were important changes, particularly in jobs programs. In its report
on the fall budget resolution, the Senate Budget Committee high-
lighted Congress' "leadership against inflation," warning that continued large deficits could not be justified indefinitely.[27]

Congressional fiscal policy, however, soon received another jolt.
Congress was forced to pass a third resolution for fiscal 1979 as
outlays ran $6.2 billion higher than estimated. Because high infla-
tion drove up revenues even more sharply, however, the deficit
turned out to be $27.7 billion, well under the level Congress had set
and more than $30 billion below the deficit in the original Carter
budget. When Carter came in with a "lean and austere" 1980 budget
that projected the smallest deficit since 1974, Congress followed
suit. In the fall it once again committed itself to holding the deficit

below $30 billion, although to do so it had to rely on inflation-boosted revenues, as well as economic assumptions and spending estimates that were, to put it generously, optimistic. Then, only two months after Congress adopted its spending ceiling for 1980, OMB estimates placed outlays some $16 billion above that ceiling.[28] By the following spring the projected deficit was approaching $50 billion, and the actual deficit for 1980 reached $59 billion, roughly double the original commitment.

Controlling Fiscal Policy Outcomes

To suggest that Congress alone has a poor record of fiscal policy management would be unfair and inaccurate. The Carter administration's original 1980 budget, for example, was some $65 billion off the mark—almost $50 billion too low on outlays and nearly $20 billion too low on revenues. Much of that difference reflected a continuing inability to predict inflation. The Carter inflation forecast for 1977 was 1.5 percent below the actual rate; in 1978 the gap was 2.9 percent; in 1979 it was 4.8 percent; and during 1980 it reached almost 7 percent.[29] Congressional estimating and forecasting errors have been substantial, but clearly not unique.

Consensus on fiscal policy remedies has also been seriously weakened. Obviously, no easy solution has been—or is likely to be—found for inflation, and the government's ability to manage the economy is no longer simply assumed. Economic theorists are divided over the inflationary effects of tax cuts and spending increases, and interest in monetary policy solutions is growing. As the Joint Economic Committee recently concluded, "Now . . . opinions about the stimulative potential of fiscal policy range from the skeptical to the exuberant."[30]

In the midst of this uncertainty, Congress' difficulty in fashioning an institutional response is not surprising. In 1978, for example, Congress approved a bewildering set of national economic goals; it passed the Humphrey-Hawkins bill, calling for a 4 percent unemployment rate and 3 percent inflation rate by 1983, along with legislation promising tax and spending reductions over the next several years and mandating a balanced budget by 1981. Sentiment for control of spending and reduction of the deficit has since increased, but Congress' ability to enforce fiscal restraint remains suspect. Moreover, just as spending shortfalls frustrated Congress' efforts to stimulate the economy, even more massive errors in the opposite direction threaten to overwhelm the current attempts at fiscal restraint.

Whether members of Congress will want to maintain responsibility for fiscal policy under these circumstances is open to question. The Senate, for example, appears to have a much stronger commitment on this score than does the House. Electoral and institutional factors may explain some of the difference. Six-year terms and statewide constituencies can help to diffuse pressures to spend, and broad policy issues are perhaps more compatible with the generalist orientation of the Senate than with the specialist orientation of the House. In addition, the coalition that passes budget resolutions in the Senate is bipartisan and moderate. A comparable coalition has never emerged in the House, and the Democratic majority is continually threatened by defections among liberals and conservatives. If either group decides that the future course of fiscal policy is unacceptable, it may finally conclude that the budget process is simply not worth supporting.

Although the congressional fiscal policy experiment is far from being the institutional boon its proponents expected, it may not be a complete failure. The decision-making process has improved. Members of Congress now routinely consider the budgetary implications of decisions on taxing and spending; they have accepted the responsibility of establishing a coherent fiscal plan and dealing with the relationship between government and the economy.

The president still enjoys the initiative, however, and Congress remains vulnerable to charges of fiscal irresponsibility, whatever the merits of those charges. Congressional liberals once saw the budget process as a way to control fiscal policy, but are no longer certain about this approach. For example, Representative Bolling now concludes that the annual budget process is unsuitable for setting long-term economic policy[31] and instead proposes an expanded role for the Joint Economic Committee in the development of congressional economic goals to guide the budgetary process, a prospect that the Budget committees view without enthusiasm.

Tax Expenditures

Congressional liberals expected the budget process to facilitate a comprehensive reexamination and resulting reduction in the use of "tax expenditures," provisions in the tax code that reduce the "normal" tax liability for an individual or a corporation. Instead, as the Senate Budget Committee recently complained, Congress has continued the "major use of tax expenditures to implement policy," adding new tax expenditures, protecting existing ones, and making "very few significant reductions."[32] In the 1978 tax bill, for example, Congress rejected most of the "reform" proposals by President Carter and the liberal bloc in Congress, and on its own initiative voted to liberalize the preferential rate for capital gains and to preserve other controversial tax expenditures.

In order to counter this trend in congressional tax policy, liberals have pushed for procedural changes. For several years they have tried to institute "sunset" requirements—mandated periodic reauthorizations for tax expenditures—an approach that the Carter administration supported. In the Senate, proposals for sunset requirements have been coupled with proposals to extend jurisdiction over tax expenditures to authorizing committees as well as the Finance Committee. Now that proposals to set limits on spending are being seriously considered by Congress, critics of tax expenditures, such as Robert Giaimo, argue that tax expenditures and direct spending should be treated equally.[33] As revenue committees, especially the Finance Committee, are strongly opposed to these changes, it is unlikely that procedural approaches will succeed.

The Language of Reform

In the area of tax policy, terminology is quite important. People who use the term "tax expenditures" maintain that these various exemptions, deductions, exclusions, credits, and deferrals are the equivalent of direct spending by government. The only difference, according to this view, is that instead of providing a benefit in the form of a payment, the government decides to allow individuals or corporations to retain funds that would otherwise be paid as taxes.

Those who argue that tax expenditures are the equivalent of direct spending want to see tax expenditures treated like regular spending programs and incorporated in the debate on budget priorities. They believe this procedure would make it easier to attack specific tax expenditures and would eventually cause them to be replaced by direct expenditures, a change they advocate on grounds of equity and efficiency. Tax expenditures, such critics claim, disproportionately benefit higher income groups, and the government could achieve the same policy goals at lower cost by direct expenditure. For opponents of tax expenditures, revenues forgone are the same as money spent, but spending is the preferred means to achieve policy goals; tax reform therefore means the closing of loopholes.

Many members of Congress do not accept this argument. For example, Lloyd Bentsen of Texas, a Democratic member of the Senate Finance Committee, prefers the term "tax incentives": "If you use [the term] tax expenditures you assume all income belongs to the government."[34] This position is shared by many antitax groups that have refused to join the movement against tax expenditures. "To equate spending with not taking," says William Bonner, treasurer of the National Taxpayers Union, "suggests the government owns everything."[35]

The very concept of tax expenditures has fuzzy outlines. In order to measure tax expenditures, a normal tax structure must first be specified—not a simple task. And the dispute over the use of tax expenditures is complicated by considerations of efficiency and equity. Senator Daniel Patrick Moynihan of New York, for example, has defended the efficiency and advisability of the tax-expenditure approach. It is, he declares, "the one way we have found to attain public purposes without Government intervention . . . a way to get markets to do what we would otherwise have bureaucracies attempt to do."[36] Even the Carter administration finally conceded that the equity issue is complex:

> The benefits of tax expenditures designed to encourage particular types of economic activity may not rest fully or even mainly with the corporations or individuals whose taxes are initially affected. Benefits often accrue to others . . . or . . . become widely diffused. For example, to the extent that the investment tax credit stimulates capital formation, productivity may increase and real wages may rise, benefiting recipients of labor income as well as capital income.[37]

The language of tax reform masks, no doubt deliberately, a host of related public policy issues. "A loophole," as Russell Long is fond of reminding the Senate, ". . . is something that benefits the other guy. If it benefits you, it is tax reform."[38]

The stakes are high. Although the figures are far from precise, because "tax expenditure estimates cannot be simply added together

Table 8.3. Estimated benefits to corporations and individuals of major tax expenditures, fiscal year 1981, by aggregated categories (in billions of dollars)

	Corporations	Individuals
Capital gains	$ 1.3	$22.3
Exclusion of interest on state and local debt	5.5	3.9
Deduction of state and local nonbusiness taxes	—	24.8
Deduction of charitable contributions	1.0	8.9
Itemized deductions	—	44.5
Deduction of mortgage interest and property tax on owner-occupied homes	—	22.3
Benefits for the elderly (exclusion of social security and railroad retirement, plus additional exemption and tax credit)	—	12.4
Investment credits	17.0	3.2
Exclusion of employer contributions for medical insurance premiums and medical care	—	15.2
Net exclusion of pension contributions and earnings, employer plans	—	14.7

SOURCE: *Special Analyses, Budget of the United States Government, Fiscal Year 1981* (Washington, D.C.: Government Printing Office, 1980), pp. 231, 234.

to obtain totals for functional areas or a grand total,"[39] the Senate Budget Committee reports that existing tax expenditures will exceed $200 billion during fiscal year 1981.[40] Roughly three-fourths of this sum is accounted for by tax expenditures for individuals, which provide benefits that are obviously distributed broadly throughout the population (see Table 8.3).

The Procedural Issue

An early version of the 1974 budget act treated tax expenditures as a form of spending. The Senate Government Operations Committee bill specified that tax expenditures would be listed by functional category in the congressional budget resolutions, just as regular spending programs would be, in order to permit Congress to make spending decisions "on a much more informed basis in each area."[41] The Senate Finance Committee strenuously opposed this proposal, as well as the requirement that total revenues be broken down by source in the budget resolutions.[42]

The Finance Committee succeeded in removing both tax expenditures and the revenue breakdown from the budget resolution procedure. The legislation that was finally enacted authorized the Budget committees merely "to devise methods of coordinating tax expenditures, policies, and programs with direct budget outlays."[43] The Budget committees could recommend changes in tax policy and tax expenditures in their reports, but they could not take the critical additional step of including such changes in the spring and fall budget resolutions.

These limitations on the Budget committees have been very significant: they make it possible for the tax-writing committees, most notably the Finance Committee, to take the position that the only binding revenue figure in a congressional budget resolution is the revenue total. As long as they reach that revenue total, claim the tax-writing committees, they enjoy full discretion in shaping tax legislation. The Budget committees have, naturally, disputed this contention. Muskie and Bellmon, for example, repeatedly tried to convince the Senate that adopting a budget resolution commits Congress to the economic assumptions and fiscal policy plan behind it. The way a revenue total is reached, they argued, is not simply a matter of the Finance Committee's discretion. And while leadership of the Senate Budget Committee has tried to downplay the intercommittee competition by casting these issues in the form of "protecting the congressional budget process," Russell Long and the Senate Finance Committee have deliberately and successfully contended that basic committee prerogatives are at stake.

The situation in the House has been less confrontational, largely because neither the House Budget Committee nor Ways and Means is as independent or influential as its Senate counterpart. The House Democratic leadership has been heavily involved in both committees, so that jurisdictional disputes have been minimized. In addition, the committee chairmen involved have tried to avoid open conflicts. Faced with shaky support for budget resolutions, House Budget Committee chairmen Brock Adams and Robert Giaimo necessarily relied on accommodation with other committees, particularly Appropriations and Ways and Means; Al Ullman, chairman of Ways and Means from 1975 to 1980, shared that approach.

Russell Long's aggressive defense of the Finance Committee's prerogatives has been aimed at maintaining the balance of influence on tax policy, which clearly would be changed if the Senate Budget Committee were involved in the specifics of tax policy or if sunset requirements were imposed on tax expenditures. Senator Edward Kennedy's proposal to extend jurisdiction over tax-expenditure legislation to authorizing committees, which he contends would provide "more effective coordination of all the various spending programs," is simply another attempt to shift the initiative away from Finance. As Kennedy acknowledges: "There is a different climate in the Senate on tax spending as opposed to direct spending . . . for spending through the tax laws than . . . for spending through appropriations."[44] By treating tax expenditures as simply another form of spending, Kennedy and his allies would alter this climate.

The Senate Budget Committee is interested in extending its power and influence, and to the extent that this ambition involves tax policy, its interests coincide with those of Finance's critics. Both want to limit the discretion and influence currently enjoyed by Finance and, not incidentally, Russell Long. As a result, the Finance Committee's strategy has been to challenge broad interpretations of the budget act, and Long has established a string of important and supportive precedents in this manner. The Senate has agreed that the only binding figures in budget resolutions are the totals, that tax legislation affecting future or out-years can be considered without Budget Committee waivers, and that effective dates of tax legislation can be manipulated to conform to budget resolutions.

The out-year issue is instructive. During the fall of 1978 the Roth-Kemp proposal for tax cuts was introduced as an amendment on the Senate floor. Neither Muskie nor Long supported Roth-Kemp. Muskie, however, maintained that the tax cuts for fiscal 1980 contained in the proposal could not be considered without a waiver from the Senate Budget Committee. Section 303(a) of the budget act would, in this case, have prohibited floor consideration of 1980 tax legislation between January 1, 1979, and adoption of the first budget resolution for fiscal 1980. Section 303(b), however, allows Congress to act on tax bills that go into effect in a fiscal year following "the fiscal year to which the concurrent resolution applies."[45] Under this provision, according to Long, Roth-Kemp could be considered without the Budget Committee's permission, and so, by implication, could any out-year proposal that the Finance Committee sponsored. Muskie presented his case in typically apocalyptic language, declaring that Long's interpretation of the budget act would "for all practical purposes [eliminate] the discipline of the budget process from the revenue side of the budget."[46] Long shifted the question from the budget process to the Budget Committee:

> It makes no sense to say that no Senator can offer a tax amendment without the consent of the Budget Committee if the amendment's effect takes place in the year after the year in which the budget resolution applies. The Budget Committee has not yet acted on the resolution for that year, they have not proposed a spending limitation, they have not proposed what the income will be—so to limit the right of Senators to offer amendments in this way makes no sense. The budget act was never intended to be interpreted in this way.[47]

By a vote of 48–38, the Senate supported Long's position; Long then called on Muskie to "speak out strongly and say 'The Budget Committee has considered this matter and we find we cannot stand the revenue loss involved in the Roth amendment.'"[48]

Long, having persuaded the Senate that the budget act was not quite so sweeping as some people suggested, was not at all reluctant to turn around and use it to buttress his own bargaining position. Thus, when amendments to Finance Committee bills were offered on the Senate floor, Long pointed to the revenue floor. When Senate amendments were traded away during conference, he explained how the budget act forced the Senate to recede. When allies were needed to dampen tax-cut largess, Long called on the Budget Committee for declarations about fiscal responsibility. It was a masterful performance, and it helps to explain why the Finance Committee is even more powerful now than it was before budget reform. Moreover, Long's demotion to ranking minority member on Finance for the 97th Congress does not mean that his influence and power are gone. Long will undoubtedly continue to be a vigorous proponent of the Finance Committee's prerogatives.

The Budget Process and Tax Policy

The first year under the new budget procedures produced few serious disputes on the revenue side of the budget. There was general agreement that the 1975 tax cut should be extended through fiscal

1976. The House version of the first budget resolution for 1976 called for partial offsetting of the tax cut by $3 billion in revenue gains through "tax-reform legislation" (reduced tax expenditures). Most of these gains were added on the House floor to cover increases in spending, and the House agreed to reduce the total to $1 billion during conference. As the second budget resolution for 1976 was being drafted, there was no sign that Congress would enact even this reduced sum. The Senate Budget Committee recommended that the revenue floor be based strictly on an extension of the tax cut, and Muskie successfully opposed a floor amendment to modify the budget resolution with a $200 million reduction in tax expenditures. The House retained its revised figure of $1 billion in increased tax revenues but then agreed to drop it during conference. The second resolution was not adopted until December, and Muskie insisted that it was unrealistic to expect Congress to act on tax revisions before the end of the fiscal year.

The 1976 Tax Bill. The Senate spent several months debating a major tax bill during 1976, including a four-day debate between Muskie and Long over the way the budget process applied to revenues. Long successfully insisted that the Finance Committee, not the Budget Committee, would decide how revenue targets should be met. He then managed to turn back most of the reductions in tax expenditures that were on the floor. A bloc of Democratic liberals prepared a $2.3 billion tax-reform package, but the Senate rejected virtually all of its key proposals. The liberals even lost when they tried to delete the word "reform" from the bill's title. Indeed, the bill that emerged from the Senate floor went well beyond even what the Finance Committee had recommended. Before the final vote, Muskie admitted that Long was once again correct: "He [Long] said that once you get into tax legislation there is always a majority for 'reform' but very seldom a majority . . . for any particular reform."[49]

Once the point about the Finance Committee's prerogatives had been made, however, Long showed how the budget process could be used to his advantage. During conference Long traded away many of the costly amendments that had been added on the Senate floor, at the same time managing to preserve the essential features of the original Finance bill. This was not a new strategy, but now the Finance chairman could announce, "In several cases, we had to recede on Senate amendments in order to meet our revenue targets."

Although the Senate amendments were meritorious, he said, some could not be afforded "in the context of the revenue goals."[50]

The 1977 Energy Tax Bill. Long took on the Senate Budget Committee again over the energy tax bill that Congress wrestled with during 1977. On October 21 the Finance Committee reported to the floor a bill that contained none of the three key tax proposals that the Carter administration had sent to Congress. Instead, the committee recommended a series of tax credits for energy production and conservation estimated to cost some $40 billion through fiscal 1985. In order to keep within the revenue floor of the recently adopted budget resolution for 1978, the Finance Committee included a provision postponing the effective date of various tax credits. Muskie charged that this maneuver violated the budget process, and he promised to challenge it on the Senate floor.

Once again Long emerged the victor. During six days of debate he persuaded other committees to drop their challenges. When James Abourezk, Democrat of South Dakota, charged a violation of the budget act, since the Finance Committee's bill allowed tax credits to be postponed as late as October 1, 1978 (the beginning of fiscal 1979, for which no budget resolution had been passed), Long sidestepped the point of order by changing the date to September 30, the last day of fiscal 1978. When other senators then used the delayed effective date to enact additional tax credits, Long promised that the eventual conference bill would preserve the revenue floor. While the House-Senate conference bogged down over a compromise, Long had ensured his committee substantial flexibility in negotiating with the House.

The Finance Committee sent other, smaller signals that the Budget Committee heeded. President Carter had proposed that general revenues be transferred to the social security fund, and the House Budget Committee was ready to accept this proposal. During July, Long had his Finance Committee explicitly reject the proposal and the Senate Budget Committee kept it out of the second budget resolution.

The 1978 Tax Bill. The $18.7 billion tax cut that Congress passed in 1978 featured a substantial reduction in the capital gains tax and was, in most other respects as well, a stinging defeat for congressional liberals. The Carter administration and its allies in Congress lost almost all of their tax-expenditure reforms and succeeded only in scaling down the size of the tax-cut package.

The Finance Committee added some $6 billion in cuts to the tax bill that had passed the House, and there were potential problems with the revenue figure in the 1979 budget resolution. During the course of committee consideration, Long used various tactics to resolve these problems, such as rejecting the administration's estimates of the potential revenue losses from specific provisions, particularly the reduction in the capital gains tax. He reduced some cuts and delayed the effective dates of others, such as the proposed minimum tax and earned income credit.

When the tax bill went to the Senate floor, the Roth-Kemp amendment was offered, and after the Budget Committee's procedural objections were overruled, Long joined Muskie in trying to protect the revenue floor against a flood of Senate amendments. The Senate did reject some amendments on budgetary grounds—including energy tax credits for the elderly and a deduction for state and local gasoline taxes, which had received overwhelming support only the year before—but it added a host of others that raised the Finance Committee's package by about $6 billion. During conference, however, the costlier Senate amendments were eliminated. Senate-passed tuition tax credits, for example, were dropped under a threatened presidential veto. Other Senate provisions were traded away or reduced until estimated revenues more than met the figure established as the revenue floor.

Recent Developments. Not all of the action on tax expenditures has been on the Senate side, nor is the Finance Committee unique in its adaptation to the budget process. In 1979, for example, the House Ways and Means Committee persuaded the House Budget Committee to bury the Carter administration's real wage insurance plan. In its March 15 report the Ways and Means Committee stated: "The Congressional Budget Act does not require the Committee to specify the precise composition of the anticipated $2.0 billion reduction in FY 1980 revenues," and no official position was taken on the real wage insurance proposal.[51] Committee members were skeptical about its utility and cost, however, and Barber Conable, Republican of New York and one of Ways and Means' representatives on the Budget Committee, moved to eliminate the revenue cushion for real

197

wage insurance in the spring budget resolution for fiscal 1980. The Budget Committee voted for Conable's motion 14–11—the only substantive Republican motion accepted that year.

On the House floor, Ways and Means suffered at least a temporary defeat on another tax expenditure, the tax credit for foreign earnings of oil companies. Elizabeth Holtzman of New York, a Democratic member of the House Budget Committee and sponsor of the proposed amendment to the 1980 budget resolution, won a 355–66 vote to close a "tax loophole" that she claimed would add over $1 billion in revenues. The chairman of the Ways and Means Committee, Al Ullman, offered the conventional Long rebuttal that specific tax provisions should not be addressed in budget resolutions and also suggested that Holtzman's revenue claims were wildly exaggerated. Although Ullman lost the vote and despite continued pressure by the House Budget Committee in the fall, the tax-credit issue remained bottled up in Ways and Means for the rest of the year.

The Ways and Means Committee did announce a series of hearings early in 1979 to review some of the larger and more controversial tax expenditures, and the Finance Committee has considered modest review procedures of its own. These moves were designed to counter any renewed attempt to impose sunset requirements on tax expenditures, but by the end of 1979 the threat from sunset proposals had largely disappeared, and so had any serious efforts to review tax expenditures. Indeed, late in 1979 the Finance Committee managed to shift attention to a series of new tax expenditures as it drafted the bill to increase taxes on the oil industry's windfall profits.

The Policy Effects of Reform

The post-1974 trends in budget policy offer little satisfaction to House and Senate liberals. Defense spending has emerged as an urgent budget priority; congressional fiscal policy has had, at best, a mixed record; and the use of tax expenditures has not been curtailed. The substantive policy changes that liberals hoped would flow from budget reform have not been realized, nor are their current prospects at all promising.

These failures are attributable to a combination of events—situational changes in the economy and international politics, ideological changes in the electorate and Congress, and a continued lack of cohesion in the congressional parties. With or without budget reform, Congress would be facing increases in defense spending, questioning conventional fiscal policy solutions, and avoiding highly redistributive tax policies.

In addition, liberals miscalculated the institutional conservatism of Congress. Congress, under what the liberals disparaged as a disorganized and antiquated budget process, had substantially shifted budget priorities for two decades. The formal and highly public priority-setting system now in existence has had the unintended consequence of stabilizing existing priorities. The functional categories have symbolic importance for their clienteles and spokesmen, and Congress has been understandably reluctant to intensify competition among the categories and among these groups.

Initially the budget process provided some protection for members who voted for large deficits. The current interest in eliminating deficits suggests that this protection has eroded. Legislators are reassessing the political costs of voting on budget totals when those totals mean deliberate deficits. They also must confront the fact that this otherwise laudable assumption of legislative responsibility has had no lasting positive effects on the prestige and reputation of Congress. The experience with the Ford administration makes it clear that Congress is extremely defensive about publicly and formally increasing a presidential deficit. This defensiveness temporarily disappeared when President Carter took office, but the advent of a new—and Republican—administration has revived it in even stronger form.

Having indexed so much of the spending side of the budget, Congress has been hesitant to limit its flexibility over one of the last remaining forms of largess, tax expenditures. The budget process has not reshaped tax policy, and liberals are now looking for other procedural means, such as sunset requirements, to attack the tax system. Here, too, the initial rush to focus attention on tax expenditures was counterproductive. Congress is willing to review tax expenditures quietly and selectively. It has no enthusiasm for doing so when all of the parties that benefit from tax expenditures have been alerted by a frontal assault.

We are forced to assess Congress' capabilities as modest. Congress can have independent influence on budget policy, and indeed, it exercised considerable influence before 1974. Congress can also sustain a fairly well-organized and coherent budget process, but it has great difficulty providing comprehensive, formal policy leadership, something the liberal policy agenda of the 1970s assumed, incorrectly, that it could provide.

Finally, the disdain for spending control demonstrated by congressional liberals has not done much for their cause or, incidentally, for Congress' credibility. When liberals in Congress were more numerous and influential, they refused to deal seriously with the growing problem of uncontrollable spending. As a result, the congressional budget process finds itself ill equipped to respond to legitimate demands for fiscal restraint. Once again Congress is on the defensive.

CHAPTER 9

Conservatives, Spending, and Deficits

Fiscal conservatives saw budget reform, first and foremost, as a means to control spending and eliminate chronic budget deficits. If deficits were to be eliminated, reform would have to provide procedural improvements, such as spending ceilings and reconciliation processes, that would facilitate control over spending. In addition, the complementary political pressures to limit spending and balance the budget would have to be brought to bear as Congress acted on budget totals and deficits. Thus conservative hopes rested on Congress' willingness to accept several necessary conditions: (1) spending ceilings in congressional budgets would have to be low—and firm; (2) budget uncontrollability would have to be reduced; (3) back-door spending routes and fiscal subterfuges would have to be foreclosed. If these things happened—and whether the new budget process could bring them about was unclear—a truly momentous change in congressional spending habits would have taken place. Needless to say, this change did not occur.

By 1979, however, spending restraint and balanced budgets were no longer the exclusive goals of conservatives. Congress, convinced that painful choices could not be indefinitely postponed, directed the Budget committees to prepare balanced budgets for the early 1980s, a move supported by both public and expert opinion. When the Carter administration recommended a deficit in its original 1981 budget, Congress seized the initiative to erase that deficit. Although the balanced budget for 1981 did not last very long, it demonstrated the enormous pressure on Congress to control spending and the excruciating difficulty of actually doing so.

For conservatives, the five-year record of budget reform has been disappointing. In their view, some spending problems have become even more intractable over the past few years as a result of congressional action or inaction. Uncontrollable spending now accounts for a larger share of the budget than it did in 1974, and spending outside the budget, in the form of off-budget activities and guaranteed loans, has proliferated. Congress' control of what the government spends each year has, in important respects, been weakened. The mounting evidence that Congress has failed to come to grips with the spending problem is at the heart of the conservative critique. Indeed, the congressional budget process will have to perform remarkably well to convince conservatives—and many moderates—that statutory or constitutional limits on spending are unnecessary.

Assessments of Budgetary Restraint

To predict what spending levels and deficits would have been under the old budgetary system may be impossible, but members of Congress show little reluctance to try to do so. The Senate Budget Committee reports each year that billions have been saved because of the new process, and Democrats on the House Budget Committee usually agree. Many Republicans, especially in the House, do not. The ranking Republican on the House Budget Committee, Delbert Latta of Ohio, states that "the budget process has been converted into big spenders' biggest ally. The Budget Committee encourages more spending by putting its blessing on many social welfare proposals so inflationary that the House, left to its own devices, would probably not approve many of them."[1] Over the years, Budget Committee Republicans have declared repeatedly that spending is "out of control," that Democratic claims of "lean and tight budgets" are fallacious; when it comes to fiscal matters, they declare, Congress is an "irresponsible Santa Claus."[2]

Procedural Complaints

Republican frustrations extend to precedents and procedures established since 1974. House Republicans specifically object to voting *seriatim* on functional spending categories before deciding on a spending total, a procedure they contend makes the Budget Committee an "adding machine committee" and "always result[s] in higher deficits and overspending."[3] Democrats have refused to reverse the sequence despite these charges—and the additional objection that the procedure biases decision making on fiscal policy.

Advocates of fiscal restraint are also convinced that Congress has been lax in designing and enforcing the second, or binding, budget resolution. When the spring and fall budget resolutions are found to be tens of billions of dollars too low on the spending side, Congress does not cut spending to meet the resolutions; it simply revises the resolutions to accommodate the spending.

In 1973 the Joint Study Committee on Budget Control recommended a single, binding resolution each year. The recommendation was attacked as inflexible and impractical, and Congress decided to require two resolutions and to allow additional ones in extraordinary cases. Now the extraordinary has become routine, and as a result, budget decisions change repeatedly during a fiscal year, just as they did in the prereform era.

Conservatives are dissatisfied with the procedural flexibility that allows Congress to ignore its own budgets, rendering spending control ineffective and contributing to the failure of the 1974 budget reforms. Although their charges sometimes lack precision, trends in spending, deficits, and revenues tend to support their general argument.

The Spending Record

The spending pattern of recent years affords conservatives no consolation. Between fiscal 1976 and fiscal 1980, outlays rose by over $200 billion, and the federal debt went up by an even larger amount (see Table 9.1). Compared with those of earlier years, these

Table 9.1. Budget outlays, deficits, and the federal debt, fiscal years 1976–80 (in billions of dollars)

Fiscal year	Outlays	Deficit	Total debt, end of year
1976	$366.4	$−66.4	$631.9
1977	402.7	−44.9	709.1
1978	450.8	−48.8	780.4
1979	493.6	−27.7	833.8
1980	579.6	−59.6	914.3

SOURCE: *United States Budget in Brief, Fiscal Year 1982* (Washington, D.C.: Government Printing Office, 1981), pp. 89, 91.

increases are not altogether startling, but neither do they suggest any break in spending's momentum. In the period 1971–75, outlays grew approximately 54 percent and the federal debt climbed 33 percent. Over the next five fiscal years, the corresponding figures were 58 percent for outlays and 45 percent for debt.

The degree of spending restraint envisioned by conservatives in 1974 has not been achieved. The budget process has no doubt had an impact on selected legislative decisions during recent years, and the Budget committees have won some battles to hold spending down. Some observers believe these successes represent a new fiscal consciousness in Congress. Analogous cases, however, in which Congress rejected proposals on fiscal grounds, could be drawn from the 1950s and 1960s, when there were no budget resolutions or Budget committees. Moreover, on three occasions in that period—1954, 1955, and 1965—budget outlays were reduced below the previous year's level, and in several other cases there was negative real growth in the budget. An accurate assessment of progress on spending restraint therefore requires an examination of several broad trends.

Spending and Gross National Product (GNP). The relationship between government spending and gross national product is a basic measure of the size of government and its impact on the economy. As might be anticipated, the federal "share" of GNP has experienced a long-term increase (see Figure 9.1). The relationship between federal spending and GNP changed only marginally between 1955 and 1965, but with greater involvement in Vietnam and Johnson's "Great Society" program, there was a definite upward swing, as the yearly average increased to approximately 20 percent. In the mid-1970s there was another upward shift, this time to the 22–23 percent range, and federal spending has subsequently remained stable at this relatively high level. (Spending for off-budget entities, which commenced in 1973, is also included in Figure 9.1 to show the true impact of federal spending.) The budget process has not forced a shift in the relative size of the federal sector to its prereform levels.[4] (Although these differences seem modest, they represent quite a substantial change. With 1 percent of GNP now amounting to almost $30 billion, a reduction in federal outlays to 20 percent of GNP, as some members of Congress have proposed, would require enormous cuts in spending over the next few years.)

Figure 9.1. Federal budget outlays as percentage of gross national product, fiscal years 1955–81

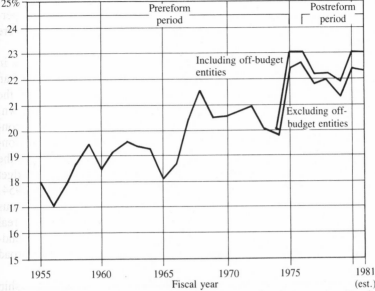

SOURCE: Figures for 1955–58 are from *Budget of the United States Government, Fiscal Year 1978* (Washington, D.C.: Government Printing Office, 1977), p. 435; figures for 1958–81 are from *Budget of the United States Government, Fiscal Year 1981* (Washington, D.C.: Government Printing Office, 1980), p. 612.

The 20 percent level may have arguable significance, but it is a key symbol in the debate over the federal budget. What lends a sense of urgency to this fiscal issue, at least for conservatives, is that combined public-sector spending—federal, state, and local—is close to the 40 percent mark when measured against GNP (see Table 9.2). Public-sector spending has risen almost 50 percent since 1950, and roughly two-thirds of the increase is a result of the growth of the federal budget. Moreover, this level was reached with virtually no public debate over the appropriate or desirable size of the public sector.

As formal limits on expenditures are discussed in Congress, this situation may change. Conservatives want to reduce the relative size of government in order to balance the budget and simultaneously to cut taxes, as well as to discourage the introduction of new programs and the expansion of old ones. Their fiscal policy goals go further than balanced budgets, since budgets can be balanced at any level of

Table 9.2. Total spending of federal, state, and local governments as percentage of gross national product, fiscal years 1950–77

Fiscal year	Total spending (billions of dollars)	Spending as percent of GNP
1950	$ 70	26.5%
1955	111	29.1
1960	151	30.4
1965	206	31.2
1970	333	34.7
1975	560	38.4
1976	625	38.5
1977	680	38.1

SOURCE: U.S. Department of Commerce, Bureau of the Census, *Statistical Abstract of the United States, 1979* (Washington, D.C.: Government Printing Office, 1979), p. 283.

GNP through increased taxes. In order to have deep and permanent tax cuts as well as balanced budgets, the relative size of the federal sector must be reduced.

Spending and Inflation. When spending is measured in current dollars, we can see little progress in efforts to curb its growth since the mid-1970s. When adjustments are made for inflation, the performance is somewhat better. From 1971 to 1975, annual increases in real spending averaged 2.9 percent (see Table 9.3). Since fiscal

Table 9.3. Percentage increase or decrease in federal defense and nondefense spending, fiscal years 1971–80 (constant 1972 prices)

Fiscal year	Overall spending	Defense spending	Nondefense spending
1971	+ 1.0%	− 10.1%	+ 8.7%
1972	+ 4.1	− 5.7	+ 9.7
1973	+ 0.6	− 8.6	+ 5.0
1974	− 0.5	− 3.0	+ 0.4
1975	+ 9.3	− 1.0	+ 13.6
Average, 1971–75	+ 2.9	− 5.7	+ 7.5
1976	+ 5.1	− 2.3	+ 7.8
1977	+ 2.1	+ 1.4	+ 2.3
1978	+ 3.6	+ 0.1	+ 4.7
1979	− 0.7	+ 4.0	− 2.2
1980 (estimated)	+ 2.3	+ 2.0	+ 2.3
Average, 1976–80	+ 2.5	+ 1.0	+ 3.0

SOURCE: *Budget of the United States Government, Fiscal Year 1981* (Washington, D.C.: Government Printing Office, 1980), p. 613.

1976 the average increase has been reduced to 2.5 percent, despite real growth in defense spending, a marked change from the sustained decline in defense spending during the early 1970s. The fact that the average rate of real growth in nondefense outlays has been more than halved suggests some measure of budgetary control.

Unfortunately, high rates of inflation have increased outlays so rapidly that this progress on real spending has received little attention. In fact, the conservative critique does not accept automatic adjustments in the budget for inflation, except perhaps in the case of defense. Since real spending has declined in only one year since 1975 (1979)—and this decline was matched in 1974—the argument is that the budget process does not impose sufficient restraint, despite the slight deceleration of increases in real spending and the greater balance between defense and nondefense spending.

Deficits

The final year under the prereform budget process ended in a deficit of more than $45 billion, the largest for any fiscal year since 1945. The first year under the new process quickly achieved even greater historical notoriety with the largest deficit since the Republic was established: $66.4 billion. Subsequent deficits have also been substantial, and fiscal conservatives have bitterly attacked Congress' failure to eliminate deficits and balance the budget. As Table 9.4 indicates, the combined deficit for fiscal years 1971–80 is more than six times that of the preceding decade. The first five years of the reformed budget process produced deficits totaling more than twice those of the early 1970s and actually exceeding the combined deficits of the preceding three decades. The comparison is even sharper when the deficits from off-budget activities are included. As a proportion of total outlays, recent deficits are also well above past levels (see Table 9.5).

The only bright spot in the deficit picture is the renewed decline in the federal debt as a percentage of GNP. Current estimates place the deficit total at the end of fiscal 1980 at about $900 billion, which represents approximately 35 percent of GNP, the lowest level in recent decades.[5] After more than twenty years of almost continuous decline in this percentage, there was a slight upturn in 1975 and another in 1976. But in 1977 the trend was reestablished, and the federal debt/GNP ratio is likely to drop below 30 percent by the

Table 9.4. Federal budget deficits, including and excluding off-budget activities, fiscal years 1961–80 (in billions of dollars)

Fiscal year	Budget deficits	Budget deficits plus off-budget activities
1961–70 (total)	$ − 60.0	$ − 60.0
1971	− 23.0	− 23.0
1972	− 23.4	− 23.4
1973	− 14.8	− 14.9
1974	− 4.7	− 6.1
1975	− 45.1	− 53.2
Total, 1971–75	$ 111.0	$ 120.6
1976	− 66.4	− 73.7
TQ*	− 12.9	− 14.7
1977	− 44.9	− 53.6
1978	− 48.8	− 59.2
1979	− 27.7	− 40.2
1980	− 59.6	− 73.8
Total, 1976–80	$ − 260.3	$ − 315.2
Total, 1971–80	$ − 371.3	$ − 435.8

SOURCE: *United States Budget in Brief, Fiscal Year 1982* (Washington, D.C.: Government Printing Office, 1981), p. 91.

*Transition quarter, necessitated by the switch in the period covered by the fiscal year from July 1–June 30 to the current October 1–September 30. The change was part of the Congressional Budget and Impoundment Control Act of 1974.

mid-1980s. Thus, even with the very large deficits of recent years, the rate of growth in the federal debt has generally been below the rate of growth in the economy. Since this is a long-term phenomenon, however, neither Congress nor the budget process can take credit for it.

In political terms (as opposed to more complicated economic judgments), failure to balance the budget is a major indictment of Congress. Large deficits cannot be justified indefinitely, and unless Congress demonstrates that it can eliminate them, it will continue to face proposals for limits on expenditures and amendments requiring balanced budgets. Until the budget process passes the test of balancing the budget, congressional conservatives—and much of the public—will consider it a failure.

Table 9.5. Federal budget deficits as percentage of total outlays, fiscal years 1961–1980

Fiscal year	Total deficit as percentage of total outlays*
1961–70 (average)	4.3%
1971	10.9
1972	10.1
1973	6.0
1974	2.3
1975	15.9
Average, 1971–75	9.0
1976	19.7
1977	13.0
1978	12.8
1979	7.9
1980	12.4
Average, 1976–80	13.2

*Includes off-budget federal entities.

Taxes

Liberals' indignation over tax expenditures is matched by conservatives' dissatisfaction with current tax rates. Spurred by high inflation, which automatically pushes individuals into higher tax brackets, as well as by substantial increases in social security taxes, federal revenues have grown at a faster rate than spending (or the economy) since 1976, and in the absence of substantial tax cuts, this trend will continue. For example, estimates issued by the Carter administration early in 1980 showed the long string of budget deficits being transformed into a $25 billion surplus by fiscal 1983, as a result not of budget restraint, but of higher taxes. Spending would rise by 37 percent over four years, while receipts would go up by almost 43 percent.[6]

Conservatives do not look on this method of balancing the budget with much favor, as it obviously depends on an increasing tax burden relative to economic growth. During the 1960s, federal receipts averaged less than 19 percent of GNP; the 1983 surplus projected by the Carter administration was based on receipts estimated to total almost 23 percent of GNP. The only way to balance the budget if spending as a proportion of GNP is not reduced, however, is to accelerate the growth of revenues.

Federal receipts are drawn from various taxes, customs duties,

Table 9.6. Amount of and increase in per capita personal income and individual income tax, 1970–79

	Personal income		Individual income tax	
Year	Amount	Increase (percent)	Amount	Increase (percent)
1970	$3,911	—	$441	—
1971	4,149	6.1%	416	− 5.7%
1972	4,513	8.8	453	8.9
1973	5,002	10.8	490	8.2
1974	5,449	8.9	561	14.5
1975	5,879	7.9	573	2.1
1976	6,420	9.2	611	6.6
1977	7,061	10.0	727	19.0
1978	7,856	11.2	828	13.9
1979	8,723	11.0	988	19.3

SOURCE: Per capita figures are calculated from data in *Economic Report of the President, 1980* (Washington, D.C.: Government Printing Office, 1980), pp. 228–29, 284–85.

and other sources. To an increasing extent, however, the federal budget dollar has become dependent on individual income tax revenues (which provide some 45 percent of the federal tax dollar) and social insurance taxes (which provide another 30 percent). The combined impact of these taxes on individuals has increased significantly in recent years, despite highly publicized tax cuts. Between 1976 and 1979, personal income in the United States rose 39 percent. Over the same period, federal receipts from individual income taxes went up 65 percent, and social insurance revenues rose 53 percent.[7] On a per capita basis, individual income taxes have risen at an annual rate of almost 15 percent since 1976, compared to about 5 percent from 1970 to 1975 (see Table 9.6). In 1977, 1978, and 1979, moreover, the rate of per capita tax increases was well above the growth in per capita income.

It was estimated that by the end of fiscal 1981, combined receipts from individual income taxes and social insurance taxes would be 16.7 percent of GNP, compared to 13.8 percent of GNP in 1976 and almost exactly the same percentage, on the average, during 1970–75.[8] Since 1976, then, the increase in the proportion of GNP represented by individual income and social insurance tax receipts has exceeded 20 percent. This increase helps to explain the high priority Republicans have assigned to large and permanent tax cuts, such as the Roth-Kemp proposal, and the indexing of tax rates to inflation. Even Senate Budget Committee Republicans have usually opposed balanced budgets that depend on increases in taxes rather than reductions in spending, and their House counterparts have been even more critical of the failure to reduce individual tax burdens.[9] The tax side of budget reform has been as disappointing for conservatives as for liberals, though for very different reasons. The budget process has not served to reduce taxes; instead, individual tax revenues and social insurance taxes have risen more rapidly than personal income or government spending or the economy. This situation has transferred a growing share of national wealth to government and supported a level of government spending that conservatives find intolerable—and which the Reagan administration has pledged itself to reverse.

The Problem of Uncontrollables

The standard assumption behind congressional budgets is that Congress can determine budget outcomes—how much is to be spent and for what. The effort at budget reform was directed, in fact, at improving the correspondence between what is budgeted and what is actually spent through comprehensive budget resolutions and procedural checks. The innovation of the budget resolution, with its binding ceilings on total spending and allocations for functional categories, was designed to improve congressional control over year-to-year spending. For congressional conservatives, greater control was the way to limit spending; for others, control was a way to establish priorities. There was agreement, however, that effective control was essential.

Despite procedural improvements and the informational services of the CBO, however, Congress may now be even less able to control budget outcomes, particularly spending, than it was in 1974. Congress faces enormous budgetary commitments each year over which it has very little control. In fact, the portion of the budget classified as "relatively uncontrollable under existing law" has actually increased over the past few years—from just under 73 percent of total outlays in fiscal 1975 to over 76 percent in 1981. More important, mandatory entitlements are now not only the dominant form of uncontrollable spending, but also the vehicle for distributing some 60 percent of the entire budget. In practical terms, such entitlements are hard to estimate on a year-to-year basis; in political terms, they are largely immune to congressional rollbacks in coverage or benefits. Spending that is both protected and unpredictable, which is the current status of uncontrollables, reaffirms that Congress has not solved its budget-control problems.

Back-door Spending and Budget Reform

Since the 1930s, various forms of back-door spending—contract authority, borrowing authority, and entitlements—have been employed by authorizing committees to circumvent the Appropriations committees and to create spending obligations that must be met. The result has been the growth of open-ended or uncontrollable spending commitments, whose impact on the budget has increased dramatically over the past two decades, primarily because of new and expanded entitlement programs.

The final version of the 1974 budget act did not entirely ignore the back-door spending issue, but it was not the tough response that the Joint Study Committee on Budget Control had originally proposed. The Appropriations committees were given increased control over two forms of back-door spending—contract authority and borrowing authority. With some limited exceptions, the law made new contract or borrowing authority subject to the annual appropriations process and thus to review by the Appropriations committees. On entitlements the solution was more complicated. Existing entitlements were exempted, but new entitlements now faced procedural limits. First, floor action on new entitlements is prohibited before adoption of the first budget resolution for a fiscal year. Second, new entitlements, once approved, cannot go into effect before the start of the next fiscal year, so that they become subject to any reconciliation process for that fiscal year. Third, if an authorizing committee reports a new entitlement that exceeds its allocation under the most recent budget resolution, the entitlement is referred to the Appropriations committees, which can report amendments that affect its size and scope. As a result of this process, Congress receives a second opinion, usually a less favorable one, on new entitlements.

These requirements appear to have discouraged additional entitlement programs. In 1978, for example, the Appropriations committees succeeded in gaining partial control of a child nutrition bill originally reported by the Agriculture committees as a complete entitlement. The following year the House turned down an entitlement for child welfare services reported by the Ways and Means Committee, although later in the year it approved an entitlement for child health services. In general, however, very few new entitlements have been created since 1975.

The growth in entitlement spending, then, is almost totally attributable to programs created before passage of the 1974 budget act and unregulated under its provisions. Some of these programs, such as social security and other retirement programs, are indexed and therefore have risen automatically with inflation. Others, such as medicaid, are not formally indexed but nevertheless respond to rising price levels. Until now, Congress has not reviewed the coverage and benefit levels of most major entitlement programs. But in its 1980 budget resolution Congress took the first step toward such a review, requiring House committees to review entitlements under their jurisdiction and to recommend ways to improve control over entitlement spending. The entitlement problem is complicated, however, and politically troublesome—and as a result, progress is likely to be slow.

Entitlement Spending

Entitlement programs mandate the payment of benefits to recipients who meet requirements established by law. (Indeed, a series of court decisions over the past two decades suggests that beneficiaries may have what amounts to a property right in their benefits.)[10] The major portion of entitlement spending is accounted for by trust funds, such as social security, which are not subject to the annual appropriations process. Entitlements that come from general revenues usually require annual appropriations, but that is essentially a technicality; the legislation that created the program, not the appropriation, dictates the amount spent. As Congress has created and expanded this type of mandatory spending, the budgetary weight of entitlements has increased dramatically. In fiscal 1967, entitlements accounted for 37 percent of total outlays and about 60 percent of all uncontrollable spending. By 1980, entitlement spending was 60 percent of total outlays and almost 80 percent of all uncontrollable spending (see Figure 9.2).

Although there are some three dozen major entitlement programs,

213

Figure 9.2. Entitlement and other uncontrollable spending as percentage of federal budget, fiscal years 1967–80

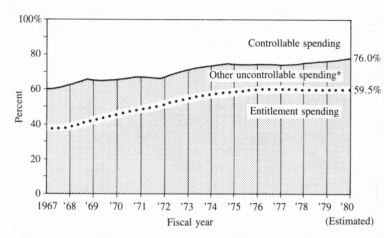

*Spending required by contracts made in past years, borrowing authority, guaranteed loans, and other obligations.

Source: *Congressional Quarterly Weekly Report,* January 19, 1980, p. 119.

primarily in the income security function, about 90 percent of entitlement spending is contained within a few program categories. The rates of increase in most of these entitlements have been extremely high even by comparison with uncontrollable spending generally (see Table 9.7). All but one—direct public assistance—have more than doubled since 1975.

Inflation accounts for much of this recent growth. Retirement programs, for example, are indexed to the inflation rate. Social security beneficiaries receive annual cost-of-living adjustments based on the rise in the consumer price index, and federal retirees have their benefits adjusted semiannually. (From 1969 until 1976, when Congress finally abolished it, federal retirees benefited from an unusual "kicker" that boosted benefits an additional 1 percent whenever the inflation rate exceeded 3 percent.)[11] Indirect benefits, such as medical care and food assistance, respond to price increases as well.

Indexing, although costly, was designed to save money by depoliticizing increases in entitlement benefits. In 1972, for example, Congress indexed social security benefits and at the same time pro-

Table 9.7. Outlays and increase in spending for selected entitlements and other uncontrollable spending, fiscal years 1975 and 1981

	Outlays (billions of dollars)		Increase (percent)
	1975	1981*	
Social security and railroad retirement	$ 68.3	$143.5	110%
Federal employees retirement, civil and military	18.4	40.8	122
Medical care	21.6	56.5	161
Public assistance			
Food and nutrition	6.2	14.9	140
Housing	2.1	6.6	214
Direct assistance and others	12.6	20.1	59
Interest (net)	23.2	67.0	189
Other uncontrollables	85.2	153.6	80
All uncontrollables	$237.6	$503.0	112%

*Estimated.
SOURCE: *Budget of the United States Government, Fiscal Year 1982* (Washington, D.C.: Government Printing Office, 1981), p. 596.

vided an immediate 20 percent boost. Initially a much more modest increase had been planned, but under the impetus of campaign politics, the Nixon administration and Congress agreed on the 20 percent jump and scheduled it to go into effect just before the election.

In case anyone missed the point, all beneficiaries received a notice signed by the president with their October checks, explaining that payments had been raised by 20 percent and that future adjustments would automatically be triggered by increases in the cost of living. The economic effect of this move was substantial—$8.0 billion of the $15.2 billion growth in personal income during October 1972 was the result of the new social security benefits.[12] Since the payroll tax to finance social security benefits did not go up until the following January, the increase was perfect election-year politics for incumbents. Social security benefits, veterans' benefits, and other transfers have followed the electoral cycle in the past, and it is possible that without indexing, Congress and the president would simply return to the old, if not exactly honorable, practice.

The political calculus is not hard to figure. Tens of millions of Americans receive benefits under one or more entitlement programs.

Because of overlapping benefits among programs, no total number of beneficiaries can be estimated for all programs, but a few numbers are illuminating:

- Nearly 36 million people receive social security benefits.
- More than 20 million people receive food stamps.
- About 23 million people receive health care under the medicaid program.
- Approximately 28 million aged and disabled individuals are covered by medicare.[13]

In all likelihood, increases in the benefits provided by most if not all entitlement programs would be hard to resist in the absence of indexing. If this picture of political timidity is accurate, however, then it makes equally good sense to index taxes or to impose formal limits on spending. If Congress cannot cope with one set of politically difficult decisions, it is hard to credit it with the ability to take a responsible approach to others.

If Congress is willing to confront hard choices, it can begin to deal with the entitlement dilemma by, for example, refusing to create new entitlements and ensuring that current ones are brought under the annual appropriations process. The Appropriations committees represent a second opportunity for oversight, and their emphasis on budgetary realities is likely to produce much tougher and more searching oversight than that conducted by the authorizing committees. House Republican leader Robert H. Michel of Illinois emphasizes that "under the appropriations process it's so much easier to get annual review." In dealing with entitlements, "you get answers that you can only get when you're talking about specific dollars. You can ask 'What went into that figure?' "[14]

Bringing entitlements under the regular appropriations process would encourage Congress to reeexamine its past policy decisions and to decide whether those decisions have "proved to be too costly in light of changing priorities."[15] Plenty of decisions would benefit from such a review—eligibility requirements, benefit levels, indexing formulas, and even some entire programs. In addition, forcing Congress to confront the long-term costs of entitlement provisions would serve a second purpose. What appear to be minor savings can heavily influence long-term costs. The 1 percent kicker in federal retirement programs that was eliminated in 1976 has saved billions. In the regular social security program, the 1972 formula for calculating future benefits overcompensated for inflation. Although the short-term costs were modest, the long-term implications were disastrous. Congress recently changed the formula, reducing the projected long-term deficit in the social security system by one-half.[16] In both cases the indexing formulas were flawed. Good intentions and fiscal realities were not being considered together.

Entitlements would not be eliminated by multiyear budgeting and inclusion in the annual appropriations process. This procedure might, however, ensure that entitlement costs would be considered in relation to other programs, that oversight would be strengthened, and that necessary legislative changes in entitlement programs could be accomplished within a reasonable period of time. Entitlement programs, which really are the government's promises to its citizens, present complicated and difficult choices. Their political constituencies are formidable, and there is general agreement that entitlement formulas and guaranteed funding are the only way to administer individual benefit programs. Entitlement spending can be controlled more effectively in the future, however, than it was in the past. For example, it was at one time probably necessary to have social security benefits outpace wage increases in the private sector. Accordingly, from 1967 to 1978, while the consumer price index rose 95.4 percent, average social security benefits went up 240 percent, compared to increases of 140 percent in the hourly earnings of teamsters and auto workers and 164 percent for steel workers.[17] The disparities that justified these differentials, however, have now been eliminated, and an overly generous indexing formula has become a luxury that Congress and the nation can no longer afford.

Entitlements, then, are not the only form of uncontrollable spending, but they present the most serious fiscal control problems. Uncontrollable spending, which represents three-fourths of the budget, increases at a faster rate than controllable spending: from 1975 to 1981, uncontrollables have risen by almost 120 percent, controllables by 80 percent. Among uncontrollable costs, entitlements are increasing most rapidly. They must be included in congressional spending reform. When the current director of the OMB, David Stockman, was a Republican member of Congress from Michigan, he warned that Congress had become "a green eye-shaded disbursement officer, who totes up the bill, writes the check, and then trundles off to the chapel to mourn."[18] Until Congress finds the courage to deal with entitlements, that unflattering portrait will stand.

Budgetary Sleight of Hand

One of the ways to keep spending down is to hide some of it, and in recent years Congress has become particularly adept at doing just that. Some $18 billion annually is now spent by off-budget agencies, new commitments for guaranteed and insured loans are over $80 billion, and loans by off-budget and government-sponsored enterprises exceed $30 billion.[19] In comparison, direct loans by on-budget agencies are expected to show a small net surplus by fiscal year 1981, and unlike the off-budget loan activities, outstanding direct loan balances have been fairly stable in recent years (see Figure 9.3).

Since fiscal year 1973, off-budget spending has risen from $60 million to over $18 billion, virtually all for credit activities. None of this spending is shown in annual budget outlays, appropriations, or

Figure 9.3. Federal and federally assisted credit outstanding, fiscal years 1970–81, by category

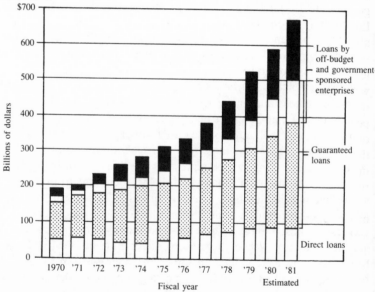

SOURCE: *Special Analyses, Budget of the United States Government, Fiscal Year 1981* (Washington, D.C.: Government Printing Office, 1980), p. 145.

budget authority, or in the budget deficit. In addition, off-budget spending is not subject to the ceilings set by the congressional budget resolutions. Eventually, however, because they are financed by borrowing, these outlays show up as equivalent increases in the federal debt. Since fiscal 1976, they have raised it over $75 billion. Although the Budget committees have attacked the concept of off-budget agencies—and Congress has refrained from creating major new ones the past few years—they have been unsuccessful in bringing the larger of these agencies, such as the Federal Financing Bank, under the umbrella of the annual budget.

Guaranteed and insured loans disguise government activity because actual outlays occur only when borrowers default. Under guaranteed loan programs, government funds are pledged to secure a lender against possible default by a borrower, and the loan guarantee is the government's contingent liability. (Insured loans are somewhat different: the government sets up a pool of assigned risks and uses accumulated premiums to protect lenders.) At one time guaranteed loans were used primarily for housing programs, but now they are spread throughout the economy. State and local governments (including New York City), businesses (including Lockheed and Chrysler), individuals, and foreign governments have all been recipients of such loans.

When housing loans were the major activity, losses and potential losses were relatively minor, as the government could protect itself with liens on marketable property and the total amounts that could realistically be directed toward assisted housing were limited. The potential losses on the newer forms of guaranteed loans are more difficult to calculate, and there appear to be few serious restraints on the totals being pledged. Guaranteed and insured loans account for more than half of the $670 billion in outstanding federal loan commitments as of fiscal 1981.[20] They are also expanding at a rapid rate: $75 billion in new commitments in 1979, $75 billion in 1980, and an estimated $81 billion in 1981.[21] During 1972–76, the total of outstanding guaranteed loans went up by a little over 20 percent. From 1977 to 1981, the total nearly doubled—from $175 billion to $339 billion.

The justifications for individual guaranteed loan programs may differ, but the programs share certain characteristics. The federal guarantee serves as an interest subsidy for borrowers and even allows many of them to obtain funds they would not otherwise be able to borrow. Federal intervention imposes additional demands on credit markets and often drives up interest rates for other borrowers, including the federal government. Economic resources are diverted, and there are economic costs to be borne in addition to possible default and administrative expenses.

For budgetary purposes, however, guaranteed loans appear to be almost cost-free. Government can avoid direct expenditures, in the form of direct loans or subsidies that show up on the outlay ledger and must be reconciled with budget totals. Instead, it pursues its policy objectives with indirect subsidies, hard-to-calculate risks, and no restraints from budget resolutions or credit ceilings. Congress can create any amount of loan guarantees it wishes; yet the real costs are largely hidden, and the only ones that show up in the budget are those caused by defaults.

The Budget committees established federal credit budgets in the 1981 budget resolutions in response to this explosive growth in credit activities. Rejecting the more limited controls proposed by the Carter administration, the Budget committees recommended ceilings on both direct loans and loan guarantees, with limitations on individual programs to be set by the Appropriations committees. If these ceilings are strictly enforced and credit budgets are included in future resolutions, Congress will have at least made its budget resolutions comprehensive. Whether this action will actually slow down the growth in credit activities is unclear, since the authorizing committees will still have an enormous stake in what is really just another form of spending.

The Conservative Verdict

During the twenty-five years that H. R. Gross served in the House of Representatives, he gained a reputation as one of the most conservative and outspoken Republicans in Congress. When Gross retired in 1974, his colleagues praised his record on fiscal matters. Gross, they said, was a "pillar of parsimony," "watchdog of the treasury," "scourge of the spenders," and "the deep-safety man against appropriations."[22] Earlier that year, however, Congress' fiscal watchdog had been singularly unimpressed with what his fellow legislators deemed a milestone in congressional history. The budget reform act was no great achievement, according to Gross, but rather "another resort of gimmickry." His skepticism was total:

> A great day is about to dawn in the House of Representatives. There has been a lack, we are told today, of will, discipline, and restraint, and this budget control bill is going to cure all things. . . . Everything and everybody is going to be reformed . . . is going to be hunky-dory, and the goose is going to hang high. If we just pass this bill, we will have brought into play all the will, all of the restraint, and all of the discipline that is necessary to balance the budget, stop inflation, and restore fiscal sanity. Do not believe it for one minute.[23]

Gross's skepticism has not altogether missed the mark. Spending restraint since 1974 has not been demonstrably stronger than it was earlier; deficits have been enormous and resistant to short-term changes, uncontrollable spending has become an even more serious problem, and Congress has complicated matters with new forms of back-door spending, such as off-budget agencies and guaranteed loans. Some people may argue that budget control has been marginally effective. From the conservative perspective, it may be difficult to concede even that much. Congress has yet to demonstrate that it can control spending firmly and over time, and is in some respects in a more vulnerable position than it was in 1974. As Robert Giaimo finally warned his colleagues in the House, "If we cannot now do the job, then the American people, led by the balance-the-budget people, will impose a discipline on us that we refuse to impose on ourselves . . . we are just asking for a constitutional amendment requiring balanced budgets."[24]

CHAPTER 10

The Politics of
Spending Control

Congress has yet to prove that it can control spending. Relations between Congress and the news media during the two years following the 1974 budget reform act were not unlike the honeymoon period that follows a presidential inauguration. The *New York Times,* for example, in 1975 expressed its belief that budget reform "could drastically alter the way Congress transacts its business and rearrange its power structure as well."[1] The current tenor of opinion is much more restrained, if not skeptical. While few journalists suggest that budget reform has failed completely, its accomplishments are viewed as modest at best. The recurrent pattern of highly publicized, controversial, "tight" budget resolutions in advance of the fiscal year, followed by quiet revisions to allow more spending once the fiscal year is under way, have become visible to many. Clearly the budget-cutting sentiments that shape spring budget resolutions wilt when actual program cuts are considered.

It may not be altogether accidental that by the time Congress abandons its so-called binding budget for one fiscal year, the Budget committees and leadership are calling attention to the austere budget being planned for the next. Congress' second and ostensibly binding budget resolution for fiscal year 1980 included language that precluded a third resolution. Nevertheless, in the spring of 1980 Congress dutifully passed a third resolution, raising the "binding" spending ceiling by some $25 billion and ignoring its commitment to keep the 1980 deficit under $30 billion. At the same time, the Budget committees proudly announced a balanced budget for 1981. Whether this plan could long survive was another matter. Paul Simon of Illinois, a member of the House Budget Committee, was

222

far from optimistic: "This Congress is grabbing at a symbol to get us past that magic date in November. And lo and behold, we're going to have a third [budget] resolution. And in fiscal 1982, we're going to be in worse shape."[2] It took even less time than Simon predicted for the 1981 balanced budget to become a phantom, yet legislators continued to boast about their accomplishment.

Members of Congress and outside observers seem to agree that congressional budgets respond to public opinion. Therefore, the apparent public displeasure with continued high spending and deficits should be enough to force Congress to cut budget growth significantly. In reality, the issues are far more complex. Public opinion on taxing and spending issues is not always clear-cut. Moreover, organized interests place direct and persistent pressures on legislators to spend, and they may be vocal enough or strong enough politically to outweigh more generalized antispending sentiments. The electoral implications of budgets thus do not necessarily strengthen congressional fiscal discipline. In fact, quite the reverse may be true.

Can Congress Control Spending?

If Congress is to turn budget making into a less debilitating and less confrontational exercise in the future, it will have to bring spending under control, a task that may prove extraordinarily difficult. As in the past, economic conditions may prove unfavorable. In addition, political factors must be considered. Can Congress be expected to support economy moves that major electoral constituencies dislike? The question applies to Republicans as well as Democrats, since income transfers and other entitlements benefit large, electorally potent groups whose support is vital to any party that aspires to majority status. The historical record shows that Congress has always found it difficult to cope with spending demands. With federal spending now directly targeted at tens of millions of Americans, the congressional dilemma has become even more serious.

What is at issue is the ability of the democratic process to resolve fiscal issues responsibly when the power of the purse is in the hands of the legislative branch. Past and present supporters of congressional budget reform believe that fiscal discipline is possible if the appropriate procedures and organization are available. But the alternative view that Congress, whatever its merits, is incapable of holding down spending if it is left to its own devices is being heard more and more often. In fact, some of its merits are seen as part of the fiscal problem. Most congressional experts agree that Congress is an extremely democratic institution—responsive to public opinion, attentive to constituents' concerns, and highly accessible to numerous groups and interests—and that its members are very much aware of their accountability to voters. Legislators' large personal staffs, their highly specialized subcommittees, and their heavy emphasis on casework and service to constituents reflect this preoccupation with the electorate.[3]

Although high levels of spending may erode Congress' institutional reputation, individual legislators may benefit from them. Members of Congress receive credit from their constituents for initiating and protecting massive income-transfer programs.[4] While the relationship between spending and the esteem of constituents may help to explain political longevity among senators and especially among representatives, it points to a definite institutional weakness.

To an increasing extent, members of Congress are individual political entrepreneurs; party labels and presidential coattails have been found to have limited electoral importance.[5] Moreover, for many members, the recent restrictions on outside income and business ties lend financial urgency to reelection, and thereby increase the influence of special-interest groups. Under these circumstances, responsible fiscal decision making is hard to sustain. Members of Congress are likely to find themselves in agreement with a former New York deputy mayor who declared, "It is better to borrow than to tax."[6] The other side of the fiscal coin is that it is better (and easier) to spend than to cut. The best of both worlds is to borrow and to spend, which is what Congress has been doing for years. And unless a way can be found to protect members against the electoral results of raising taxes and cutting programs, the budget process is unlikely ever to succeed.

The idea that what Congress does is determined by political considerations is hardly original, but it applies with special force to budget decisions. A Democratic leader in the House notes that the talk in the cloakrooms among members of Congress "is about personalities, strategies, election prospects and the like; discussion of

224

policy options or the future of the congressional budget process, for example, is generally out of bounds."[7] Congress' distressing ambivalence in supporting proposals to balance the budget and then voting for more spending is rooted in the almost complete dissociation between the institutional reputation of Congress and the political survival of its members. In fact, a fascinating contemporary phenomenon has been the degree to which congressional incumbents attack Congress as part of their reelection campaigns. The electorate appears to respond positively to the juxtaposition of heroic individual legislators and institutional failure.[8]

Clearly, political factors must be taken into account when the difficulties of controlling spending are examined. The conflicting signals that emerge from public opinion surveys also help to explain the annual congressional contortions over the budget.

Public Opinion

The 1980 elections seem to represent a conservative mandate, but the nature of this mandate, at least with respect to the budget, is not entirely clear. Under the new administration, defense spending is certain to increase substantially. Regulatory efforts might be curbed, but the direct budgetary costs associated with them are minor. How, then, can the government respond to the public's apparent demand that it cut spending and deficits? Would the public support, for example, cutbacks in *major* entitlements? Public opinion does not provide unambiguous guides to Congress on how to deal with spending. The public's response reveals a great deal of ambivalence and contradiction, so we should not be at all surprised to find these same characteristics as Congress decides spending issues.

Budget-Cutting Sentiments

Poll after poll reveals that Americans have become extremely dissatisfied with the costs and consequences of "big government." In 1958, 42 percent of the respondents in a national survey believed "the government wastes a lot of tax money."[9] By 1978, 84 percent of those who had an opinion thought that the government was spending too much money.[10] Public responses to the imposing specter of big government are similar. In 1978, three out of four Americans felt the government in Washington was too powerful.[11] That same year, a substantial majority of the public agreed that the government had gone too far in regulating business and interfering with the free-enterprise system.[12]

Since the 1950s the public's trust and confidence in the federal government have declined sharply. In 1958 some three-fourths of the public said they trusted the government to do the right thing all or most of the time. By 1970 only about half agreed with this assessment, and six years later less than a third did so.[13] The poor performance of government, which rarely entered the public's perception of the nation's most important problems in the 1950s and 1960s, had become by the 1980s a measurable and growing concern.[14]

The apparent buildup of antigovernment opinion finds further expression in the ideological labels that Americans prefer. In the mid-1960s, equal numbers of Americans described themselves as liberals and as conservatives.[15] The advantage today lies with the conservatives. In 1978, 42 percent of the public chose a conservative designation as opposed to 23 percent who picked the liberal label.[16]

Not unexpectedly, the polls show overwhelming public support for balancing the budget. Sentiment favors reductions in spending and taxes, of course, but substantial support exists for postponement of tax cuts if such action is necessary to ensure a balanced budget.[17] The public is also firmly behind a constitutional amendment that would require balanced budgets (see Table 10.1). The public seems to want a smaller, less costly, less intrusive government.

When the questions are general, fiscal conservatism appears triumphant. How, then, does one explain the enormous growth of the federal budget, especially over the past several years?

The Welfare State

The American public is at one and the same time against big budgets and the welfare state and in favor of the programs that the welfare state advances and that big budgets finance. The apparent contradiction between abstract and specific opinions can be attributed to the limitations of public opinion polls. Despite the advances in the accuracy of sampling and other technical matters, the polls simply cannot answer precisely or definitively many of the public policy questions to which they are applied. When we examine the

Table 10.1. Public support for and opposition to a constitutional amendment requiring balanced federal budgets, 1976–80 (percent)

	Favor	Oppose	Don't know/ no opinion
April 1976	78%	13%	9%
July 1978	81	11	8
February 1979	78	12	10
March 1980	67	13	20

NOTE: The question asked in 1976, 1978, and 1979 was: "Would you favor or oppose a constitutional amendment that would require Congress to balance the federal budget each year—that is, keep taxes and expenditures in balance?" The 1980 question was different: "A proposed amendment to the Constitution would require Congress to approve a balanced federal budget each year. Government spending would have to be limited to no more than expected revenues, unless a three-fifths majority of Congress voted to spend more than expected revenue. Would you favor or oppose this amendment to the Constitution?"

SOURCE: *The Gallup Poll: Public Opinion* for 1976–77, 1978, and 1979 (Wilmington: Scholarly Resources, 1978–80); *the Gallup Opinion Index,* 176 (March 1980), 4.

specific types of governmental responsibility that characterize the modern welfare state, we find that the public today is firmly behind activist government. Support for government intervention in such areas as the health-care system, education, assistance for the elderly, disabled, and disadvantaged, and employment has grown substantially among virtually all income, education, and occupational subgroups.

For example, a government mandate to ensure "that everybody who wants to work has a job" was supported by 63 percent of the public in 1960 and 74 percent in 1978. In 1960, 64 percent agreed that "the government ought to help people get doctors and hospital care at low cost"; by 1978 the level of agreement reached 81 percent. The public today seems more rather than less predisposed toward substantial governmental assistance for the unemployed, the elderly, and the poor than it was two or three decades ago: "Americans seem to have developed an irreversible commitment to basic government welfare programs. . . . It is now as natural to them as getting up in the morning."[18]

This commitment is not just an abstraction; it embraces support for actual spending. For example, the National Opinion Research Center's 1978 general social survey reported that most Americans felt too little was being spent to improve health and education and to

Table 10.2. Public attitudes toward amount being spent nationally on health, education, and crime prevention, 1978 (percent)

	Too much	Too little	About the right amount
Improving health care	7%	57%	35%
Improving educational system	11	54	35
Crime prevention	6	67	26

NOTE: The question asked was: "We are faced with many problems in this country none of which can be solved easily or inexpensively. I'm going to name some of these problems, and for each one I'd like you to tell me whether you think we're spending too much money on it, too little money, or about the right amount . . . Halting the rising crime rate; improving and protecting the nation's health; improving the nation's education system."

SOURCE: National Opinion Research Center, General Social Survey, 1978, reported in *Public Opinion*, 3 (December/January 1980), 21.

reduce crime (see Table 10.2). In each case, the percentage that felt "too much" was being spent was negligible.

A series of surveys during the 1970s shows remarkable stability in such pro-spending responses (see Figure 10.1). Current or increased levels of spending are widely favored for the major domestic initiatives of the past two decades—improving and protecting the nation's environment, as well as its health and educational systems; assisting cities in solving their problems; and improving the conditions of blacks. Attitudes are less favorable toward expenditures for foreign aid, welfare, and space research, but the only one of these programs actually to lose support during the 1970s was welfare.

The national consensus in favor of most domestic spending programs, particularly the very large income security and health programs, means that there are few major differences among population subgroups. Self-described liberals, moderates, and conservatives have almost identical opinions on the health, education, and environmental expenditures examined in Figure 10.1. The same is true of different educational subgroups and even racial groups. On some issues, notably welfare, liberals and conservatives take opposing positions, as do blacks and whites, but the overall pattern is clear "Most Americans want 'big government,' if the latter means a high level of government-provided services."[19]

Even the responses to questions about welfare vary greatly depending on wording. "Welfare" is a negative cue word for most

228

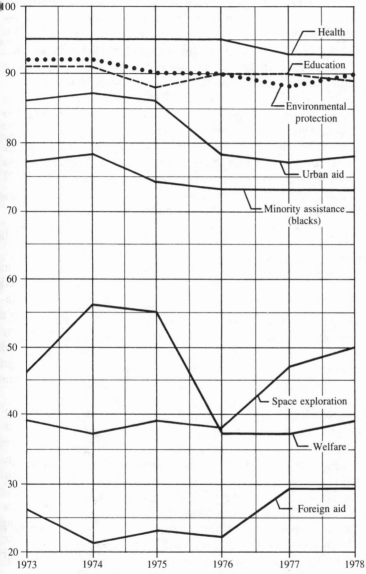

Figure 10.1. Public responses in agreement that "about the right amount" or "too little" is being spent on various federal programs, 1973–78, by category (percent)

SOURCE: Adapted, by permission of the publisher, from Everett Carll Ladd, Jr., et al., "The Polls: Taxing and Spending," *Public Opinion Quarterly*, 43 (Spring 1979), 132. Copyright © 1979 by The Trustees of Columbia University.

people, and the reactions to survey questions that use the term reflect this bias. When a question refers instead to help for the poor or the needy or the disadvantaged, the public's hostility disappears.

Finally, the alleged antispending mood of recent years does not apply to defense. In 1969 a majority of the public felt that defense spending was too high, but by 1976 an abrupt change was taking place (see Figure 10.2). Between 1978 and 1980, an even more profound change occurred, and by the latter year, more than half of the public agreed that defense spending was too low.

Americans want the benefits and "good purposes" of the welfare state but are uneasy with certain of the consequences, including the costs. They want money spent for "good things" but find the totals frightening. And while there is probably a good deal of government waste and fraud, as the public suspects, most experts agree that waste and fraud represent only a small percentage of the federal budget. The simple fact is that there is no widespread support for elimination or sharp curtailment of large domestic programs or defense spending.

Taxes

Dissatisfaction with the structure of the tax system and the level of current taxes seems to be widespread. Harris polls in 1977 and 1978, for example, reported that almost three-fourths of the public considered the federal income tax to be too high.[20] Similar polls during the past few decades indicate that although this level of resentment may be a historical peak of sorts, it certainly is not an anomaly. Gallup surveys show almost equally high levels of resentment after World War II and on into the years of the Korean war.[21] During the late 1950s and early 1960s the level of negative opinion declined; in 1962, for example, for almost every person who felt his federal income taxes were too high, someone else felt his federal incomes taxes were about right.[22] The mid-1960s saw a rise in negative opinion that continued through the 1970s.

Just as the public wants lower spending, at least in the abstract, it also wants lower taxes. A 1977 Gallup poll reported that over 85 percent of respondents who had an opinion favored a cut in federal income taxes. But when that same survey went on to ask those who favored the cut, "Would you still favor a cut in federal income taxes even if that meant a huge government deficit?" the pro-cutting margin was less than 4 to 3.[23]

Figure 10.2. Public responses to questions concerning defense spending, 1969–80 (percent)

Question: "There is much discussion as to the amount of money the government in Washington should spend for national defense and military purposes. How do you feel about this: do you think we are spending too little, too much, or about the right amount?" ("Don't know"/"No opinion" responses are not charted.)

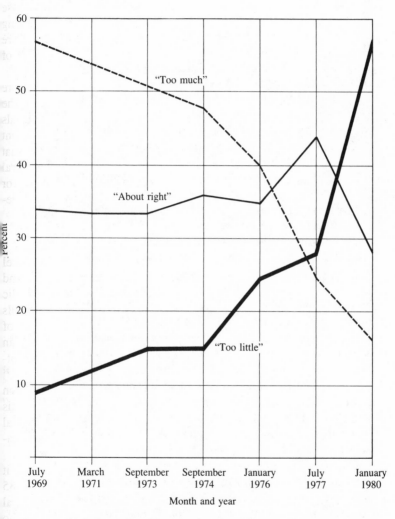

SOURCE: *The Gallup Poll: Public Opinion, 1935–1971* (New York: Random House, 1972), pp. 2210, 2298; *The Gallup Poll: Public Opinion, 1972–1977* (Wilmington: Scholarly Resources, 1978), pp. 183, 362, 664, 1164; *The Gallup Opinion Index*, 175 (February 1980), 10.

During 1978 Gallup asked respondents whether it was "more important to work toward balancing the budget or to cut taxes at this time." In January a balanced budget was favored over a tax cut by 58 to 42 percent. In April, a sensitive time for questions about taxes, a balanced budget was still favored by half of the respondents who had an opinion. In 1978, when tax cuts were weighed against inflation control, 90 percent of the public agreed that "controlling inflation is more important than cutting taxes."[24]

Politicians are really not under serious pressure to enact permanent, steep cuts when they have imposing economic evils to show the public to counter the normal aversion to paying taxes. The lack of any significant public response to the Republican party's Roth-Kemp tax-cut plan should not be a surprise. Democrats have been able to argue that the Republican plan would increase the deficit and fuel inflation. In response, Republicans are left with the arguable merits of supply-side economics, an intellectually intriguing theory but not one altogether appropriate for a mass electorate.

Moreover, the political benefits of tax cuts may be exaggerated. Herbert Stein, a member of the Council of Economic Advisers during the Nixon administration, says that "tax reduction is politically a loser." Tax reduction is believed to be popular, and Stein agrees that it is "in general terms. But every specific tax bill makes more enemies than friends, because everyone thinks he got less than he deserved while others got more."[25] Figure 10.3 illustrates Stein's theory. In January 1978 the Gallup poll asked a national sample who would benefit most from tax cuts proposed by President Carter. Various income groups differed on who would receive the greatest benefits, although the differences were small. Twenty-four percent of the respondents in the bottom income category and 40 percent of those in the top income category, for example, felt that low-income people would receive the most benefits. The striking finding was that only 3 percent of the respondents felt that people like themselves would benefit most from the proposed tax cut. Stein concludes that this attitude is not so irrational as it seems: "If 'benefit' was an objective fact, measurable in dollars of tax reduction or percentage of tax reduction, the answers would be paradoxical. But 'benefit' means amount of tax reduction *relative to my just deserts*. A tax reduction that is less than my just deserts is not a benefit but an insult. And, of course, no one ever thinks he gets his just deserts."[26]

Figure 10.3. Public perceptions of who benefits most from tax cuts, 1978, by income group (percent)

Question: Of these groups, low-income people, high-income people, middle-income people, businesses, and people like yourself, which do you feel would benefit the most [from President Carter's proposed tax cut]?"

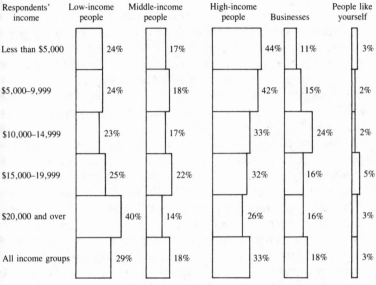

Respondents' income	Low-income people	Middle-income people	High-income people	Businesses	People like yourself
Less than $5,000	24%	17%	44%	11%	3%
$5,000–9,999	24%	18%	42%	15%	2%
$10,000–14,999	23%	17%	33%	24%	2%
$15,000–19,999	25%	22%	32%	16%	5%
$20,000 and over	40%	14%	26%	16%	3%
All income groups	29%	18%	33%	18%	3%

SOURCE: Survey by American Institute of Public Opinion, January 20–26, 1978; adapted from *Public Opinion,* 1 (May/June 1978), 24.

Implications for the Parties

The public's response to taxing and spending issues is not always consistent, but it does show some clear tendencies that help to explain current taxing and spending levels. Federal budgets are large because most spending programs, including the most expensive ones, are quite popular. There are no compelling *political* reasons to cut spending drastically or even to reduce taxes.

As noted earlier, party labels have become less and less important to politicians over the years. To the extent that party labels are important, politicians will take into account the fact that the public does see differences between the parties on the questions of spending and taxing. A 1978 *New York Times*/CBS poll found that over half the public thought that the parties differed on tax reform, while a considerably smaller proportion saw differences on other domestic or foreign policies.[27] A survey conducted for the National Republican Congressional Committee in preparation for the 1980 election campaign found that the Republican party had a slight edge when people were asked which party would do a better job of controlling government spending, holding down taxes, and even controlling inflation.[28] The government-spending question showed an impressive Republican advantage of almost 2 to 1. The Democratic party, however, was perceived to be better able to handle almost a dozen other problem areas. When the questions were phrased in terms of providing help to specific groups—equal opportunities for minorities, financial assistance for the elderly, assistance for first-time home buyers, jobs for the unemployed—the Democratic party far outdistanced the Republican party.

Furthermore, the distributions of opinions on some issues—spending, taxing, inflation—are not stable. As recently as 1978 a Gallup survey found that when people were asked which party was better able to reduce spending and hold taxes down, more people named the Democratic party than the Republican.[29] As far as general economic prosperity is concerned, the Democratic party has been considered the better bet for most of the past three decades. Even if taxing and spending issues did produce stable, long-term Republican opinion preferences, the size of the budget or level of taxation (or both) has generally not been salient enough to overcome Democratic strengths on other issues. The Republican party may be able to capitalize on its recent electoral gains and convert taxing and spending policies into a firm base of popular support. Its ability to do so, however, is likely to depend on the state of the economy rather than specific budgetary initiatives. If the Republicans manage to enforce fiscal austerity, and if fiscal austerity happens to coincide with healthy economic growth, they will probably receive major electoral benefits. But if the economy fails to grow appreciably, fiscal austerity may be discredited as a political appeal and abandoned by Republicans as well as Democrats in Congress. In effect, spending control over the next few years appears to depend on broad economic trends rather than clear and unmistakable public mandates.

Who Wants More Spending?

Some twenty years ago the *Congressional Quarterly* tried to explain that congressional spending was likely to increase regardless of he public's concern over the costs:

> The fact that economy moves prevailed in 1958—a recession year— on only 24 percent of the clear-cut floor tests affecting spending may be compared with a score of 33 percent in 1957—a year when the public demand for reduced Federal spending was unusually strong. Given the relatively small difference in the outcome, despite the greatly different situations . . . , one may conclude that the odds against efforts to reduce Federal spending or to prevent it from rising are preponderant.[30]

The major reason the odds are against a decline in federal spending is the limited nature of public support for cuts in programs. Fiscal restraint can be enforced only if the electorate defeats those politicians who it decides spend too much. In the past, increases in government spending have usually facilitated the reelection of members of Congress and strengthened Democratic control of Congress. The public does not see—or perhaps does not wish to see—the connection between unacceptable budget totals and deficits and the "worthy" efforts of senators and representatives to secure government benefits and services for constituency groups.

In addition, there is more than one public. The millions of Americans who say they want fiscally responsible government are the same millions who are current or potential beneficiaries of federal programs. Many of them, moreover, are organized into interest groups that zealously defend their claims on the public purse.

The interest-group system in Washington encompasses a bewildering number and variety of organizations that engage in legislative lobbying and other activities aimed at influencing public policy. The major business, labor, and agricultural interest groups are well known, and have been around for a long time. Many other large and highly effective organizations represent a variety of beneficiary groups—the aged, veterans, teachers (and educational institutions), minorities, even state and local governments. The three largest senior citizens' groups, for example, have over 11 million members and a combined staff of nearly 800. The American Legion, the Disabled American Veterans, and the Veterans of Foreign Wars have over 5 million members. The National Education Association, which is only one of hundreds of education groups, has approximately 1.7 million members.[31] The explosive growth of the federal health budget has been accompanied by a proliferation of health associations representing recipients and providers of health care.

None of this is new, of course. The fight for federal money has been going on for a long time and shows no signs of lessening. Some new twists, however, are affecting the lobbying game. Lobbying tactics are changing. Recipient groups continue to perform traditional lobbying activities in Congress, but many are also resorting to sophisticated grass-roots campaigns to increase pressure on individual legislators. Recipient lobbies can quickly organize their large constituencies to flood Capitol Hill with letters and telegrams, and even to march on it. The size of these lobbies ensures campaign resources and, of course, votes, neither of which is easily ignored by legislators. As one lobbyist explains, "We are putting the screws to politicians back home. You need a Washington presence, but what counts is pressure from folks who vote for a politician."[32] And if all else fails, the interest group can turn to the federal courts, which have already provided impressive legal protections for many entitlements. The chances of lobbying failure, however, are remote, as no antispending group has the organization, resources, or expertise to counter the efforts of recipient groups.

The lure of federal spending has encouraged the formation of formidable lobbying coalitions. The Committee for Full Funding of Education Programs and the Coalition for Health Funding are two of the oldest and most effective of the targeted spending groups. A recent coalition, the Umbrella Group, was initiated by the AFL-CIO and includes almost 150 organizations representing health, environmental, minority, labor, women's, and urban interests. Its efforts are aimed at a broad range of domestic spending programs, and one of its main objectives is to ensure that these programs are not cut or set against each other in the current climate of budget cuts and balanced budgets. Proponents of spending, in sum, are finding that cooperative efforts are helpful.

Moreover, even business lobbying groups, which usually support balanced budgets and spending cuts as general goals, have a fondness for government assistance—and all want business tax cuts with or without a deficit. The National Association of Realtors, for example, spent $200,000 in April 1980 on a national newspaper advertising campaign for a balanced budget and a "2 Percent Solution"—a 2 percent cut in the Carter and congressional budgets for 1981.[33] More than 1,700 realtors came to Washington for the association's annual legislative conference, and they proceeded to march on the Capitol and spread the gospel of the 2 percent solution. The citizen-lobbyists were not totally selfless, however; along with the reduced budgets, many argued for a $1 billion housing subsidy bill and better tax treatment for residential real estate.

Those who cry "no cuts anywhere" or "balance the budget but not at our expense" do not depend solely on reasoned argument and congressional goodwill for victory; electoral reprisal is their major weapon. As Robert Giaimo said: "The people you vote against never forget you. The teacher, the nurse, the union member—they are organized and can work against you in a reelection campaign."[34] Members of Congress must judge the electoral potential of antispending moods against these organized demands, which for obvious reasons usually seem to pose a greater threat.

The budget process and Budget committees are less susceptible to the interest groups' lobbying efforts, for the members of the Budget committees do not have the direct legislative ties to interest groups that members of authorizing committees do. Individual members who also serve on authorizing committees may have such ties, but they are not shared by the entire membership of the Budget committees. At the very least, this is yet another group of legislators that an interest group must lobby, and many of them are not sympathizers or program experts in the policy area the group covers. It is possible that a budget-cutting committee may be able to establish spending targets or ceilings that hinder the interest group's efforts to get the funding it wants from the authorizing and appropriations committees.

But the Budget committees have no control over funding for indexed entitlements. They simply estimate the required outlays and adjust their estimates periodically to match the automatic funding. Until entitlements are deindexed, the Budget committees are effectively restricted to a narrowing, controllable portion of the budget, and the recipient groups and spending committees are certain to do everything possible to preserve their protected programs.

For those groups whose programs are either in the controllable category or not indexed, the fight for benefits and funding is obviously more difficult. Thus far, however, Congress has been willing to loosen its budget resolutions as the year goes on, thus keeping the door open for groups that do poorly in the early rounds. In the eighteen months between Congress' adoption of its first budget resolution until the fiscal year covered by that resolution ends, antispending attitudes inevitably diminish. General public pressures may force legislators to vote for tight budget resolutions and balanced budgets, but unless those votes are enforced later on, they are merely symbolic.

The problems associated with depending on public pressures to control budgets are numerous. Public sentiment is diffuse and unorganized; it provides no guidance to legislators who are seeking to determine where and how cuts should be made; and it provides no protection for those legislators who attempt to make budget cuts. Organized interests, with their specific and immediate demands and their resources and commitment, do not become bored or inattentive as the budgetary process wears on. If anything, their efforts increase and produce more insistent pressure, which usually prevails.

A House Divided

The disagreements between the House and Senate on spending go further than the obvious difficulties now associated with divided party control. Antispending moods may have less relevance for the House than for the Senate. In a sense, the 1980 congressional election results were somewhat paradoxical from the standpoint of budget policy. Amidst an apparent conservative victory, Democrats managed to hold on to an almost fifty-seat margin in the House. On two central budget policy issues—defense and spending control—the House has been less conservative than the Senate. Indeed, since the budget process was put into place, the Senate has consistently pushed for lower spending levels than the House.

This contrast in the spending preferences of the House and Senate represents a reversal of earlier patterns. Richard Fenno, for example, describes the pre-1960s Senate as a "court of appeals," counted on by administrations to restore the budget cuts imposed by a more conservative House.[35] Several congressional studies of the 1950s and 1960s offered similar interpretations of a liberal Senate and a conservative House, with explanations for this phenomenon that usually emphasized the larger, more diverse, more urban constituencies that make up the Senate.[36]

Recent studies have offered various explanations for the shift in the relative ideological positions of the House and Senate, at least on budgetary matters. The bipartisan nature of the budgetary process in the Senate and the unity and strength of the leadership of the Senate Budget Committee—especially when Muskie and Bellmon were in charge—have received a great deal of credit for strengthening the budget process and restraining spending.[37] Another explanation focuses on the six-year terms and large, diverse electorates that make it easier for senators to resist pressures for specific expenditures, at least in comparison with their colleagues in the House.

Visibility may also help to explain the different responses to electoral concerns over spending: senators appear to be considerably more visible to the electorate than members of the House.[38] They receive greater media exposure and hence greater scrutiny. Services to constituents are considered generally less important in elections for the Senate, policy positions more so. In highly publicized senatorial races, then, the electorate is more likely to have information on the policies advocated by the competing candidates. And during periods when fiscal issues are considered critical, the candidates' stands on federal spending may affect voters' choices. Moreover, the public believes that senators are high enough on the political ladder and few enough to be able to do something about national issues. Public opinion about national issues thus tends to be more important in Senate races than House races, and senators must therefore take into account national sentiments, such as the anti-spending phenomenon.

The effects of these differences in visibility are confirmed by recent electoral results. Incumbent senators who run for reelection face much more volatile electorates than incumbents of the House. The reelection rate for House incumbents has been at or near 90 percent since the 1950s.[39] Between 1970 and 1980, the success rate for House incumbents who sought reelection was *over* 90 percent. With few exceptions, House members have managed to turn away challenges in primary and general elections, and they have done so by growing electoral margins.[40]

The Senate's incumbency record looks quite different. Although senators have usually lagged behind House members in reelection success rates, the gap has widened dramatically, from about 10 percent during the 1960s to more than double that since 1970. In 1978 and 1980, incumbents' success in the Senate averaged approximately 55 percent.

The dilemma faced by senators was described by Democrat William D. Hathaway, a four-term House member who defeated Republican Margaret Chase Smith for one of Maine's Senate seats in 1972 and was in turn defeated by Republican William Cohen in 1978. After his defeat Hathaway remarked, "I was just as liberal in the House as I was in the Senate, but I wasn't criticized for it then because I got the grants and whatever else it took."[41]

The fiscal conservatism of the Senate in recent years, at least in comparison to the House, may therefore reflect greater wariness about the national temperament on government spending. Members of the House have been more insulated and secure, free to support the spending programs that benefit so many of their constituents directly without fear of being held accountable for the resulting totals. Thus the Senate worries about widespread public concern over the amount the government is spending, while the House is more likely to respond to the groups that benefit from that spending.

The Spending Dilemma

In the past, Congress manipulated budgets for electoral purposes, in response either to calls for economizing or, more frequently, to the demands of spending constituencies.[42] Short-term manipulation, particularly to hold down spending growth, has become increasingly difficult as more and more of the budget is expended on uncontrollables. To keep expenditures down, Congress must take positive steps to reverse automatic increases. Such steps mean cuts in ongoing programs. The trimming of programs requires a policy consensus among members, effective organization, and leadership; most important, it requires a willingness to challenge organized spending constituencies.

Most members of Congress have apparently come to believe that federal spending has grown too quickly and that chronic deficits must be eliminated.[43] Whether they can put the brakes on government spending, however, is another matter. Congress responds to political realities, and most Americans either directly benefit from or support major spending programs. The spending pressures generated as a result have thus far managed to overwhelm the transient and diffuse public moods for economy in government. The budget process, by itself, is thus not likely to resolve Congress' dilemma.

A Formula Solution

Budget reform has come on hard times. Congressional budgets, hammered out after great investments of time and energy and with considerable acrimony, have been upset by changing economic conditions and, more important, political pressures. As spending and deficits have mounted steadily, attacks on Congress have become sharper. Many legislators believed that Congress might regain its institutional credibility if it could balance the fiscal 1981 budget and keep it balanced. But even if this budget-balancing effort were sincere, the prospects for its success were never very good. Moreover, the problem Congress faces goes far beyond one or two budgets. Lawmakers are now being confronted with serious proposals to limit their powers to tax and spend. Over the past few years, dozens of plans have been introduced in Congress to reform, once again, the budgetary process. While some of these plans represent only minor modifications in procedure or organization and would leave congressional discretion intact, others provide formulas—statutory or constitutional—that would determine the size of the budget or the balance between spending and revenue.

The debate promises to be lively and protracted. Richard Bolling, the Rules Committee chairman who claims much of the credit for the 1974 budget act and whose committee has jurisdiction over proposed changes in it, opposes all formula solutions as "mindless." According to Bolling, Congress is fully capable of disciplining itself under existing procedures: "Teeth are not what you need in this kind of internal discipline. What you need is will."[1] Others doubt Congress' ability to achieve fiscal responsibility on its own. Robert Giaimo, the former House Budget Committee chairman, believes

242

that a statutory spending formula is needed to defend "Congress' preordained ceiling against individual temptations."[2] It is an interesting commentary on the spending problems in the House that several Budget Committee members, including Giaimo, have introduced spending-control statutes that would take some of the pressure off their committee. The Senate Budget Committee, which leads a less troubled existence, has generally disclaimed the need for any spending formulas, but even there some of the instinctive dislike of formulas appears to have softened.

Proposals for constitutional amendments, which would impose even more formidable limits on congressional powers, predictably give rise to more impassioned rhetoric. In order to decide which reform route is best, we must examine the way Congress has exercised its power of the purse in the past and the political factors that have shaped its decisions on spending and taxing. All that can be expected from Congress in the future, in the absence of some type of effective formula solution, is what it has done in the past.

Process and Policy

The congressional budgetary process that was so widely heralded *MAJOR PREMISE* in 1974 has had a very limited impact on budget policy. Spending has not been greatly affected. There is no evidence of dramatic shifts in spending priorities or tax policy, nor have we any reason to suspect that congressional fiscal policy decisions would have been greatly different if the budget-reform act had not been passed.

All the 1974 budget act did was put into place a new decision-making process. It did not prescribe, nor could it, certain policy results. There was no reason to believe that procedural and organizational changes would restrain spending or balance budgets or reverse the growth of the public sector unless Congress' policy preferences took a sudden and unlikely turn in that direction. The new process was superimposed on a powerful and resilient system of spending committees, which took great pains to circumscribe the authority of the Budget committees and to protect their own influence and prerogatives. Many members of Congress are dissatisfied with the high spending totals of the past few years, but it would have been difficult for any *incremental* reform to produce results more to their liking—and anything beyond the limited and relatively neutral modifications of 1974 would probably have been rejected.

On the other side, according to congressional liberals, budgets have been too tight, hurting the poor and the elderly. Liberals believe fiscal policy has been insufficiently stimulative and budget priorities wrong—especially the new emphasis on defense spending. Finally, liberals are unhappy with the healthy growth in tax expenditures and the continued independence and power of the tax-writing committees, especially the Senate Finance Committee. But even if we accept these complaints as valid (a difficult thing to do given recent spending patterns), they simply indicate that Congress has not followed the precise policy route that liberals believe desirable.

The question is: What has budget reform accomplished? As far as the decision-making process is concerned, some improvements have been made. Congress now operates in a more orderly and coherent fashion, paying more attention to fiscal policy issues and the long-term consequences of spending legislation. The CBO gives Congress direct access to budget data and analysis, which are used in committees and on the floor. Budget resolutions and scorekeeping encourage better planning and coordination among the authorizing and appropriations committees. Butler Derrick, a South Carolina Democrat who once served on the House Budget Committee, vigorously defends these accomplishments, maintaining that Congress is "making better, more careful decisions based on a better understanding of the numbers and the long-term consequences."[3] It is true that Congress can no longer ignore spending totals or deficits or other embarrassments that once were conveniently hidden from public view. If nothing else, the reforms have made legislators more accountable for what they do because what they do is far more visible. Greater care and accountability, however, do not ensure better decisions.

In fact, the most valuable, if unintended, lesson that emerges from the budget-reform experience is that changes in decision-making processes do not alter political realities. Budgets grow because there is widespread public and congressional support for spending programs. Congressional procedures and organization may facilitate this growth, but the uncoordinated budgetary process that allowed spending to get out of control during the early 1970s managed to keep it well under control when there was a consensus on the need for balanced budgets. In the absence of any such consensus in 1974, and with massive electoral groups benefiting from income security and assistance programs, it was naive to expect Congress suddenly to take a new tack on spending. The political forces that had boosted spending were the same. Budget reform provided a minor check on these forces by requiring votes on spending totals, but members of Congress quickly demonstrated that electoral success was quite compatible with large deficits and high totals.

The 1974 reforms also affected presidential influence on spending. Presidents are hard pressed to overcome Congress on spending issues, at least over time. A president may be able to prevent some new spending programs, but he cannot change the momentum of past spending commitments, especially now that impoundments for reasons of policy are no longer feasible, and he lacks an item veto. And since so little spending comes in the form of annual, controllable appropriations, his leverage is reduced still further. Budget reform, by reducing presidential influence over spending, has weakened a potential source of restraint on spending.

In addition, congressional spending ceilings have proved remarkably flexible, leaving the rules of the congressional spending game unchanged. Groups that benefit from government spending do not have to compete against each other, because everyone understands that the totals will eventually be adjusted to accommodate them all. Spending thrives in the absence of centralized control and firm leadership in Congress, since coordination of actions is not necessary to raise spending but is very necessary indeed to reduce it. The "democratized" Congress born in the 1970s does not place a premium on discipline or internal cohesion. Its entrepreneurial members (with their very substantial staffs) are indirect beneficiaries of a massive public sector, and show no inclination to run the political risks of reducing that sector by changing the way Congress operates.

In sum, congressional spending does not increase in spite of public demands, but because of them. No one is being duped, although everyone professes astonishment and dismay when the costs of individually popular programs are added up. If Congress is to be blamed for anything, it is for failing to provide leadership to address this collective problem, while at the same time holding up the legislative power of the purse as somehow sacrosanct. In fairness, however, this failure is not unique to the modern Congress.

The fact remains that the collective problem cannot be avoided forever. Serious issues of public policy—the shift of resources from the private to the public sector, the impact of government budgets on the economy, a large proportion of the population dependent on government for some or all of its income,[4] and the removal of most of the budget from annual review or control—are tied to current spending levels. And *spending* is the key; virtually everyone agrees that it is too high, but there is sharp disagreement on how to reduce or control it.

Spending-Control Options

Further reforms in the congressional budgetary process designed to control spending now appear unavoidable.[5] In this regard, the next round of budget reform will be different from its policy-neutral predecessor. Congress will eventually have to decide whether to complement modifications of its current process with statutory or constitutional formulas.

Modifications

The first steps toward increased control of spending were taken early in 1980, as the Budget committees prepared the first budget resolution for fiscal year 1981. Emboldened by broad congressional agreement on the need for a balanced budget, the House and Senate Budget committees decided to force spending cuts on other committees by attaching reconciliation instructions to the initial budget for 1981. The Budget committees have pushed for additional changes, such as holding up final action on spending bills that exceed the targets in the first resolution unless and until Congress adopts a revised resolution permitting the added spending. The reconciliation initiative, however, probably represents the most important step that the Budget committees have taken. Predictably, it has been attacked by the spending committees. In the House, for example, most committee chairmen demanded the elimination of reconciliation instructions:

> Invoking reconciliation in the first step of the congressional budget process undermines the committee system, reposing in the Budget Committee authority to legislate substantively with respect to the nature and scope of federal activities. Such a procedure, which infringes on the legitimate roles of authority and appropriations processes, is not required in achieving a balanced budget.[6]

And some reactions were far less temperate. A staff spokesman on the House Education and Labor Committee likened the Budget Committee's approach to "guidance like that of Hitler or Stalin."[7] Amidst the hysteria, the lesson the House Budget Committee had received on the responsibility of spending committees in 1979 was scarcely mentioned. When the House Budget Committee decided to oppose reconciliation in the second 1980 resolution, it hoped that spending committees would continue to report out spending cuts in line with the congressional budget. Of the almost $6 billion in legislative savings initially requested by the Budget panel, the spending committees responded with a not so grand total of just over $200 million in cuts.[8]

The aggressive course taken by the Budget committees may be promising, but the circumstances in the spring of 1980 were, after all, unusual. An extraordinary inflation rate focused attention on the deficit when an election was just around the corner, and congressional Democrats were nervous. Even more stringent spending controls had considerable support; for example, in March the Senate Judiciary Committee managed to keep a constitutional amendment calling for a balanced budget from going to the floor by only a one-vote margin. The Democrats' only response to Republican proposals for spending limits and balanced budgets were those measures sponsored by the Budget committees.

The Budget committees are not likely to have much success with reconciliation or moral suasion when electoral attention subsides, even if they finally manage to keep the fiscal 1981 budget under reasonable control. The spending committees have never tolerated centralized spending control, and they are not about to let "supercommittees" emerge at this point. The leadership commitment and political management needed to hold a centralized spending process together are not staples of congressional operations. As an example of the problem, Speaker Tip O'Neill has already complained about "dismantling the programs that I've been working for as an old liberal" and predicted there will not be "discipline in the House to actually make those cuts [to balance the budget]."[9] One assumes that O'Neill is not speaking just for himself.

At any rate, modification of the present budgetary process is at best a temporary expedient. The same assessment can be applied to other proposals that would leave congressional discretion unfettered. For example, Joseph Biden, a member of the Senate Budget Committee, has proposed eliminating most of the automatic spending (and automatic increases) that now occurs by ending permanent appropriations and requiring that spending be approved annually in appropriations bills. Biden's plan would bring a good portion of uncontrollable spending under the year-to-year restraints of the budgetary process and force Congress to make decisions it now avoids.

Richard Gephardt of the House Budget Committee would like to see less flexible budget resolutions. Gephardt has proposed that the Federal Reserve recommend to Congress spending and revenue levels that would then be used by the Budget committees when they prepared budget totals for the fiscal year. He also suggests that Congress be required to adopt a binding resolution by March 15. The concept of an early, binding budget resolution was promoted by the Joint Study Committee on Budget Control back in 1973, and something along these lines is needed if the budget resolution procedure is to gain credibility. Unfortunately, no resolution can be binding unless spending estimates are reasonably accurate and Congress insists on enforcing them. With the large amount of automatic spending now contained in the budget, accurate estimates and strict enforcement are difficult. Unless Congress brings entitlement spending under control, it cannot realistically expect to stay within spending totals. Thus the Gephardt proposal would probably suffer the same fate as past resolutions. Congress would agree to low initial totals, then economic conditions or other events would place pressure on these totals, and Congress would respond by abandoning them.

The chairman of the Senate Budget Committee, Pete Domenici, has complained loudly and often that the budget process "isn't self-policing and hence not credible."[10] Domenici is also unwilling to count solely on political changes in Congress to strengthen the process. He has advocated much stronger enforcement of the budget resolutions and suggested that enforcement measures be available for use against individual spending bills *before* the overall spending ceiling is breached. He has also acknowledged, however, that any substantial success in efforts to control spending will require continuous pressure on Congress by the president.

Incremental changes in the budgetary process cannot solve the spending problem. All that procedural obstacles can do is make it more difficult or embarrassing for Congress to get the spending it wants. Procedures do not create incentives for lawmakers to limit spending. What is needed to bring congressional spending under control is something that will control Congress' political weakness; clearly, the only way to combat this political weakness is less rather than more congressional discretion over spending.

Statutory Limits

One option for controlling congressional spending that appears to have strong support in Congress is a statutory limit on expenditures that would tie the size of the federal budget to a fixed percentage of GNP. A bill introduced in the 96th Congress by Representative Giaimo, for example, limited direct spending and tax expenditures to 27.5 percent of GNP by fiscal 1983. Two other members of the House Budget Committee, Democrat Jim Jones of Oklahoma and Republican Marjorie Holt of Maryland, introduced separate bills to limit direct spending only, placing it under a 21 percent GNP cap in fiscal 1981 and a 20 percent cap thereafter. (The Giaimo and Holt proposals also required budgetary controls on federal credit and loan programs.) With Jones moving up to the Budget Committee chairmanship for the 97th Congress, statutory limitation of expenditures will continue to have a forceful and influential spokesman.

Statutes limiting expenditures differ in scope and in the percentage of GNP set as a ceiling. Credit and loan programs should be subject to effective fiscal checks, either through controls on appropriations or through ceilings in budget resolutions, but whether or not they should be part of an expenditure limit is arguable. Connecting direct spending and tax expenditures also raises objections. The conceptual weakness of tax expenditures is well understood, and Congress has thus far refused to accept them as equivalent to direct spending. The purpose of a limit on expenditures is to control spending, not to force unspecified "reforms" in the tax code.

An expenditure limit should incorporate what can be defined fairly clearly—direct spending and GNP. It should make those definitions permanent, solving the problem of direct spending and leaving such matters as tax expenditures and credit and loan programs to the budget process. The precise level to be set for spending with respect to GNP is a more complicated problem. The 20 percent limit, which rests on a historical base of spending during the late 1950s and

249

1960s, has received the most attention. Such a limit would have to be phased in gradually, since Congress will have to hold spending within absolute limits. Setting the precise percentage of GNP, however, is not nearly so important as fixing the relative size of the federal sector, at least in terms of spending. There would be, finally, a connection between national wealth and the resources available to the federal government. And so long as that connection is secure, it does not matter whether the spending limit is based on this year's GNP estimates, last year's actual GNP, or some weighted average over a period of several years.

The proposed statutes setting limits on expenditures do not present serious technical problems, but they all have a glaring political weakness. Congress can, if it wishes, waive or override them. Virtually all such proposals provide that if the president recommends that the limit for a particular year be suspended, a majority of the House and Senate can set it aside. Proponents of the statutory approach believe that legislators would be reluctant to go on record as voting to suspend an expenditure limit. Although it conceivably might be more difficult to explain such votes than it is to maneuver around the votes on multiple budget resolutions each year, to expect this consideration to alter congressional behavior substantially is foolish. Over the past several years, Congress has readily ignored its own binding budgets when it has been confronted with the alternative of major cuts in spending. In 1979 it even went so far as to adopt language prohibiting a third budget resolution for fiscal 1980, only to raise spending dramatically through just such a third resolution several months later. When faced with the choice between symbolic totals and real spending programs, Congress finds it much less painful to sacrifice the totals. Unless the electorate were suddenly to exhibit a newfound propensity to discipline legislators on fiscal issues, Congress is likely to continue to disregard totals, even if they are prescribed by statute.

Some legislators argue that statutory formulas would enable Congress to resist pressures more effectively. Jones claims that "unless there is some artificial limit under which politicians can take cover, you aren't going to get the specific cuts"[11]—a peculiar justification, at least for a statutory limit. It assumes that members of Congress know what they should do (that is, cut spending) but are somehow forced by political pressures to go against their better judgment. But it is equally likely that most members are committed advocates of spending programs, not reluctant spenders. Unless members of Congress believe that a fixed percentage of GNP is the only spending level the public will accept—and they are not likely to do so without overwhelming evidence—spending advocacy will not be greatly affected by a ceiling. Moreover, even if Jones is correct, the logical solution would be a constitutional rather than statutory limit, since political timidity will always threaten the latter's effectiveness.

Those opposed to statutory formulas do not always object on the same grounds. First, there is the question of congressional prerogatives. Such congressional veterans as Bolling and, while he was in the Senate, Muskie argue that Congress has demonstrated in the past the ability to handle spending issues and that the recent problems are merely aberrations. In fact, spending issues have always frustrated Congress, which has never found a satisfactory mode of internal organization to accommodate both spending demands and fiscal discipline. To maintain, as Bolling does, that the failure is one of will requires an admission that strong-willed antispending Congresses have been historical oddities.

Statutory spending formulas also come under attack because of the proposed link to GNP, which some people believe might result in such spending patterns as decreases when the GNP slumps during economic difficulties and increases when the economy is healthy or inflation is high. An additional objection is that the GNP is subject to error or actual manipulation in estimating and reporting and that the estimating agency would be subject to immense political pressures. The fiscal policy objections cannot be entirely dismissed, but spending limits would not prohibit adjustments in tax rates to provide economic stimulus or restraint. In fact, one of the most important contributions of the spending-limit approach would be to separate decisions about the necessity or desirability of various spending programs from decisions about economic stimulus. It is politically and practically much easier to move tax revenues up or down than it is to reduce spending programs once the need for stimulus disappears. If congressional fiscal policy options were limited to the tax side of the budget, one of the current biases for increased spending would be eliminated.

The estimating difficulties are not a serious liability. While the definition of GNP is not without some fuzziness, all that is required

251

is to fix permanently the current basis of measurement, thus eliminating conscious manipulation. Past GNP is known, and forecasts are no more prone to error than other economic assumptions that are routinely used to project budgetary costs and revenues. Whether Congress would somehow be able to exploit these technical weaknesses to evade spending limits or find some other opportunities for avoidance appears to trouble mainly the opponents of formulas; perhaps their real concern is that formula limits might actually be effective. They probably have little to fear, since Congress can simply vote to ignore statutory limits if a spending crunch develops. If recent experience is any guide, such congressional behavior would seem to be almost inevitable.

Statutory formulas to limit taxes are another option for controlling congressional spending—though the control would be indirect. Most such formulas feature indexing provisions that would require adjustments in federal tax brackets to account for inflation. This option would keep taxpayers from moving into higher brackets because of nominal increases in income and prevent the inflation-boosted revenue increases that have been so conspicuous over the past several years. The overall effect of such proposals depends on how far they extend beyond the actual tax brackets to such matters as the computation of capital gains, or depreciation and other allowances, but the common goal is to reduce and fix the level of federal revenue as a proportion of GNP. If these reductions in revenues are not accompanied by reductions in spending, deficits will mount.

Indexing plans have never made much headway in Congress. Some people claim that indexing effectively institutionalizes inflation by removing one of the incentives to combat it. With a good portion of the spending side of the budget already indexed, so this line of reasoning goes, neither taxpayers nor beneficiaries will be greatly discomfited by inflation. Since Congress ordinarily enacts periodic tax cuts to offset at least some of these inflationary effects, however, it is difficult to see how indexing would seriously alter the response to inflation, although it definitely would eliminate the political credits that legislators receive for reducing taxes. More to the point, statutory tax formulas would have no direct effect on spending growth or deficits. Proponents of tax-limit formulas suggest that spending would be indirectly restrained by the reduction in revenue growth, so that Congress would be forced to vote for large deficits to maintain spending. But in the past, deficits have not proved to be at all unpalatable as a means of financing spending increases, and there is no indication that this situation has changed.

Constitutional Limits

Constitutional formulas are the final resort for those who are convinced that statutory formulas are ineffective. Two major types of constitutional solutions have been introduced in Congress: amendments that require balanced budgets and amendments that set limits on spending. Both types would limit congressional discretion on taxing and spending, but their direct objectives—and probable effects—differ. A balanced-budget amendment would eliminate deficits; a spending-limit amendment would fix the relative size of the public and private sectors by preventing government spending from growing more rapidly than the economy.

The Balanced-Budget Amendment. The National Taxpayers Union has coordinated a national effort behind a constitutional amendment that would require balanced federal budgets. Some thirty states, four short of the required two-thirds, have petitioned Congress to approve such an amendment and submit it to the states for ratification, or to call a constitutional convention in order to propose it. Late in 1979 the Constitution subcommittee of the Senate Judiciary Committee narrowly approved a constitutional amendment requiring the president to recommend and Congress to adopt a balanced budget each year. (The proposed amendment also provided that revenues in a fiscal year would be limited to the same proportion of GNP as the previous year. A so-called emergency waiver provision was included to allow Congress to lift these restrictions by three-fifths votes of the House and Senate.) In March 1980, however, the full Judiciary Committee voted to keep this measure off the floor. The Republican majority on the Senate Judiciary Committee may force Senate action during the 97th Congress, but with the House Democratic leadership and Judiciary Committee chairman adamantly opposed to a balanced-budget amendment, the prospects for floor consideration in the House are dim. There is no real possibility, moreover, that Congress will convene a constitutional convention. Even if the required number of states do submit petitions, challenges to their validity, uniformity, and effect will no doubt delay action indefinitely.

The most common objection to the balanced-budget amendment is that the Constitution is not an appropriate forum for deciding fiscal issues. Since this objection would apply to any constitutional solution, the balanced-budget approach is not uniquely objectionable. A more specific objection is that it might cripple the budget as a tool of economic management. Since deficits would be prohibited (except during "national emergencies"), spending would have to decline during economic slumps in order to keep in line with reduced revenues. Spending would also increase most rapidly when economic growth was highest. Both responses to economic trends are reversals of conventional fiscal policy.

A constitutional requirement of balanced budgets would lead to creative bookkeeping, some people say, with perhaps separate capital and operating budgets or other devices employed by state and local governments to get around such restrictions. In addition, unless a balanced-budget requirement is accompanied by restrictions on revenues (which would complicate matters immensely), budgets can simply be balanced at high tax levels. Balancing the budget and limiting the growth of spending are not the same thing, and it is risky to assume that public resistance to increased tax burdens would outweigh the pressures toward spending.

A balanced-budget amendment might prevent deficits, but it would not directly halt the growth in the relative size of the public sector, and it would not ensure restraint in spending. The goal of eliminating deficits, which changes the rules of the spending game so that increases in spending cannot be financed and hidden by borrowing, is important because it restores direct confrontations between taxpayers' costs and benefits. It assumes, however, that a balanced budget is the country's foremost economic policy goal. Most experts on fiscal policy agree that the economic issue is more complicated. Moreover, the real political problem is posed by spending, not by deficits. A balanced-budget amendment would not directly limit the rate of growth in spending or fix the relative size of the federal sector. It would treat, in effect, an unpleasant manifestation of fiscal irresponsibility, not the source of that irresponsibility.

Spending-Limit Amendments. Constitutional limitations of expenditures, like statutory ones, would restrict the rate of growth in federal spending to the rate of economic growth by setting a ceiling on the share of GNP that could be absorbed by the federal sector.

The GNP caps for both types of proposals are similar. Many of the constitutional or statutory limits on expenditures would reduce federal spending to 20 percent of GNP within one or two years, and fix it at that level. Less stringent plans would allow spending at 21 or 22 percent of GNP.

There is an important difference, however, between the constitutional and statutory approaches. Constitutional limits cannot be readily waived or ignored. Most of the proposed constitutional amendments to limit expenditures contain an escape clause—a one-year suspension of the spending limit during a national emergency declared by the president and affirmed by an extraordinary majority of both houses of Congress. Without a genuine national emergency, however, the political branches of the government could not suspend a constitutional expenditure limit. Unlike a statutory limit, the loophole is relatively narrow and difficult to exploit.

A constitutional expenditure limit would not guarantee a balanced budget and would be subject to the same fiscal policy constraints and technical problems that apply to statutory spending limits.[12] Its advantage over other solutions is that, unlike the balanced-budget amendment, it preserves a major fiscal policy option (the revenue side of the budget), and unlike a statutory spending limit, it is likely to result in effective control over spending. At the present time, Congress does not control the spending side of the budget, primarily because of entitlements. All that Congress can do with entitlement spending is hope to make accurate estimates, and when it fails, to ignore or work around spending ceilings.

Despite the obvious inconsistency between indexed entitlements and spending control, Congress has refused to consider any comprehensive review of the indexing problem, refused even to eliminate the semiannual cost-of-living adjustment for civil service retirees. With this protective response toward one of the least defensible indexing schemes, it is hard to imagine that Congress would willingly enact less generous indexing formulas for social security and other major benefit programs.

Members of Congress know full well that spending control is impossible without limits on entitlement spending. The political factors that insulate such spending, however, virtually guarantee that nothing will be done unless Congress is forced to act, and that is what an irrevocable expenditure limit would accomplish. A fixed ceiling on spending would mean that entitlements would have to be considered alongside other government programs. If Congress decided to keep indexing formulas in place, funding for controllable programs would suffer, and Congress would no longer have the option of simply raising the spending ceiling. The result is likely to be modification if not elimination of indexing and other forms of automatic increases. At that point, government programs would compete for funds, and increases, on an equal basis.

With the maximum resources available determined in advance, the current budget process would be credible. Budget resolutions would be serious spending plans. Priorities would embrace the entire budget. Supplementals would be integrated into Congress' spending priorities and fiscal policy plans. Congress would, at last, be forced to take budgeting seriously—to reexamine the commitments it has made, to decide what it can realistically afford, and to make the painful choices between what is essential and what is merely desirable.

Spending Limits and Budget Reform

Several years ago most policy experts and public officials considered spending limits of any kind unthinkable—mere "easy answers" that thoughtful people understood could not possibly resolve complicated issues of public policy. Although some people in Congress and the CBO still insist that spending is under control or almost under control, that multiyear budgeting and planning are the answer to spending problems, and that huge budget margins and surpluses are just around the corner, more and more policy makers are beginning to think the unthinkable. The simple and inescapable lesson of the six years of the congressional budget process is that Congress has failed to control spending, and the situation is not likely to change. Indeed, it is likely to become even more serious as uncontrollable spending continues its upward drift.

For a growing number of skeptics, budget resolutions, multiyear projections, reconciliation, rescissions, and the various other appurtenances of the congressional budget process do not add up to spending control. The result has been a more searching examination of spending limits generally and a serious exploration of the merits of a constitutional limit.[13] In particular, a debate is developing over such issues as effectiveness, flexibility, and constitutional propriety.

Effectiveness

An essential criterion for any constitutional rule is clarity of purpose. In the case of a constitutional limit on expenditures, that purpose is to link federal spending and economic growth, thereby substituting an economic constraint on the size of the public sector for the traditional political constraint. If an expenditure amendment is to make sense both to the public and to its representatives, its purpose must be set forth in clear, straightforward, and workable constitutional language.

Unfortunately, some of the expenditure proposals that have received widespread publicity over the past few years do not meet this standard. The long and complex amendment sponsored by the National Tax Limitation Committee (and Milton Friedman), for example, contains numerous formulas as well as detailed provisions related to inflation, debt reduction, state and local governments, and judicial discretion.[14] The broad scope of this and similar proposals has a certain intellectual fascination, but it does not conform to what we customarily consider the bounds of constitutional reality.

Less complex, shorter amendments have also been set forth by, among others, William Niskanen and Aaron Wildavsky.[15] The Niskanen amendment contains an admirably concise key provision: "The percentage increase in total outlays in any fiscal year shall not exceed the percentage increase in the gross national product in the last calendar year ending prior to the beginning of said fiscal year."[16] Beyond this limitation, it is necessary only to provide for emergencies by allowing the president and Congress (perhaps by a two-thirds vote of the House and Senate) to suspend the expenditure ceiling in any year. As with most of the recent amendments to the Constitution, the details of implementation and enforcement can be left to subsequent legislation.

Simplicity and clarity do not ensure, of course, that an expenditure limit will work. Implementation does present problems, since all contingencies cannot be foreseen or all evasions protected against. While a number of states have adopted constitutional expenditure limits in recent years, it is too soon to generalize about the

257

impact of limits. Naomi Caiden reports that until now, compliance in such states has been reasonably good: "Budgets have been below the limitations. . . . Cash flow problems [have been] managed. . . . Cases of illegality or deliberate overspending appear exceptional and are easily detected."[17] Since "these limits have not yet exerted serious pressure on government spending,"[18] however, concerns about evasion have not been dispelled. Under a different set of legal controls, the state of New York <u>evaded</u> budgetary restrictions through independent agencies and "moral obligation" bonds, while New York City contributed an extraordinary and disastrous lesson in creative bookkeeping. While these examples are decidedly atypical, they do discourage blind faith in the efficacy of government expenditure limits. Proponents of constitutional limits must deal with this issue since evasions might create even more serious and intractable spending problems than those that now exist. It might be helpful, however, to distinguish first between inadvertent and deliberate budgetary pitfalls.

Inadvertent Overspending. Over the past few years, federal spending control has been seriously weakened by estimating error and supplemental appropriations. Neither would be eliminated by constitutional expenditure limit, but their effects could probably be controlled without great difficulty. Since the spending limit for fiscal year would be set in advance (the best reason for using the growth rate of the previous year's GNP is that it eliminates the need for an estimate and thus sets a firm limit), contingencies or margins can be established to accommodate unanticipated spending increases. If these margins proved insufficient, Congress could authorize transfers of unspent funds or grant the president limited authority to impound them. The latter move is perhaps inevitable if spending limit must be enforced, but Congress can easily protect against abuses by establishing a maximum percentage reduction in programs, which would eliminate the possibility of terminations and crippling reductions of the kind Nixon made. Congress could, moreover, mitigate if not entirely avoid the need for transfers or impoundments by improving its estimates and maintaining adequate margins. A constitutional spending limit would impose a discipline on estimates and supplementals that is now missing. If Congress had to pay a price for its mistakes, in the form of large contingency funds

258

or greater executive discretion in regard to spending, its insistence on accuracy would no doubt increase.

Keeping *direct spending* within a limit determined by the GNP would therefore present no serious technical or definitional problems. Indeed, it would provide compelling incentives to improve the accuracy of estimates, discourage automatic increases in spending, and encourage serious review of past spending commitments.

Evasions and End Runs. Whether a constitutional expenditure limit would encourage extrabudget forms of spending is problematical. Off-budget entities and credit activities already represent large gaps in budget control, and Congress may respond to an expenditure limit by using them even more extensively or by creating new and more imaginative evasive techniques. But Congress is already under growing pressure to eliminate the off-budget fiction and impose appropriations controls on federal credit activities, and the economic costs of fiscal irresponsibility may have sufficiently chastened elected officials to make budgetary end runs seem less attractive in the future whether or not a constitutional spending limit is passed.

A constitutional spending limit does not and cannot solve any and all fiscal problems. Unless the public and its elected representatives share a serious commitment to solving spending problems and are willing to live with the self-restraint that commitment implies, a constitutional check or any other solution cannot be expected to work. Whatever respect for restraint now exists, however, is clearly undermined by a system that fixes no limits. Under the current congressional budget process, a spending constituency's appetite is whetted by the knowledge that, whatever a budget resolution says, more money can always be obtained. The eventual reward for a group that willingly accepts some sacrifice is not the knowledge that totals will decline but the realization that other groups will take advantage of the spending slack. If totals are never fixed, restraint is difficult to achieve. With a constitutionally determined spending limit in place, however, restraint is reinforced rather than subverted, both for Congress and for the spending interests with which it must deal.

The spending problem has not arisen because members of Congress are uniquely cynical or irresponsible, but rather because the pressures exerted on them to spend are intense, unyielding, and indeed proliferating. Internal reforms to control these pressures have repeatedly failed. A beleaguered Appropriations Committee chairman pleaded with his colleagues a century ago, "We ought to have some way . . . to protect us from ourselves."[19] But Appropriations committees have proved unequal to that task, as have presidential budgets, legislative budgets, omnibus appropriations, and, more recently, Budget committees and budget resolutions. A constitutional limit on expenditures would provide an unprecedented degree of protection, clearly distinguishable from earlier reforms, with greater prospects for success in pushing Congress toward fiscal responsibility.

Evasions and end runs are potential worries, but uncontrolled spending is a serious, immediate, and undeniably real fiscal problem. And in the absence of a perfect and guaranteed solution to all of government's fiscal dilemmas, a constitutional expenditure limit is a prudent alternative. In the final analysis, nothing can prevent the public and Congress from deliberate and possibly even disastrous evasions, but a constitutional expenditure limit assumes that spending decisions in a democracy can, with modest assists, proceed in responsible rather than destructive directions.

Flexibility

Defenders of congressional prerogatives also fear that if constitutional expenditure limits are effective, they will limit Congress' discretion in regard to policy. Congress would no longer determine the size of the public sector, at least in terms of spending. Congress could not resort to the wholesale use of spending stimulus in nonemergency situations. Congress would lack the flexibility to respond to the changing needs served by the public sector.

The flexibility argument is disingenuous if not actually dishonest. Congress has never deliberately debated the appropriate size of the public sector, nor has it paid much attention to the economic and political consequences of its expansion. Congress did not base its spending decisions on a carefully thought-out vision of the relationship between the public and private sectors. That relationship was defined over time by a series of discrete spending decisions. A constitutional expenditure limit would not remove the public-sector issue from the political agenda, for the simple reason that the issue has always been deliberately ignored by Congress. Moreover, a 20 percent GNP limit would not impoverish government, but would ensure that budget growth was in line with economic growth. Any lack of flexibility thereby implied would be easily outweighed by the enforced fiscal discipline.

The objection to constraint in regard to fiscal policy is a relevant consideration. Congress would have to depend largely on tax policies rather than spending to stimulate or restrain the economy. Although tax cuts may not be the only effective fiscal policy response to an economic slowdown, the economics profession is no longer quite so certain that spending is indeed a preferred form of stimulus. Economic policy merits aside, the advantage of tax cuts over spending stimulus is that they do not confuse the need for economic stimulus with the desirability of jobs programs or subsidized employment in the public sector or other spending programs. Economic stimulus and defensible government programs are entirely different matters. Fiscal policy decisions that affect primarily the revenue side of the budget would end this confusion.

Constitutional Propriety

The argument that fiscal decisions should not be enshrined in the Constitution is not very substantial. The purpose of a constitution is, after all, to limit government. By controlling the amount of public-sector spending, a constitutional expenditure limit does exactly that. The widespread notion that fiscal matters are not elevated enough to deserve constitutional resolution deliberately ignores the fact that the federal Constitution already treats them in some detail. In addition, many state constitutions have incorporated spending or taxing limitations as well as balanced-budget requirements. As Alexander Hamilton explained in *The Federalist* 30, "Money is, with propriety, considered as the vital principle of the body politic. . . ."[20] Since the Constitution has provided the federal government with bountiful access to revenue, there appears to be nothing in the least remarkable about a parallel constitutional limit on spending.

A constitutional solution merely acknowledges that the democratic process has limitations, something that has been recognized in other policy areas. In the past the nation has agreed that certain individual rights and liberties need protection against possible abuse by the political process. The legislative power of the purse and the democratic process produce collective results that *most* citizens find distressing. At the same time, neither Congress nor the electorate has been able to fashion an effective solution to the spending problem.

Expenditure Limits and Congress

A constitutional expenditure limit would represent a substantial but clearly defined change in the budgetary process. Congress would begin with a spending total that was not politically determined and one that could not be evaded. Thereafter, however, Congress would retain full discretion over allocations and priorities. With a fixed total, it is even possible that Congress might conduct more vigorous oversight of existing programs. There would be incentives to effect economies and to view impoundment as something more than an institutional affront. An expenditure limitation would be fully compatible with the congressional budget process—indeed, it should actually enhance that process. The Budget committees would be less vulnerable to attacks by spending committees; budget resolutions would be binding; and budget analysis would necessarily become a more integral part of the legislative process.

Congress would not be transformed by a constitutional expenditure limit, but its persistent and serious failure to bring spending under control would finally be solved. It would be solved, moreover, without resort to the elusive notions of "better" legislators or a "more informed" electorate, which often pass for political reform. Instead, there would be a direct, limited, and effective response to the lack of fiscal discipline in politics. We lack fiscal discipline not because we fail to appreciate its importance, but rather because we do not know how to reconcile it with the legislative power of the purse. A constitutional amendment that set a limit on expenditures would provide this reconciliation, correcting a political flaw in the democratic process and an institutional weakness of Congress. And such a constitutional amendment would protect both the electorate and Congress against the consequences of uncontrolled spending by the federal government.

Notes

1. Introduction: Congressional Budget Reform

1. *Congressional Record*, 119 (December 4, 1973), 39344, 39348.

2. Ibid., p. 39344.

3. On this point, see James M. Buchanan and Richard E. Wagner, *Democracy in Deficit* (New York: Academic Press, 1977).

4. U.S. Department of Commerce, Bureau of the Census, *Current Population Reports*, ser. P-60, no. 115, *Characteristics of the Population below the Poverty Level: 1976* (Washington, D.C.: Government Printing Office, 1978).

5. One estimate is that corrections for in-kind benefits and for the underreporting of income by respondents in census surveys would reduce the poverty rate to less than half its official level (John L. Palmer and Joseph J. Minarik, "Income Security Policy," in *Setting National Priorities: The Next Ten Years*, ed. Henry Owen and Charles L. Schultze [Washington, D.C.: Brookings Institution, 1976], pp. 519–27).

6. One recent estimate is that recipients of federal income transfers and pensions, together with beneficiaries of other government programs, total approximately 76 million, or roughly one-third of the population (Donald M. Ogilvie, "Constitutional Limits and the Federal Budget," paper presented at the American Enterprise Institute Conference on the Congressional Budgetary Process, Washington, D.C., October 22, 1979, p. 26).

2. The Legislative Power of the Purse

1. *The Federalist Papers* (New York: Mentor Books, 1961), p. 359.

2. *United States Statutes at Large*, 88 (Washington, D.C.: Government Printing Office, 1975), 298.

3. On presidential involvement in the budgetary process during this period, see Louis Fisher, *Presidential Spending Power* (Princeton: Princeton University Press, 1975), chap. 1.

4. See Lucius Wilmerding, *The Spending Power* (New Haven: Yale University Press, 1943), chap. 5.

5. Ibid., p. 99.

6. Ibid., pp. 205, 223.

7. Ibid., p. 205.

8. *Congressional Globe,* pt. 2, 1864–65 (March 2, 1865), p. 1312.

9. Ibid., p. 1315.

10. These were the appropriations bills for the Army, Navy, Military Academy, Post Office, Indian affairs, and consular and diplomatic affairs (Fisher, *Presidential Spending Power*, p. 22).

11. *Congressional Record,* 17 (December 14, 1885), 172, 199 (emphasis added).

12. Ibid. (December 17, 1885), 286.

13. These bills included those for the Army and Military Academy, Navy, Indian, Post Office, agriculture, and pensions (Fisher, *Presidential Spending Power*, p. 24).

14. Fisher, *Presidential Spending Power*, pp. 24–26.

15. Nelson W. Polsby, "The Institutionalization of the U.S. House of Representatives," *American Political Science Review*, 62 (March 1968), 146.

16. Randall B. Ripley, *Congress: Process and Policy* (New York: W. W. Norton, 1975), p. 36.

17. Joseph P. Harris, *Congressional Control of Administration* (Washington, D.C.: Brookings Institution, 1969), p. 54.

18. See Wilmerding, *Spending Power,* chap. 7.

19. Quoted in Fisher, *Presidential Spending Power*, p. 30.

20. *Congressional Record,* 59 (June 1, 1920), 8109.

21. Ibid., p. 8116.

22. Ibid., p. 8117.

23. See Fisher, *Presidential Spending Power,* p. 36.

24. *Congressional Record,* 92 (July 25, 1946), 10040.

25. Ibid., p. 10041.

26. Ralph K. Huitt, "Research Study Seven, Congressional Organization and Operations in the Field of Money and Credit," in Commission on Money and Credit, *Fiscal and Debt Management Policies* (Englewood Cliffs, N.J.: Prentice-Hall, 1963), p. 441.

27. See James P. Pfiffner, "Congressional Budget Reform, 1974: Initiative and Reaction," paper presented at the 1975 annual meeting of the American Political Science Association, San Francisco, September 2–5, 1975, p. 7.

28. Ibid., pp. 6–7.

29. See Richard F. Fenno, Jr., *The Power of the Purse: Appropriations Politics in Congress* (Boston: Little, Brown, 1966), p. 122.

30. *Congressional Record,* 95 (February 7, 1949), 880–81.

31. Ibid., 96 (March 3, 1950), A1616–18.

32. On the differences between the House and Senate Appropriations committees, see Fenno, *Power of the Purse*, chap. 12.

33. See Aaron Wildavsky, *The Politics of the Budgetary Process*, 3d ed. (Boston: Little, Brown, 1979), pp. 160–65.

34. See John R. Gist, "'Increment' and 'Base' in the Congressional Appropriations Process," *American Journal of Political Science*, 21 (May 1977), 348–50.

3. Redefining Budget Control

1. *Congressional Record*, 113 (September 27, 1967), 26956–57.

2. "Special Message to the Congress on Federal Government Spending," *Public Papers of the Presidents, 1972* (Washington, D.C.: Government Printing Office, 1974), p. 742.

3. *Budget of the United States Government, Fiscal Year 1973* (Washington, D.C.: Government Printing Office, 1972), p. 15.

4. Joint Committee on Reduction of Federal Expenditures, *1973 Budget Scorekeeping Report No. 9—Revised* (Washington, D.C.: Government Printing Office, 1972), pp. 1–9.

5. *Weekly Compilation of Presidential Documents*, 8, no. 44 (October 30, 1972), 1578.

6. *Budget of the United States Government, Fiscal Year 1974* (Washington, D.C.: Government Printing Office, 1973), pp. 3, 4, 16, 5 (emphasis in original).

7. U.S. Congress, Joint Study Committee on Budget Control, *Interim Report, Improving Congressional Control over Congressional Budgetary Outlay and Receipt Totals* (Washington, D.C.: Government Printing Office, February 7, 1973), p. 4.

8. *Congressional Quarterly Weekly Report*, 31 (May 19, 1973), 1211.

9. Ibid. (April 28, 1973), p. 1013.

10. Senator Ervin was also chairman of the Government Operations Committee.

11. *Congressional Record*, 119 (July 24, 1973), 25572–73.

12. U.S. House of Representatives, Committee on Rules, *Report No. 93-658, Budget and Impoundment Control Act of 1973* (Washington, D.C.: Government Printing Office, 1973), pp. 21, 29.

13. U.S. Senate, Committee on Rules and Administration, *Report No. 93-688, Congressional Budget Act of 1974* (Washington, D.C.: Government Printing Office, 1974), p. 2.

14. Ibid., pp. 91–97.

15. Ibid., p. 4 (emphasis added).

16. As the committee report emphasized, "It is not intended that the Budget Committee diminish the responsibilities of any other committee. By performing effectively the new tasks required by the congressional budget process, functions that no other legislative committee now performs, it will enable other committees, such as Appropriations and Finance, to work within a comprehensive framework of congressional budget and priority decisions" (ibid., p. 31).

17. *Public Papers of the Presidents, 1974* (Washington, D.C.: Government Printing Office, 1974), p. 586.

18. There are two views on policy-neutral budget reform. In the first edition of his seminal work on budgetary politics, Aaron Wildavsky argued that "there would be no point in tinkering with the budget machinery if, at the end, the pattern of budgetary decisions was precisely the same as before. On the contrary, reform has little justification unless it results in different kinds of decisions" (*The Politics of the Budgetary Process* [Boston: Little, Brown, 1964], p. 132). Allen Schick has recently declared that policy-biased budgetary reform—for example, an arrangement that favors "spending cuts over increases"—would curb "the legislative power of Congress by making future outcomes dependent on budget procedures rather than on majority will" (*Congress and Money: Budgeting, Spending, and Taxing* [Washington, D.C.: Urban Institute, 1980], pp. 72–73). Schick's position may have some theoretical validity, although one could point to congressional procedures that deliberately make it difficult for majorities to act or at least to act quickly.

4. The Budget Committees

1. Interview with House Budget Committee member, September 8, 1978. The two Republicans who voted to report the resolution were Barber Conable of New York and Elford A. Cederberg of Michigan.

2. *Congressional Record*, 121 (April 30, 1975), 12568.

3. Ibid., p. 12545.

4. Interview with former senior staff member, House Budget Committee, August 22, 1978.

5. The initial Democratic margins in the House since 1975 have been 291–143 (94th Congress), 289–143 (95th Congress), and 276–157 (96th Congress). The corresponding figures for the Senate are 61–39 (94th Congress), 62–38 (95th Congress), and 59–41 (96th Congress). The 97th Congress lineups are 53R–47D in the Senate and 243D–192R in the House.

6. *Congressional Quarterly Weekly Report*, 39 (January 10, 1981), 79.

7. The average annual percentage of party unity votes in the Senate from 1970 to 1980 was about 42 percent; the average annual percentage for the House was approximately 37 percent (compiled from data presented in *Congressional Quarterly Almanac*, various years).

8. In 1976, 1978, and 1980, the percentage of party unity votes in the House averaged slightly over 35 percent; the average for 1975, 1977, and 1979 was over 45 percent *(Congressional Quarterly Weekly Report,* 39 [January 10, 1981], 79).

9. The Democratic party success rate on party votes in the House averaged approximately 73 percent between 1975 and 1980; in the Senate, the average was just under 72 percent (compiled from *Congressional Quarterly Almanac,* various years).

10. *Congressional Quarterly Almanac, 1979,* p. 35-C.

11. Lance T. LeLoup, "Process versus Policy: The U.S. House Budget Committee," *Legislative Studies Quarterly,* 4 (May 1979), 244–46.

12. U.S. Senate, Committee on the Budget, *Report No. 96-654, First Concurrent Resolution on the Budget FY 1981* (Washington, D.C.: Government Printing Office, 1980), pp. 274–336.

13. *Congressional Quarterly Weekly Report,* 37 (May 26, 1979), 996.

14. See Joel Havemann, *Congress and the Budget* (Bloomington: Indiana University Press, 1978), pp. 93–96.

15. Interview with House Budget Committee senior staff members, August 23, 1978.

16. *Congressional Record,* 121 (May 1, 1975), 12794–95.

17. Ibid., p. 12770.

18. *New York Times,* June 17, 1980, p. 12.

19. *Congressional Quarterly Weekly Report,* 37 (May 12, 1979), 879.

20. Ibid.

21. Staff members on the House Budget Committee agree that multiyear budgeting is attractive conceptually, but they doubt that it can be permanently implemented in the House (interview with senior staff members, House Budget Committee, October 22, 1979).

22. *Congressional Quarterly Weekly Report,* 36 (April 15, 1978), 901.

23. U.S. Senate, Committee on the Budget, *Report No. 95-739, First Concurrent Resolution on the Budget FY 1979* (Washington, D.C.: Government Printing Office, 1978), p. 5.

24. *Congressional Record,* 122 (April 9, 1976), 10280.

25. Ibid. (June 16, 1976), p. 18847.

26. Ibid., p. 18852.

27. Interview with House Budget Committee member, September 8, 1979.

28. Interview with Senate Budget Committee staff member, February 22, 1980.

29. Interview with Senate Budget Committee member, October 23, 1979.

30. *Congressional Quarterly Weekly Report,* 38 (September 6, 1980), 2635.

31. *Congressional Record,* 126 (September 18, 1980), H 9127, H 9128.

32. U.S. Senate, Committee on Government Operations, *Report No. 93-579,*

Federal Act to Control Expenditures and Establish National Priorities (Washington, D.C.: Government Printing Office, 1973), p. 12.

5. Congressional Budget Policy

1. P.L. 93-344, 88 Stat. 310.
2. This is the phrasing used in budget resolutions.
3. *Congressional Record,* 123 (February 23, 1977), H 1343.
4. *Congressional Quarterly Weekly Report,* 35 (May 7, 1977), 842.
5. Ibid. (April 30, 1977), p. 777.
6. Ibid., p. 776.
7. Ibid., 37 (May 5, 1979), 815.
8. *Congressional Record,* 123 (September 8, 1977), S 14323.
9. Ibid., 126 (November 20, 1980), S 14578.
10. *Congressional Quarterly Weekly Report,* 38 (May 31, 1980), 1460.
11. Ibid.
12. U.S. Senate, Committee on the Budget, *Report No. 96-654, First Concurrent Resolution on the Budget FY 1981* (Washington, D.C.: Government Printing Office, 1980), pp. 41–42, 269–73.
13. *Congressional Record,* 126 (June 12, 1980), S 6807.
14. *Congressional Quarterly Weekly Report,* 38 (November 1, 1980), 3250.
15. *Congressional Record,* 126 (November 20, 1980), S 14573, S 14757.

6. The Congressional Budget Bureaucracy

1. See Joel Havemann, *Congress and the Budget* (Bloomington: Indiana University Press, 1978), pp. 104–5. On the lobbying effort undertaken by Rivlin to promote her candidacy, see Tom Bethell, "Fooling with the Budget," *Harper's,* October 1979, p. 48.
2. Aaron Wildavsky, *The Politics of the Budgetary Process,* 3d ed. (Boston: Little, Brown, 1979), p. 246. See also Mary Paul, "The CBO—Specialists in Budget-Cutting," *Nation's Business,* January 1979, pp. 49–52.
3. U.S. House of Representatives, Subcommittee on Legislative Branch Appropriations, Committee on Appropriations, *Hearings, Legislative Branch Appropriations for 1980* (Washington, D.C.: Government Printing Office, 1979), p. 613.
4. U.S. Senate, Government Operations Committee, *Legislative History, Congressional Budget and Impoundment Control Act of 1974* (Washington, D.C.: Government Printing Office, 1974), p. 2000.
5. Subcommittee on Legislative Branch Appropriations, *Hearings, Legislative Branch Appropriations for 1980,* p. 645.
6. Interview with Congressional Budget Office official, August 23, 1978.

7. Wildavsky, *Politics of the Budgetary Process*, p. 244.

8. Subcommittee on Legislative Branch Appropriations, *Hearings, Legislative Branch Appropriations for 1980*, pp. 603, 605.

9. U.S. House of Representatives, Subcommittee on Legislative Branch Appropriations, Committee on Appropriations, *Hearings, Legislative Branch Appropriations for 1981* (Washington, D.C.: Government Printing Office, 1980), p. 151.

10. Linda E. Demkovich, "The Numbers Are the Issue in the Debate over Welfare Reform," *National Journal*, 10 (April 22, 1978), 633–37.

11. Ibid., p. 637.

12. Subcommittee on Legislative Branch Appropriations, *Hearings, Legislative Branch Appropriations for 1980*, p. 606.

13. Congressional Budget Office, *Advance Budgeting: A Report to the Congress* (Washington, D.C.: Government Printing Office, March 1977).

14. *Congressional Quarterly Weekly Report*, 38 (March 8, 1980), 642–44.

15. U.S. House of Representatives, Committee on the Budget, *Federal Budget Outlay Estimates: A Growing Problem* (Washington, D.C.: Government Printing Office, 1979). This report was prepared by the General Accounting Office rather than the CBO.

16. See, for example, Preston J. Miller and Arthur J. Rolnick, "The CBO's Policy Analysis: An Unquestionable Misuse of a Questionable Theory," paper presented at the American Enterprise Institute Conference on the Congressional Budgetary Process, Washington, D.C., October 22, 1979.

17. Ibid., p. 8.

18. Interview with Senate Budget Committee member, October 23, 1979.

19. William J. Beeman, "Macroeconomic Policy Analysis at CBO: A Response to Miller and Rolnick," paper presented at the American Enterprise Institute Conference on the Congressional Budgetary Process, Washington, D.C., October 22, 1979, pp. 2–4.

20. Interview with Congressional Budget Office official, August 23, 1978.

21. Subcommittee on Legislative Branch Appropriations, *Hearings, Legislative Branch Appropriations for 1980*, pp. 544–45, 637, 641.

22. Congressional Budget Office, *Controlling Rising Hospital Costs* (Washington, D.C.: Government Printing Office, September 1979).

23. *National Journal*, 11 (December 1, 1979), 2039.

24. Ibid. (November 17, 1979), p. 1952.

25. Congressional Budget Office, *Reducing the Federal Budget: Strategies and Examples* (Washington, D.C.: Government Printing Office, February 1980).

26. Havemann, *Congress and the Budget*, p. 118.

27. U.S. House of Representatives, Subcommittee on Legislative Branch Appropriations, Committee on Appropriations, *Hearings, Legislative Branch*

Appropriations for 1979 (Washington, D.C.: Government Printing Office, 1978), p. 1040.

28. Interviews with House and Senate Budget Committee staff members, October 1, 1979.

29. There have been no formal oversight hearings since those held in June 1977 by the House Budget Committee Task Force on the Budget Process. The Senate Budget Committee staff conducted an informal review and requested background information during 1978 (Subcommittee on Legislative Branch Appropriations, *Hearings, Legislative Branch Appropriations for 1980*, p. 560). Robert Giaimo, former chairman of the House Budget Committee, testified that he sometimes met weekly with Rivlin but little direct supervision was required: "We don't get in and try to tell them what to do. They [CBO] are undoubtedly more independent than any other staff, Committee staff or any other kind of staff in the Congress, but they were set up that way. Being a staff of both Houses, I guess of necessity they would continue in that regard" (U.S. House of Representatives, Subcommittee on the Rules and Organization of the House, Committee on Rules, *Hearings on Congressional Procedures* [Washington, D.C.: Government Printing Office, April 26, May 3–4, 1978], p. 17).

30. Subcommittee on Legislative Branch Appropriations, *Hearings, Legislative Branch Appropriations for 1980*, p. 620.

31. There is no clear legislative history on this point, but the figure of 100 appears to have been the upper limit even among most senators who advocated establishment of the CBO. See Havemann, *Congress and the Budget*, p. 108. The House figure of 75–100 comes from interviews with House Budget Committee staff members.

32. *National Journal*, 12 (March 31, 1979), 535.

33. *Congressional Quarterly Weekly Report*, 37 (March 31, 1979), 584; U.S. House of Representatives, *Report of the Clerk of the House from January 1, 1979, to March 31, 1979* (Washington, D.C.: Government Printing Office, 1979), p. 1062.

7. Managing the Budget

1. According to Joel Havemann, the relationship is even stronger: "For years supplemental appropriations had been enacted to meet spending needs that developed after regular appropriations had been completed. Rescissions became the mirror image of supplemental appropriations; they provided the President and Congress with . . . a new tool for managing the federal budget" (*Congress and the Budget* [Bloomington: Indiana University Press, 1978], p. 188).

2. The evolution of Title X is described in Chapter 3.

3. U.S. Senate, Committee on Government Operations, *Report No. 93-579*

(Washington, D.C.: Government Printing Office, 1973), p. 23, quoted in Louis Fisher, "Supplemental Appropriations, Fiscal Years 1964–1978," paper presented to the 1979 meeting of the Midwest Political Science Association, Chicago, April 20, 1979, p. 24.

4. Aaron Wildavsky, *The Politics of the Budgetary Process*, 3d ed. (Boston: Little, Brown, 1979), pp. 240–41.

5. Quoted in James P. Pfiffner, *The President, the Budget, and Congress: Impoundment and the 1974 Budget Act* (Boulder, Colo.: Westview Press, 1979), p. 123.

6. Highway trust fund impoundments were challenged, and a federal appeals court ruled them illegal in 1973 (Missouri v. Volpe, 479 F. 2d 1099 [8th Cir. 1973]).

7. *United States Statutes at Large*, 64 (Washington, D.C.: Government Printing Office, 1952), 765–66 (emphasis added).

8. Louis Fisher, *Presidential Spending Power* (Princeton: Princeton University Press, 1975), p. 156.

9. U.S. Senate, Committee on Government Operations and Committee on the Judiciary, *Hearings, Impoundment of Appropriated Funds by the President* (Washington, D.C.: Government Printing Office, 1973), p. 395.

10. See Pfiffner, *The President, the Budget, and Congress*, p. 41.

11. See Dennis S. Ippolito, *The Budget and National Politics* (San Francisco: W. H. Freeman, 1978), pp. 138–39.

12. 420 U.S. 35 (1975).

13. Louis Fisher, *Court Cases on Impoundment of Funds: A Public Policy Analysis* (Washington, D.C.: Congressional Research Service, March 15, 1974), pp. 83–86.

14. Quoted in U.S. House of Representatives, Committee on the Budget, *The Congressional Budget and Impoundment Control Act of 1974, A General Explanation* (Washington, D.C.: Government Printing Office, 1975), p. 18.

15. Louis Fisher reports that Senator Ervin, floor manager for the impoundment legislation, expected no more than "a few dozen policy impoundments a year" ("Effect of the Budget Act of 1974 on Agency Operations," paper presented to the American Enterprise Institute, Washington, D.C., October 22, 1979, p. 8).

16. Ibid., pp. 4, 6.

17. Allen Schick, *The First Years of the Congressional Budget Process* (Washington, D.C.: Congressional Research Service, June 30, 1976), pp. 31–38.

18. Fisher, "Effect of the Budget Act of 1974," p. 11.

19. Havemann, *Congress and the Budget*, pp. 185–86.

20. U.S. Senate, Committee on Appropriations, *Hearings, Budget Rescissions and Deferrals*, pt. 1 (Washington, D.C.: Government Printing Office, 1975), p. 283.

21. See Office of Management and Budget, *Cumulative Report on Rescissions and Deferrals* (September 30, 1977), esp. p. A-1.

22. *Congressional Quarterly Weekly Report,* 35 (October 1, 1977), 2092.

23. Office of Management and Budget, *Cumulative Report on Rescissions and Deferrals* (September 30, 1978), p. 1.

24. *Congressional Quarterly Weekly Report,* 35 (February 26, 1977), 378.

25. Ibid.

26. *Congressional Record,* 123 (March 10, 1977), S 3884.

27. Office of Management and Budget, *Cumulative Report on Rescissions and Deferrals* (1977), Table A; ibid. (1978), Table A; ibid. (September 30, 1979), Table A.

28. Fisher, "Effect of the Budget Act of 1974," pp. 9–11.

29. See Fisher, "Supplemental Appropriations, Fiscal Years 1964–1978," for a discussion of executive and legislative controls on supplementals.

30. Ibid., p. 1.

31. Ibid., p. 1, Appendix A.

32. Lucius Wilmerding, Jr., *The Spending Power* (New Haven: Yale University Press, 1943), chap. 7.

33. Quoted in ibid., p. 141.

34. Fisher, "Supplemental Appropriations, Fiscal Years 1964–1978," pp. 4–6.

35. Joint Committee on the Organization of Congress, *Final Report, Organization of Congress* (Washington, D.C.: Government Printing Office, July 28, 1966), p. 33.

36. Quoted in Charles O. Jones, "How Reform Changes Congress," in *Legislative Reform and Public Policy,* ed. S. Welch and J. Peters (New York: Praeger, 1977), p. 11.

37. U.S. Senate, Committee on Appropriations, *Report No. 96-224, Supplemental Appropriations Bill, 1979* (Washington, D.C.: Government Printing Office, 1979), p. 5.

38. *Congressional Record,* 125 (November 16, 1979), S 16878.

39. Ibid.

40. Ibid. (June 6, 1979), H 4109.

41. Senate Appropriations Committee, *Supplemental Appropriations Bill, 1979,* p. 3.

42. Fisher, "Supplemental Appropriations, Fiscal Years 1964–1978," p. 27.

8. The Liberal Agenda

1. *Congressional Record,* 120 (March 19 and June 18, 1974), 7175, 19684.

2. Measured in constant fiscal 1972 dollars (*Budget of the United States Government, Fiscal Year 1980* [Washington, D.C.: Government Printing Office, 1979], p. 578).

3. A 1974 Gallup poll found that only 12 percent of the public believed defense spending was too low; almost four times that percentage believed that it was too high. And these attitudes were unrelated to accurate information, for neither group had a realistic idea of how much was being spent on defense (*Gallup Opinion Index,* Report no. 129 [April 1976], pp. 19–20).

4. See Barry M. Blechman, Edward M. Gramlich, and Robert W. Hartman, *Setting National Priorities: The 1976 Budget* (Washington, D.C.: Brookings Institution, 1975), chap. 2., esp. pp. 203–4.

5. *Budget of the United States Government, Fiscal Year 1977* (Washington, D.C.: Government Printing Office, 1976), p. M4.

6. *Budget of the United States Government, Fiscal Year 1978* (Washington, D.C.: Government Printing Office, 1977), p. M5.

7. U.S. Senate, Committee on the Budget, *Report No. 94-1204, Second Concurrent Resolution on the Budget, FY 1977* (Washington, D.C.: Government Printing Office, 1976), p. 6.

8. These comparisons are based on the president's January budgets and the first congressional budget resolutions for fiscal years 1976–78.

9. *Budget of the United States Government, Fiscal Year 1979* (Washington, D.C.: Government Printing Office, 1978), p. 68.

10. *National Journal,* 11 (November 24, 1979), 1970–71.

11. *Congressional Record,* 120 (June 18, 1974), 19673.

12. *United States Statutes at Large, 1974,* 88 (Washington, D.C.: Government Printing Office, 1976), 306, 308.

13. U.S. Senate, Committee on the Budget, *Seminars, Macroeconomic Issues and the Fiscal Year 1976 Budget, February 3, 4, and 5* (Washington, D.C.: Government Printing Office, 1975), p. 33.

14. U.S. Senate, Committee on the Budget, *Hearings, The Economy and Fiscal Policy, 1974, December 11, 12, 17, 18, and 19* (Washington, D.C.: Government Printing Office, 1975), pp. 1–2.

15. Senate Budget Committee, *Seminars,* p. 185.

16. *Congressional Record,* 121 (May 1, 1975), 12656, 12657.

17. U.S. Senate, Committee on the Budget, *Report No. 94-77, First Concurrent Resolution on the Budget—Fiscal Year 1976* (Washington, D.C.: Government Printing Office, 1975), p. 5.

18. U.S. Senate, Committee on the Budget, *Report No. 94-453, Second Concurrent Resolution on the Budget—Fiscal Year 1976* (Washington, D.C.: Government Printing Office, 1975), pp. 9–13.

19. U.S. House of Representatives, Committee on the Budget, *Report No. 94-608, Second Concurrent Resolution on the Budget—Fiscal Year 1976* (Washington, D.C.: Government Printing Office, 1975), p. 7.

20. Senate Budget Committee, *Second Concurrent Resolution on the Budget—Fiscal Year 1976,* pp. 15–16.

21. For example, Richard B. Cheney, White House chief of staff, said, "The

budget process has been beneficial" (*Congressional Quarterly Almanac, 1975,* p. 904).

22. U.S. Senate, Committee on the Budget, *Report No. 94-731, First Concurrent Resolution on the Budget—Fiscal Year 1977* (Washington, D.C.: Government Printing Office, 1976), p. 2.

23. *National Journal,* 8 (May 29, 1976), 743.

24. *Congressional Quarterly Weekly Report,* 36 (July 15, 1978), 1790.

25. *Budget of the United States Government, Fiscal Year 1979* (Washington, D.C.: Government Printing Office, 1978), p. 4.

26. *Congressional Quarterly Weekly Report,* 36 (January 28, 1978), 152.

27. U.S. Senate, Committee on the Budget, *Report No. 95-1124, Second Concurrent Resolution on the Budget, Fiscal Year 1979* (Washington, D.C.: Government Printing Office, 1978), pp. 4–5.

28. *Budget of the United States Government, Fiscal Year 1981* (Washington, D.C.: Government Printing Office, 1980), p. 614.

29. *National Journal,* 11 (December 22, 1979), 2163.

30. *Congressional Quarterly Weekly Report,* 37 (January 6, 1979), 16.

31. Ibid., p. 18.

32. U.S. Senate, Committee on the Budget, *Report No. 96-68, First Concurrent Resolution on the Budget, Fiscal Year 1980* (Washington, D.C.: Government Printing Office, 1979), p. 52.

33. Giaimo's proposal, introduced during the 96th Congress, would have decreased federal spending from a statutory limit of 28.5 percent in fiscal 1981 to 27.5 percent in 1983. Included in this ceiling were both direct spending and tax expenditures.

34. *Congressional Quarterly Almanac, 1977,* p. 185.

35. *Congressional Quarterly Weekly Report,* 37 (February 24, 1979), 342.

36. *Congressional Record,* 124 (October 7, 1978), S 17495.

37. *Special Analyses, Budget of the United States Government, Fiscal Year 1981* (Washington, D.C.: Government Printing Office, 1980), p. 207.

38. *Congressional Quarterly Almanac, 1977,* p. 185.

39. *Special Analyses, Fiscal Year 1981,* p. 216.

40. U.S. Senate, Committee on the Budget, *Report No. 96-654, First Concurrent Resolution on the Budget, Fiscal Year 1981* (Washington, D.C.: Government Printing Office, 1980), p. 33.

41. U.S. Senate, Committee on Government Operations, *Report No. 93-579, Federal Act to Control Expenditures and Establish National Priorities* (Washington, D.C.: Government Printing Office, 1973), p. 24.

42. Joel Havemann, *Congress and the Budget* (Bloomington: Indiana University Press, 1978), pp. 128–30.

43. *United States Statutes at Large, 1974,* pp. 300, 301.

44. *Congressional Record,* 124 (October 7, 1970), S 17483–84.

45. *United States Statutes at Large, 1974*, p. 309.

46. *Congressional Record*, 124 (October 5, 1978), S 17420.

47. Ibid., p. S 17239.

48. Ibid., p. S 17245.

49. *Congressional Quarterly Almanac, 1976*, p. 51.

50. *Congressional Record*, 122 (September 16, 1976), S 16014, S 16013. When the Finance Committee came under heavy criticism for numerous narrow-purpose provisions, Long held a special meeting to reconsider 73 specific amendments. During reconsideration, the committee voted to drop 20 of them. Long later promised to open tax-bill markings to the public and to make written transcripts public as well.

51. U.S. House of Representatives, Committee on the Budget, *Views and Estimates of Committees of the House and Joint Committees on the Congressional Budget for Fiscal Year 1980* (Washington, D.C.: Government Printing Office, 1979), pp. 701–2, 768.

9. Conservatives, Spending, and Deficits

1. *Congressional Quarterly Weekly Report*, 37 (January 6, 1979), 12.

2. U.S. House of Representatives, Committee on the Budget, *Report No. 94-145, First Concurrent Resolution on the Budget—Fiscal Year 1976* (Washington, D.C.: Government Printing Office, 1975), p. 85; *Report No. 95-1055, First Concurrent Resolution on the Budget—Fiscal Year 1979* (Washington, D.C.: Government Printing Office, 1978), pp. 210, 211; *Report No. 95-1456, Second Concurrent Resolution on the Budget—Fiscal Year 1979* (Washington, D.C.: Government Printing Office, 1978), p. 164.

3. House Budget Committee, *First Concurrent Resolution on the Budget—Fiscal Year 1979*, "Additional Minority Views of Congressman Clair W. Burgener," p. 229.

4. A regression analysis of the upward trend in the growth of federal expenditures as a percentage of GNP indicates that the expected annual increase has not changed significantly in the postreform period. Moreover, neither war nor recession appears to have had any significant impact on this long-term trend. Regression results corresponding to Figure 9.1:

$$Y = 17.44 + 0.23X_1 - 0.70X_2 - 0.05X_3 - 0.02DX_1$$
$$ (0.07) \quad\; (0.74) \quad\;\; (0.52) \quad\;\; (0.05)$$
$$\text{d.w.} = 1.55 \quad R^2 = 0.82$$

Where Y = budget outlays as a percentage of GNP

$\; X_1$ = trend

$\; X_2$ = 1 if during the time of war

$\; X_2$ = 2 if not during time of war

X_3 = 1 if recession year (negative real growth in GNP from preceding year)

0 if not recession year

D = 1 if post-1974

0 if pre-1974

5. *Budget of the United States Government, Fiscal Year 1981* (Washington, D.C.: Government Printing Office, 1980), p. 612.

6. Ibid., p. 614.

7. *Economic Report of the President, 1980* (Washington, D.C.: Government Printing Office, 1980), pp. 228, 285.

8. Ibid., p. 285 (receipts data); *Budget of the United States Government, Fiscal Year 1981,* p. 612 (GNP estimates).

9. See U.S. Senate, Committee on the Budget, *Report No. 96-68, First Concurrent Resolution on the Budget, Fiscal Year 1980* (Washington, D.C.: Government Printing Office, 1979), pp. 334–39.

10. See "Legal Status of Entitlement Programs," *Congressional Quarterly Weekly Report,* 33 (January 19, 1980), 122.

11. *Congressional Quarterly Weekly Report,* 38 (Jaunary 19, 1980), 124.

12. Edward R. Tufte, *Political Control of the Economy* (Princeton: Princeton University Press, 1978), pp. 32–36.

13. *Budget of the United States Government, Fiscal Year 1981,* pp. 245, 261, 271.

14. *Congressional Quarterly Weekly Report,* 38 (January 19, 1980), 124.

15. *National Journal,* 12 (March 1, 1980), 369.

16. Dennis S. Ippolito, *The Budget and National Politics* (San Francisco: W. H. Freeman, 1978), p. 175.

17. *National Journal,* 12 (February 23, 1980), 321.

18. *Congressional Quarterly Weekly Report,* 38 (January 19, 1980), 117.

19. *Budget of the United States Government, Fiscal Year 1981,* pp. 597 and 614; *Special Analyses, Budget of the United States Government, Fiscal Year 1981* (Washington, D.C.: Government Printing Office, 1980), p. 144.

20. *Special Analyses, Fiscal Year 1981,* p. 184.

21. *Budget of the United States Government, Fiscal Year 1981,* p. 597.

22. *Congressional Record,* 120 (December 9, 1974), 38672–80.

23. Ibid. (June 18, 1974), p. 19685.

24. *National Journal,* 11 (March 24, 1979), 464.

10. The Politics of Spending Control

1. Quoted in Aaron Wildavsky, *The Politics of the Budgetary Process*, 3d ed. (Boston: Little, Brown, 1978), p. 222.

2. *Congressional Quarterly Weekly Report*, 38 (March 15, 1980), 708.

3. See David R. Mayhew, *Congress: The Electoral Connection* (New Haven: Yale University Press, 1974); Morris P. Fiorina, *Congress: Keystone of the Washington Establishment* (New Haven: Yale University Press, 1977).

4. Fiorina, *Congress*, pp. 39–49.

5. The number of competitive House seats, for example, has substantially declined. Stability in congressional elections since the mid-1950s has coincided with extreme volatility at the presidential level. See Fiorina, *Congress*, pp. 5–11.

6. Quoted in *National Journal*, 11 (April 14, 1979), 610.

7. Quoted in Richard E. Cohen, "A Bum Rap for the House," *National Journal*, 11 (May 19, 1979), 832.

8. See Richard F. Fenno, Jr., "If, as Ralph Nader Says, Congress Is the 'Broken Branch,' How Come We Love Our Congressmen So Much?," in *Congress in Change*, ed. N. Ornstein (New York: Praeger, 1975), pp. 277–87.

9. Seymour Martin Lipset and Earl Raab, "The Message of Proposition 13," *Commentary*, September 1978, p. 43. The figure was the result of a Gallup poll.

10. *The Gallup Poll: Public Opinion 1978* (Wilmington: Scholarly Resources, 1978), p. 198.

11. As reported by the Center for Policy Studies in *Public Opinion*, 3 (December/January 1980), 20.

12. As reported by a *New York Times*/CBS poll in ibid.

13. Everett Carll Ladd, Jr., "The Polls: Taxing and Spending," *Public Opinion Quarterly*, 43 (Spring 1979), 129.

14. *Public Opinion*, 1 (May/June 1978), 30–31.

15. Lipset and Raab, "Message of Proposition 13," p. 43.

16. *New York Times*/CBS survey, cited in ibid.

17. *Gallup Poll: Public Opinion 1978*, pp. 74, 122.

18. Lipset and Raab, "Message of Proposition 13," p. 44.

19. Ladd, "The Polls," pp. 132–33.

20. Ibid., p. 127.

21. *The Gallup Poll: Public Opinion 1935–1971*, vols. 2 and 3 (New York: Random House, 1972).

22. Ibid., vol. 3, p. 1777.

23. *The Gallup Poll: Public Opinion 1972–1977*, vol. 2 (Wilmington: Scholarly Resources, 1978), pp. 986–87.

24. *Gallup Poll: Public Opinion 1978*, pp. 74, 122.

25. *Public Opinion,* 1 (May/June 1978), 25.

26. Ibid.

27. Ibid., 3 (February/March 1980), 36.

28. Ibid., p. 35.

29. *Gallup Poll: Public Opinion 1978,* p. 244.

30. *Congressional Quarterly Almanac, 1958,* p. 770.

31. These membership and staff figures are from *Encyclopedia of Associations,* ed. Margaret Fisk, 11th ed. (Detroit: Gale Research, 1977).

32. *U.S. News & World Report,* January 29, 1979, p. 24.

33. This account is based on Bill Keller, "A Cutting Mood in Congress Forces Major Lobby Groups to Budget 'Battle Stations,'" *Congressional Quarterly Weekly Report,* 38 (April 12, 1980), 939–46.

34. Quoted in *National Journal,* 11 (March 24, 1979), 269.

35. Richard F. Fenno, Jr., *The Power of the Purse* (Boston: Little, Brown, 1966), pp. 537–39.

36. See, for example, Lewis A. Froman, *Congressmen and Their Constituencies* (Chicago: Rand McNally, 1967), chap. 6.

37. See, for example, John W. Ellwood and James A. Thurber, "The New Congressional Budget Process: The Hows and Whys of House-Senate Differences," in *Congress Reconsidered,* ed. Lawrence C. Dodd and Bruce I. Oppenheimer (New York: Praeger, 1977), pp. 163–92, and Joel Havemann, *Congress and the Budget* (Bloomington: Indiana University Press, 1978).

38. Christopher Buchanan, "Senators Face Tough Re-election Odds," *Congressional Quarterly Weekly Report,* 38 (April 5, 1980), 905–9.

39. Ibid.

40. See Fiorina, *Congress,* pp. 5–11.

41. Quoted in Buchanan, "Senators Face Tough Re-election Odds," p. 905.

42. An argument for deliberate linkage of the electoral cycle and economic policy is presented in Edward R. Tufte, *Political Control of the Economy* (Princeton: Princeton University Press, 1978).

43. See, for examples, surveys reported in the *National Journal,* 11 (March 24, 1979), 467, and *U.S. News & World Report,* January 22, 1979, p. 31.

11. A Formula Solution

1. *Congressional Quarterly Weekly Report,* 38 (March 8, 1980), 642.

2. Ibid.

3. Ibid., 37 (January 6, 1979), 12.

4. See Donald G. Ogilvie, "Constitutional Limits and the Federal Budget," paper presented at the American Enterprise Institute Conference on the Congressional Budgetary Process, Washington, D.C., October 22, 1979, p. 26.

5. The second resolution for fiscal 1981 stated "the sense of Congress that . . . the time is right for considering revisions and modifications to the Budget Act so as to improve the congressional budget process" *(Congressional Record,* 126 [November 11, 1980], H 11012).

6. *National Journal,* 12 (April 12, 1980), 593.

7. Ibid.

8. Ibid., p. 590.

9. *Congressional Quarterly Weekly Report,* 38 (March 8, 1980), 641.

10. *Wall Street Journal,* December 1, 1980, p. 26.

11. *Congressional Quarterly Weekly Report,* 38 (March 8, 1980), 641.

12. The confusion between balanced budgets and spending limits is evidenced in the Republican party's 1980 platform. At various points the platform states that "the Congressional budget process has failed to control federal spending," promises "to place limits on federal spending as a percent of the Gross National Product," and, if other initiatives fail, to push for adoption of a "Constitutional amendment to limit federal spending and balance the budget."

13. See, for example, Aaron Wildavsky, *How to Limit Government Spending* (Berkeley: University of California Press, 1980).

14. Ibid., pp. 127–33. The amendment's text is as follows:

Section 1. To protect the people against excessive governmental burdens and to promote sound fiscal and monetary policies, total outlays of the Government of the United States shall be limited.

(a) Total outlays in any fiscal year shall not increase by a percentage greater than the percentage increase in nominal gross national product in the last calendar year ending prior to the beginning of said fiscal year. Total outlays shall include budget and off-budget outlays, and exclude redemptions of the public debt and emergency outlays.

(b) If inflation for the last calendar year ending prior to the beginning of any fiscal year is more than three percent, the permissible percentage increase in total outlays for that fiscal year shall be reduced by one-fourth of the excess of inflation over three percent. Inflation shall be measured by the difference between the percentage increase in nominal gross national product and the percentage increase in real gross national product.

Section 2. When, for any fiscal year, total revenues received by the Government of the United States exceed total outlays, the surplus shall be used to reduce the public debt of the United States until such debt is eliminated.

Section 3. Following declaration of an emergency by the President, Congress may authorize, by a two-thirds vote of both Houses, a specified amount of emergency outlays in excess of the limit for the current fiscal year.

Section 4. The limit on total outlays may be changed by a specified amount by a three-fourths vote of both Houses of Congress when approved by the Legislatures of a majority of the several States. The change shall become effective for the fiscal year following approval.

Section 5. For each of the first six fiscal years after ratification of this article, total grants to States and local governments shall not be a smaller fraction of total outlays than in the three fiscal years prior to the ratification of this article. Thereafter, if grants are less than that fraction of total outlays, the limit on total outlays shall be decreased by an equivalent amount.

Section 6. The Government of the United States shall not require, directly or indirectly, that States or local governments engage in additional or expanded activities without compensation equal to the necessary additional costs.

Section 7. This article may be enforced by one or more members of the Congress in an action brought in the United States District Court for the District of Columbia, and by no other persons. The action shall name as defendant the Treasurer of the United States, who shall have authority over outlays by any unit or agency of the Government of the United States when required by a court order enforcing the provisions of this article. The order of the court shall not specify the particular outlays to be made or reduced. Changes in outlays necessary to comply with the order of the court shall be made no later than the end of the third full fiscal year following the court order.

15. Wildavsky, *How to Limit Government Spending,* pp. 135–36.

16. Niskanen, however, includes additional provisions to protect state and local governments from having federal spending programs dumped back on them. Such protection may be desirable, but the problem can be handled in implementing legislation, especially since the major protection is short term in Niskanen's plan.

17. Naomi Caiden, "Problems in Implementing Government Expenditure Limitations," *How to Limit Government Spending,* p. 159.

18. Ibid., p. 147.

19. *Congressional Record,* 17 (December 14, 1885), 199.

20. *The Federalist Papers* (New York: Mentor Books, 1961), p. 188.

Index

Index

Index

Congressional Spending

Designed by Richard E. Rosenbaum.
Composed by Eastern Graphics
in 10½ point Linotron 202 Times Roman
with display lines in Times Roman.
Printed offset and bound by Vail-Ballou Press, Inc.

Library of Congress Cataloging in Publication Data

Ippolito, Dennis S.
  Congressional spending.

  "A Twentieth Century Fund report."
  Includes bibliographical references and index.
  1. United States—Appropriations and expenditures.
  2. Government spending policy—United States.
  I. Twentieth Century Fund. II. Title.
  HJ2052.I77   336.3'9'0973   81-67971
  ISBN 0-8014-1463-6 (cloth)
  ISBN 0-8014-9230-0 (pbk.)   AACR2